AUGUST '39

Books by Stephen Howarth

The Koh-i-Noor Diamond
The Knights Templar
Morning Glory: A History of the Imperial Japanese Navy
(published in America as *The Fighting Ships of the Rising Sun*)

Books by Stephen Howarth and David Howarth

The Story of P & O:
The Peninsular and Oriental Steam Navigation Company
Nelson: The Immortal Memory

AUGUST '39

THE LAST FOUR WEEKS OF PEACE

STEPHEN HOWARTH

Mercury House, Incorporated
San Francisco

Published in the United States by
Mercury House
San Francisco, California

Distributed to the trade by
Consortium Book Sales & Distribution, Inc.
St. Paul, Minnesota

Library of Congress Cataloging-in-Publication Data

Howarth, Stephen.
  August '39 : the last four weeks of peace / Stephen Howarth.
    p. cm.
  ISBN 0–916515–67–2 : $18.95
  1. World War, 1939-1945 — Causes.   2. Europe — Politics and government —
1918-1945.   3. Peace.   I. Title.   II. Title: August 'thirty nine.
D741.H64   1989
940.53'11 — dc20   89-3395
                                                                       CIP

For my beloved sons
Christopher and Liam

*with the hope that, like me, they will be fortunate enough
to grow up in peace*

Contents

Illustrations

(between pages 130 and 131)

21. Filling sandbags outside the Royal Eye Hospital. *(Popperfoto)*
22. Nurses in uniform, with gas masks. *(Popperfoto)*
23. September 1: The Stock Exchange is closed. *(Popperfoto)*
24. Men from the Royal Artillery score off Hitler. *(Popperfoto)*
25. August 23: Stalin watches air exercises, with other high-ranking Soviet officials. *(Popperfoto)*
26. September 1: The King leaves Downing Street after visiting Chamberlain. *(Popperfoto)*
27. August 30: The SS crouch with a grenade thrower beside the Polish border. *(Popperfoto)*
28. September 2: the German cruiser *Schleswig-Holstein* in Danzig Harbor. *(Popperfoto)*
29. September 3: newspaper seller on London street. *(Imperial War Museum)*
30. Henry Moore: *September 3, 1939* (HMF 1551), pencil, white wax crayon, watercolor, crayons, pen and Indian ink. *(Private Collection,* photograph, Michel Muller, © Henry Moore Foundation, by kind permission of the Henry Moore Foundation)

Endpapers: September 2: A crowd waits outside Downing Street. *(Imperial War Museum)*

The newspaper headlines reproduced in the text were supplied by John Frost Newspaper Library and the *Daily Telegraph.*

Picture research by Julia Brown.

Preface

This is not so much a history as a story: a story of a time which for many people, including myself, *is* history—and yet which for millions of others is an unforgettable part of their lives. Because of that, I have been particularly concerned to convey an accurate sense of the moods, as much as the objective facts, of the period. In this I have been greatly helped by interviews, either in person or by letter, with many "witnesses" of August 1939. Conducting these interviews was both a privilege and an enormous pleasure for me; my only regrets are that time prevented me from carrying on the process *ad infinitum,* and that space has prevented me from using all the personal information I was given so freely and kindly.

Very little in this book is invented, and where invention has been necessary it is always closely based on factual authority. Scenes and conversations between private individuals are reconstructed from their memories, supplemented by diaries, letters, and personal photographs. Others in public life, now dead, left copious diaries and correspondence that have provided me with further sources of authentic thought and dialogue. The same is true for those many private people (some certainly dead, some perhaps still living) whose diaries form the core of the Mass-Observation Archive in the University of Sussex. I am very grateful to Curtis Brown Ltd and to the Trustees of the Mass-Observation Archive for permission to use extracts from these unpublished diaries; to Shepheard-Walwyn (Publishers) Ltd and to Janine Phillips for permission to use extracts from her diary of a Polish childhood; to William Collins, Sons and Co., for permission to use extracts from the diaries of Harold Nicolson, edited by Nigel Nicolson; to C & T Publications Ltd, copyright holders and to William Heinemann Ltd, publishers for their permission to reprint extracts from "The Companion," Part 3, to Volume V of Martin Gilbert's biography of Churchill; to Ernest Kroll, poet, for permission to use parts of his written notes; to William Heinemann Ltd, and to Malcom Muggeridge, editor, for permission to use passages from the diaries of Count Ciano, Mussolini's Foreign Minister; to Macmillan Inc., and to the Executors of the Estate of Sir Alexander Cadogan, for permission to use extracts from his diaries; and to Opera Mundi, Editions Robert Laffont, for permission to use passages from the memoirs of Paul Schmidt, *Hitler's Interpreter*. I regret that some copyright holders have been untraceable. I am also indebted to the London Library, for their long loans of various crucial volumes; and to the Meteorological Office, Bracknell, for their patience concerning an extremely long loan of the weather records of the period, and to the Royal Greenwich Observatory, Herstmonceux, for settling a question of time: In August 1939, Great Britain was working on British Summer Time, an hour ahead of G M T, while Germany was operating on its own standard time, also an hour ahead of G M T. Thus, for example, 9 A.M. in Britain was also 9 A.M. in Germany, a small but important factor in a story of this sort.

Notes at the end of the book indicate the major published sources for each chapter. Without those, this would have been a very different kind of book; but I cannot help feeling that its most important sources are the living witnesses of August 1939. On request, some of their names have been changed, and sadly, I have not been able to make use of all the memories I have been given. However, among those included in this book are Oscar Baker; Molly Brown (née McAndrew); Catherine (Kit) Clifton (née Dennis) and her husband Joseph; Tom Elliott; Dorothy Emanuel (née Williams); Barkley Goodrich, his wife Libby (née Tufts) and her mother Mrs. Annie H. Tufts; Colonel Denis Harding and his brother Frank; my father, David Howarth; Mrs. Eleanor Kennerley; John Landells; Revd. Professor Robert Leaney and his wife Elizabeth; Dr. and Mrs. Michael Haigh; Zofja Olszolwska and her late husband Tadeusz; Reginald Panting; James ("Sandy") Powell; Richard Richter; John Scott and his wife Elspeth (née Harmes); Mrs. Stella Sutherland (née

Smith), and her sisters Nanette (my mother) and Jessamine; Lionel Tomlinson; my father-in-law Francis Vanek; Mike War-breck-Howell; and Nicholas Winton. I am grateful to them all, and to all those I could not include.

For some mysterious reason it is conventional for authors to relegate thanks to their immediate families to the very end. Considering that without their support few books would be written, this seems odd; certainly without my darling wife Marianne I would get little done, and without our beautiful boys Christopher and Liam I would have little reason for doing it. Yet in this case it may be appropriate to leave them all to the end. The others named above are from the past, and are owed an unrepayable debt by my generation for the chance to grow up in peace; but my wife and sons are the present and future.

Prologue

No one who heard the Prime Minister's speech ever forgot it, or where they were and what they were doing at the time. He spoke very carefully and deliberately; there could be no mistake about his words.

"This morning the British Ambassador in Berlin handed the German Government a final note, stating that, unless the British Government heard from them by 11 o'clock that they were prepared at once to withdraw their troops from Poland, a state of war would exist between us. I have to tell you now that no such undertaking has been received, and that consequently this country is at war with Germany."

In parlors and kitchens and drawing rooms throughout Britain, the moment crystallized: a quarter past eleven in the morning, September 3, 1939, a bright, warm day, placid and tranquil. Because it was a Sunday, many people were told the news in church. There, the interruption of age-old ceremonies heightened the sense of unreality, so that afterward it seemed to have happened in slow motion—someone coming in from outside, whispers to the vicar, the hymns faltering and fading, and then, with the congregation stock-still, the awful announcement from the pulpit, from a figure suddenly shrunken and older—in the house of God, the house of peace, the news that war had come.

Whether the listeners were in church or at home, it was a moment that seemed to last an eternity. Some people, after the weeks and months of uncertainty, felt a sense of relief so intense it was almost thrilling; others felt nauseous and dizzy with a depth of horror they had never known before; still others, stunned into numbness, felt nothing at all.

The time of real fear had been twelve months earlier, during the Munich crisis. Since then—ever since the Prime Minister,

1

Neville Chamberlain, had returned in triumph from his negotiations with Hitler — there had indeed been evacuation exercises
in Britain; in various parts, gas masks had been issued and
blackouts practiced; and, especially in the cities, there had been
endless debates over different types of air-raid shelter. But,
throughout those twelve months, many British people had honestly believed there would be unbroken peace in their time, and
finally, after a week of humid, thundery weather over Britain,
August 1939 had become a summer to remember: brilliant
sunshine, temperatures comfortable in the high seventies, daily
work for some, but summer holiday for others and Bank Holiday
for all. Seeing walls of sandbags growing outside public buildings had been unsettling, but watching searchlights being hauled
into position had been interesting, and trying on gas masks had
been comical and embarrassing: They made a nasty farting noise
if they did not fit. Now, though, after the Prime Minister's
speech on September 3, it felt as if the preparations had been
only half-serious — tiresome additions to the daily round, innocent diversions of children playing with the idea of war. Now no
one could predict what would happen; war was reality, while, all
around, the sunshine, the breezes, and the birdsong seemed
unreal, as though they belonged to another era.

They did. As the weight of the Prime Minister's dreadful
message sank into the souls of the people, men and women
wondered if they would ever live to see such a splendid summer
again, and they understood that nothing they had known would
be the same; for in that moment the world had been altered
forever.

This story is an echo of the world that had vanished.

THE FIRST WEEK

August 2–8, 1939

1

Take your gas mask with you

Near Plymouth in Devon, in the orchard at the back of Winsor Farm, a half-grown lamb stared up at an open bedroom window and bleated restlessly. There was no reply. A lean-to roof reached from just under the window almost down to the ground. The lamb was impatient to start the day, so it trotted away from the house, turned, ran, and leaped onto the roof. Picking its way carefully up the gentle slope, it reached the window and looked in. Inside, all was neat and tidy: rugs on the linoleum-covered floor, a couple of wooden chairs, a small fireplace and a big wardrobe, a chest of drawers with a china basin and a ewer of water on top, and two beds, each with a young woman asleep in it—everything just as the lamb had expected. It put its front legs onto the windowsill, pulled itself up, and jumped lightly in. Its small hooves, clicking on the linoleum, were silent on the rug next to Catherine's bed. She had not heard it come in, and so, as it did every morning when the weather was fine and her window open, the lamb reached up to awaken her and very softly nibbled her cheek. The time was a quarter to seven on a warm, humid, cloudy morning, with only a hint of a breeze from the west. Wednesday, August 2, 1939, was beginning.

Catherine Dennis, or Kit—she was only called Catherine if someone was annoyed with her—was twenty-one years old, the youngest of six children, and had been born and brought up on Winsor Farm. Many people would have said it was an idyllic place, and most of the time Kit would have agreed with them. The 300-acre farm was tucked away (if you can tuck away 300 acres) down a narrow winding lane outside the village of Yealmpton. To the north rose the brown wild hills of Dartmoor; to the south lay Winsor's own fields and woods and streams in the valley below the house, and past that the English Channel,

hidden from view by the valley's opposite side where the protect-
ing hills came up again. Plymouth, only seven miles west, was
another world — busy, crowded, noisy, and visited only for farm
business or trips to the theater and cinema. A crow flying
eastward, way beyond the orchard, would pass over eighteen
miles of gentle hills and valleys, many farms, and a few villages,
before arriving at Dartmouth — much too far away for Kit to
consider. Isolated but self-contained, Winsor, like most such
farms in agricultural Britain, supplied almost everything the
family needed.

As the nation awakened, people of every condition made ready
to face the day. On his dairy farm at Plympton, seven miles from
Winsor, Joseph Clifton had already been up for an hour and a
half and, with two men to help him, had almost finished the
morning milking, coaxing the warm frothy liquid by hand from
the udders of fifty cows. In south Wales, the members of the
Swansea amateur soccer club were looking forward to an outing
together; they were to drive fifty miles, all the way to the pretty
seaside resort of Tenby, on the other side of Carmarthen Bay.
Near the center of England, at 102 Southwell Road East in the
Nottinghamshire village of Rainsworth, Oscar Baker heard his
father's alarm clock ring at 7:00 sharp and the immediate daily
reaction: a thump, a clatter, a burst of cheerful whistling, then
energetic footsteps rattling down the stairs and the sound of the
kettle going on and tea being made. Across the ridge of the
Pennines, in Cheshire, while the kitchen of a house named
Westgate also came to life, Mike Warbreck-Howell slumbered
contentedly upstairs, knowing that breakfast would be ready
when he felt like it; the maids, Hetty and Sarah, would see to
that. At 54 Falton Street in Byker, a suburb of the northeastern
shipbuilding city of Newcastle, Molly McAndrew came into the
kitchen from the bedroom she shared with her mother — the
only other room they had — and began to make porridge, using
water from the setpot, a primitive brick-insulated boiler. Its fire
had gone out, but the bricks kept the heat in quite well, so it
saved on the gas. In northern Ireland, alone in a cottage called the
Porter Lodge, twelve miles outside Belfast and half a mile from

Strangford Lough, David Howarth began shaving, and wondered whom he would get to talk about what today; as head of the Talks Department of BBC Belfast, he had to have new ideas all the time. In the most distant north of Great Britain, on the island of Bressay in the treeless Shetlands, Lollie Anderson — one of the island's three postmen — looked out from the Old Manse across the Sound to see if the ferry had started over. And, far south again in the leafy Weald of Kent, punctually at 8:00, Winston Churchill, Member of Parliament for Epping, sat upright in bed, pulled his black sleeping mask from his eyes, and rang for his valet.

★   ★   ★

This Great Britain is a long thin country; many of its people, having traveled very little, never think of quite how long and thin it is. But from Winsor Farm in Devon to the Old Manse in Bressay is something more than 700 miles. Draw a circle of that radius around Winsor Farm, and it shows some curious things. Norway, neutral Sweden, and most of Denmark lie outside it. Inside the circle, however, all of the Republic of Ireland is encompassed and nearly the whole of France and Switzerland, while Belgium, Luxembourg, and the Netherlands are comfortably included. The entire North Sea, a slice of the Atlantic, the Bay of Biscay, and even the Mediterranean Gulf of Lions all fall within its range. And while its northern arc divides the Shetlands, its southern arc touches Oporto in Portugal and the Spanish capital, Madrid. To the southeast it comes close to Milan in Italy, and its eastern arc runs through the center of Germany. In 1939, on a steep hill called Obersalzburg in the Bavarian Alps, not far beyond the limit of the circle's arc, stood a house called the Berghof — in English, the Mountain Court. As Britain awoke on the morning of August 2, so did the Berghof's builder, owner, and main occupant, Adolf Hitler, the leader of Nazi Germany, recently back from a brief visit to Berlin. Whatever else the day brought for the millions of people within the circle, for Hitler, just outside it, it was to be a day of pleasure; he was on holiday and already keenly anticipating the evening. By then he would be in Bayreuth's elaborate Festspielhaus, the opera theater, enjoying the final performance of that year's Wagner festival.

Like Bressay, Oporto, and Madrid, Bayreuth lies exactly on the line, 700 miles from Devon. Kit Dennis would have been amazed and amused to realize that Winsor Farm, the center of her world, was also the center — geographically, at least — of such an extraordinary ring.

★ ★ ★

"It may look like a lamb," said her mother with mock disapproval, "but it thinks it's a dog." Kit giggled and held out another slice of bacon for Mary. The lamb's duty as alarm clock done, it had skittered back down the lean-to roof, and now, during breakfast, it stood by the kitchen window, popping its head through the bars and eagerly gobbling bacon and fried potatoes. Far from the center of public life, Kit was one of the few ordinary people who kept a daily record of their private life. Somehow, years later, Kit lost her diary; but she was blessed with a good memory, and August 1939 was a month that stuck fast, as much for the small private innocent events as the great public ones.

Life on Winsor Farm was not hectic, but it was always busy and never more so than during August, the harvest month. Her eldest brother John had joined the Royal Navy; his visits home were rare now. William, the second brother, had married and ran his own farm less than five miles away; Alice, the eldest sister, had married a farmer and lived five miles in the other direction. That left at home, as well as Kit, her parents, another brother, Henry, and another sister, Margaret. With three laborers to help, it was a small group for 300 acres.

Kit's own first jobs of the day were light. After her pet lamb had awakened her, she had gone down to feed the hens and the calves; then, while Henry and two of the men did the morning milking, she went to the farm's dairy and skimmed the cream from last night's milk. The dairy was designed to be as naturally cool as possible: Facing north, its single window was shaded by a high hedge; its floor and its wide slab shelves were all of slate. The skimming process was simple but effective: The fresh milk was poured into wide stone troughs, like shallow sinks, and left for twelve hours. During that time, the cream rose to the surface, until the milk below could be drained off directly into the churns. A thick layer of sweet yellow cream remained, to be ladled into butter churns. But then the easy part of the day was over; after a pause for breakfast, the hard work began.

★   ★   ★

In Kent, as in Devon, it was a stuffy, oppressive day. While Kit Dennis rode out to harvest, leading a team of four heavy horses harnessed to a baler, Winston Churchill was being driven from Chartwell, his country home, to London. At the same time, from all parts of the capital and country, nearly 400 other members of the House of Commons were heading toward Westminster. The sky was overcast, with low, ragged clouds foretelling bad weather, and the afternoon debate promised little better. A year ago, acting as his own Foreign Secretary, Prime Minister Neville Chamberlain had brought out of Munich Hitler's signed promise of lifetime peace — "symbolic," said the note, "of the desire of our two peoples never to go to war with one another again." The British nation, in a more pacifist mood than ever in its history, had hailed Chamberlain as a great statesman. But since then, many changes. Now war seemed imminent; yet, this afternoon, Chamberlain was going to propose that Parliament should adjourn at the end of the week for two months' summer holiday.

Churchill, for one, was convinced it should not; three weeks was the maximum he felt should be allowed. He had prepared his speech explaining why in detail and had tried it out at home the day before on his friend and fellow Conservative, General Louis Spears, the member for Carlisle. He had also written to another friend — Viscount "Top" Wolmer, the member for Aldershot — asking him to be sure and vote against the motion, or at least to abstain. Wolmer felt it was a waste of time; Chamberlain's majority was so big, he would be able to follow whatever policy he chose.

Nothing daunted, Churchill, after lunch on August 2, took his habitual corner seat in the lofty Commons chamber; and, in a style already quaint and archaic, it was recorded in Hansard — the official account of proceedings in Parliament — that "the House met at a Quarter before Three of the Clock, Mr. SPEAKER in the Chair."

First for this afternoon were some routine home affairs: the third readings of the London Gas Undertakings (Regulations) Bill and of the Hamilton Burgh Order Confirmation Bill. Such things had always been the bread and butter of the Commons and always would be, as long as the House and nation retained their independence. But in 1939, "third year of the reign of His Majesty King George VI," much of Parliament's time was spent in a way that would soon be only a memory. The Prime Minister himself put it in a roundabout fashion: "There is a special responsibility resting upon Parliament, acting through the Secretary of State, for the welfare and progress of the British Colonies and Dependencies." Another member was more forthright: "We are Members of Parliament for the Colonial Empire." And thus, next on the agenda were matters relating to the West Indies, Cyprus, Sierra Leone, Ceylon, Trinidad, Jamaica, East Africa, Guiana, Honduras, Barbados, Gambia, and South Africa — every one, at that time, a British territory. The South Africans in particular were irritated by a German radio station broadcasting what they called "fictitious statements" about them, and the question was "whether all statements of this kind are brought to the notice of the BBC to ensure that proper corrections are made in the Empire broadcasts." The Prime Minister skirted smoothly around that one: The BBC was not an organ of government, but he was confident that the corporation's policy was appropriate. And with that, at 3:46 P.M., he opened the debate that all had come to hear: Should Parliament adjourn, and if so, for how long? He proposed adjournment until October 3. Home and imperial business had been dispatched in a single hour; the adjournment debate took nearly six hours more.

★ ★ ★

In peace and solitude, Paul Schmidt was on holiday. The island of
Norderney suited him ideally, for it was small, sparsely popu-
lated, and very, very quiet. Just nine miles long and a mile and a
half wide, it was one of the East Frisian chain that stretched like
vertebrae for 150 miles around the north coasts of Holland and
Germany, from Den Helder to the mouth of Jade Bay. It was not
far from the naval port of Wilhelmshaven, but, without actually
going outside Germany, it was just about as far from the Berghof
as possible. Wherever Schmidt went on the island, the only
sounds were the sea birds, the sea breezes, and the constant sigh
of the sea itself. He could swim, walk, or simply sit and reflect
without being obliged to talk to anyone at all. For Paul Schmidt,
the silence of Norderney was perfection; as he sometimes
explained to people, his work as Hitler's interpreter involved an
incredible amount of talking.

Schmidt had been in the German Foreign Office since 1923
and had worked for almost every Chancellor and Foreign Minister. For the past four years he had been the Foreign Office's
senior interpreter. Four hectic years, unlike anything he had
known. Very exciting, but very wearing. The first time he had
interpreted for Hitler, March 25, 1935, had been a time of crisis;
and overall, since then, the crisis had done nothing but escalate.
Schmidt neither liked Hitler nor approved of his politics; despite
pressure, he had not joined the Nazi party, though the time
would come when he could no longer avoid it. As a German, he
could understand (and sometimes share) his compatriots' common resentment of the terms imposed on them by the Allies in
1919. But as an interpreter, he was far better able than most
Germans to understand other countries' thinking, and he could
see that, from foreign points of view, the mounting crises of the
past four years looked as though they were mostly the fault of the
three Fascist states of Europe—Spain, Italy, and Germany.

After an hour of debate in the Commons, that was exactly
what Churchill was telling the House. "If you wish to check this
by examination," he observed, "see how oddly they have timed

various strokes." It seemed to him that something nasty always happened when Parliament was in recess. "Take the latest of all, the Albanian outrage at Easter." That was when Italian forces had seized independent Albania — "nicely timed," said Churchill, "for the moment when it was known that Parliament was scattered, when the Ministers were scattered — and when the Mediterranean Fleet, unfortunately, was scattered, too." He pointed out that, when Parliament had adjourned in the previous year, large troop movements had begun in Germany; that there were now 2 million men in the armed forces in Germany; that by the end of the month this number would have increased by half a million more; and that German troops were massed all along the Polish border. "This is an odd moment for the House to declare that it will go on a two months' holiday. It is only an accident that our summer holidays coincide with the danger months in Europe, when the harvests have been gathered, and," he added ominously, "when the powers of evil are at their strongest."

Standing on an empty beach, Paul Schmidt gazed out over the gray North Sea. Somewhere out there, only two or three hundred miles away, was the coast of England. It occurred to him that, just then, he was probably physically closer to Chamberlain, whose words he had translated so often, than he was to the Führer. For a moment he wondered what each of them might be doing, and then he thrust the thought away: He had an uneasy feeling that, much sooner than he wanted, he would be extremely busy and would know the answer in detail. Before that time came, he was determined to savor every moment of his holiday. He sat down on the sand, lit his pipe, and listened to the sea.

". . . It is a very hard thing," Churchill continued, "for the Government to say to the House, 'Begone! Run off and play. Take your gas masks with you . . .'" That made the honorable and right honorable members laugh: "Take your gas mask with you" had been the constant refrain in newspapers, on posters, and on the wireless for the past year. They were glad enough to have a reason to laugh.

★   ★   ★

Teatime. At Winsor Farm, it was only a short pause in the exhausting afternoon; harvesting had to carry on as long as the light lasted. Pasties and orange squash made up Kit's lunch; now it was time for sandwiches and a flask of tea. Her father did not stop. He drank quantities of strong cider throughout the day but never got drunk; once, when she had asked, he had laughed and said, "I sweat it out, girl." Not everyone could do the same; last year, a farmhand who had had too much had fallen headlong from the top of a wagon and broken his arm.

As Kit rested briefly and her father sweated on, a more decorous tea took place in London. With fine china and sweet biscuits between them, Herbert von Dirksen and Lord Kemsley had much to talk about. Von Dirksen was Germany's Ambassador to Britain; Kemsley was literally a newspaper baron — proprietor of the *Sunday Chronicle* and *Sunday Empire News,* proprietor and editor in chief of the *Sunday Times,* he was recently ennobled and just back from a visit to Germany. It had been, he felt, most instructive and enjoyable, and he was pleased to tell the ambassador his impressions. After a day in Berlin, he had motored to Bayreuth via Leipzig, visiting a labor camp on the way. It was most impressive how keen and enthusiastic all the German public men were, even down to the minor officials — Gauleiter Waechtler in particular, who had shown him new construction work at Nuremberg. Lord and Lady Kemsley had attended a performance of *Parsifal* and, during the interval, had been introduced to the Führer, who looked very vigorous and healthy and with whom Kemsley had subsequently had an hour's conversation. Both agreed that a dangerous state of tension prevailed and that something had to be done to break it. Reichsleiter Rosenberg — charming personality, said Kemsley — had been much struck by his lordship's remark that Chamberlain was, in his way, the Führer of England; at the same time, Kemsley could not avoid feeling that Joseph Goebbels, the Minister for Propaganda, was a clever and broadly educated man. Naturally, Kemsley had spent a long time with the Reich Press Chief, Otto Dietrich, discussing a proposed exchange of newspaper articles; they had, in fact, agreed that it was not the proper political moment but that no doubt a more favorable opportunity would come soon. With a little luck, Kemsley might be able to accept an invitation to the Party congress; he hoped so, but he was a very busy man. Indeed, said von Dirksen amiably, and wished his lordship luck. Kemsley then departed, amid mutual expressions of esteem; the tea things were removed; and the ambassador, left alone, wrote the conversation down. One could never completely rely on memory.

★ ★ ★

In the House of Commons, the debate continued in a courteous, even a courtly manner; yet all the members knew that underneath its purpose was deeply serious — perhaps even deadly serious. There was some strong support for Churchill: "Today," said Vyvyan Adams, "Parliament is being invited to suspend completely its animation for two months, which the blindest and most deaf of individuals knows beyond question are going to be the two most critical months for a quarter of a century," and he warned that "at any moment this war of nerves, of which the dictator countries are boasting, may develop into a war of guns." Talking to the German ambassador, Lord Kemsley had been right in one thing: In his own way, Chamberlain could be as autocratic as any European ruler. The debate had begun on a nonparty basis; around a quarter past seven, however, the Prime Minister said bluntly, "The question is whether you trust the Government or distrust the Government. If you distrust them, and show it by your vote, very well; it is a vote of no confidence in the Government, and no confidence in the Prime Minister in particular." That changed the debate's whole foundation. It had already been going on for three and a half hours, and members were tired, frustrated, and cross. Like Churchill, Ronald Cartland was a member of the ruling Conservative party who found himself in deep disagreement with Chamberlain. He could not understand why the Prime Minister would not agree to an earlier recall — no one was suggesting that the House should stay in permanent session — and with sudden passion he jumped up and shouted, "We are in the situation that within a month we may be going to fight, and we may be going to *die!*" Sir Patrick Hannon, another Conservative, could not take him seriously and burst out laughing. Flaming with indignation, Cartland turned on him: "It's all very well for you to laugh — there are thousands of young men at this moment in training in camps . . ." He sat down bitterly. The House was galvanized. In a moment, Cartland's acid rebuke had conjured up the horrors of the Great War, of old generals far behind the lines sending the young, in wave on wave, to their deaths.

★ ★ ★

Hours passed before the decision was made. From some point high above the turning world, it could all be seen clearly. Over the British army camp at Mingaladon in Burma, deep night had settled; it was already into the early hours of the next morning, 4:00 A.M. on August 3. Apart from the pacing and shuffling of duty guards, the barracks were quiet. Reg Panting, twenty-six-year-old lance corporal in the First Battalion of the Gloucester Regiment, slept but no longer dreamed of home, five and a half thousand miles away in the Forest of Dean — or, if he did, he had learned, after nearly seven years in the army, to forget those dreams before he awoke. The regiment was his family now, and he knew that a good soldier was a man who could keep his kit clean.

Only two or three hundred yards away — but otherwise infinitely separated from the other ranks — Lieutenant Denis Harding sighed in his sleep and turned over. The mosquito net twitched. For him, too, the regiment was becoming his family, but it had been less than a year since he had last seen England and Biddy, the girl he loved. The lieutenant was only twenty-four years old; he would have to wait six years before the army would allow him to marry. Meanwhile, Biddy's letters arrived regularly, and a young, contented officer in love had good reason to dream.

At the same time, far westward, the European night of August 2 was beginning. On the shores of the Baltic in the port of

Gdynia, close to the northernmost point of the Polish Corridor, it was 10:30 in the evening, and Tadeusz Olszolwski was at home in the Villa Sadyba with his wife Zofja. He was thirty-two years old; she would soon be thirty. Their fifth wedding anniversary was only two months off. From a bedroom came the tranquil, rhythmic breathing of their two sons—Stefan, aged three, and Andrew, just one year old. Tadeusz had no brothers, and though he and Zofja would have been content whether God had sent them a boy or a girl, to the young parents the sound of their sons was still a special joy, by night or day.

The Olszolwskis had many sources of pride: their family, their work, their nation. Like all parents, they were proud of their children; like all Poles of gentle birth, they were proud of their backgrounds. Both came from landowning families, the top 1 percent of the population, with large estates in central Poland; moreover, Tadeusz's uncle had been a diplomat who had taken part in the negotiations at Versailles in 1919, when Poland had gained its corridor to the Baltic Sea. Given such ancestors, Tadeusz felt that his own work was a particular satisfaction: Less than a year ago, with six partners, he had formed the Baltic Shipping Company—the first private shipping company in the country—and it was already successful. In 1930, when he had announced to his mother that he was going into shipping, she had been shocked. "Is that an honest career?" she had asked. Zofja's family had felt the same; landowners had always married landowners. To them, entrepreneurs—who made up only 2 percent of the Polish population—were slightly suspect. But the business had prospered, and the Olszolwskis had a right to be proud.

In fact, there was no such thing as a humble Pole. A census in 1921 had shown that nearly two-thirds of the population were still peasants; yet, whatever their individual circumstances, everyone who called himself Polish did so with a fierce affection and pride, deeply conscious that the nation was simultaneously one of the oldest and one of the youngest in Europe. Some Poles—Tadeusz was not one of them—were tempted to say that it was easier for an Englishman to understand Japan than Poland.

There was much truth in this, for in 1939 the conditions of Britain and Poland could hardly have been more different: Britain, the island mistress of the largest empire the world had ever known, its language spoken all around the globe: Poland, landlocked except for the artificial corridor, without any natural frontier, its language barely pronounceable by anyone else, even in Europe. Britain had known no serious invasion for the better part of 900 years; the last time Poles had been obliged to fight in order to secure their borders was in 1920 against Bolshevik Russian incursions from the east.

It was true, however, that some similarities also existed between Britain and Poland, including a love of legend. Thirty-nine years into the twentieth century, British people still some-times thought fondly of Alfred the Great as the founder, in the ninth century, of their kingdom. Poles gave the same honor to Alfred's contempoary, Piast, whose dynasty lasted 500 years. Both nations looked back to the sixteenth century as a golden age: The Tudor era in Britain had been a time of renaissance and religious reformation in Poland, too; it was then that Mikotaj Kopernik — the Pole whom people in the West call Copernicus — had shaken the heavens and stated that the Earth moved around the sun. Others muddled his nationality and thought he was Italian or Danish; Poles never forgot that he was Polish.

But after that time, the histories of Poland and Britain had taken different tracks. While England had fought its civil war and laid the foundation for parliamentary democracy, Poland had called itself "the Noble Republic" and for more than 200 years had been ruled by elected kings. It was a system that, ever after, would seem to Poles to have been ideal; yet in 1795 the country had ceased to exist. By 1939 only the most educated Poles knew all the reasons for that catastrophe, but even the simplest knew the effect. Russia, Prussia, and Austria had divided Poland among them; the nation's very name had been scrubbed from the map, its use forbidden anywhere; and for five generations the ancient cities, the towns and villages, and the vast beautiful plains surrounding them had been ruled by foreigners.

Every Pole knew all this, even if only in a vague way; they had all grown up with it. British people might have known it too, but only as an idea, a piece of information. Except for those prepared to try a prodigious leap of imagination, it did not and could not form part of their emotional world, and there was no particular reason why it should. The time when there had been no Poland — the nineteenth century — had brought to Britain the great flowering of the Empire abroad and, at home, the wonder and squalor of the industrial revolution. Britain had been and was still great; even its name said so. Every Briton knew *that*. By 1939, the contrast was enormous; since the Great War, the republic of Poland had been remade, reidentified, almost as an afterthought. Once it had been great; perhaps it could be again. Twenty years of newfound freedom were merely a blink in history. But they were all Poland had — apart from proud memories and a deep-seated, bred-in-the-bone distrust of Russia and Germany alike. And Poland was not going to let go easily of its memories, its distrust, or its freedom.

This was the mental background that had helped shape the lives of Tadeusz and Zofja Olszolwski. It was a background of absolute insecurity only recently made secure, of complete foreign domination only recently overcome; a background where, in little more than twenty years, national identity had changed from a romantic remembered idea into a reality — or at least the beginning of a reality. And, in that short time, so much had been done, so much was promised. Tadeusz, Zofja, and their millions of compatriots would not easily give it up.

Even so, as August 1939 began, they had little reason to feel either content or safe. The Olszolwskis did not need reminding, but if they had walked out for some fresh air by the seashore on the evening of August 2, and looked south, they would have seen, only ten miles beyond the lights of Gdynia, the glow of the lights of Gdansk.

Albert Förster lived there. He was not the direct cause of the Poles' fear, but he stood for that cause. As proud as any Pole of the history and achievements of his race, and of his personal achievements, Albert Förster was German and had become district political leader of the National Socialist party, the Nazi Gauleiter of Danzig. As Hitler's representative in one of the most sensitive areas of the political world, he held a key position, and he carried out his responsibilities in a commendably vigorous, thorough, and conscientious manner. He had already had the honor of several personal meetings with his Führer, and in two days he would travel again to Hitler's Mountain Court. Tonight, therefore, Gauleiter Förster was busy making ready; and as he did so, Hitler himself was sitting in the opera house in Bayreuth, gazing raptly at the stage as Wagner's heroic masterpiece approached its climax: *Götterdämmerung,* the Twilight of the Gods.

★ ★ ★

Thus, at that one moment, the Far East slept soundly; Europe prepared for sleep; and in London, lights glittered on the Thames as, at last, the House of Commons voted on the Prime Minister's motion. Forty members abstained; 129 said no; 245 said yes. So, on Friday next, the House would adjourn. It could be summoned at forty-eight hours' notice if necessary; otherwise, it would not meet again until October 30.

The little group of Conservatives who had supported Churchill's wish for an earlier recall shuffled out disconsolately. The lobbies were humming with conversation. "Ronnie Cartland's ruined his chances with the Party," said one Liberal member to a Conservative friend, "but he's made his parliamentary reputation." Cartland himself felt utterly depressed. Turning to Churchill, he said with a sigh, "Well, we can do no more." A glint came into Churchill's eye; he had not given up. "Do no more, my boy?" he echoed. "There is a lot more we can do. This is the time to fight — to speak — to attack!"

★ ★ ★

It had been a long day. But evening in London was afternoon on America's East Coast, and somewhere, on the way across the wide Atlantic, one might pass through the sunset, toward a place where August 2 was far from finished: Long Island and, in particular, Nassau Point, languidly stretched under the afternoon sun that shone on Great Peconic Bay. Here, with concern and some reluctance, the most famous scientist in the world was preparing to write a letter to the President of the United States.

Albert Förster and Albert Einstein had only two things in common: the coincidence of their first names and the fact that both were born German. Otherwise, even if they had stood side by side, they could not have been farther apart. Förster delighted in being German; his self-esteem increased each time he thought of the journey he would make to the Berghof the next weekend. He could not understand the theory of relativity, which had made Einstein such an international celebrity; he certainly never gave Copernicus a second thought—Polish intellectuals, past or present, did not interest him. But he did grasp that Einstein could have brought great intellectual luster to Germany, and he would have been glad of that, if only because other nations respected intellectuals. In contrast, Einstein, now fifty years old, found their native country's way of life—"the overemphasized military mentality of the German State"—so repressive that even as a teenager, he had decided to change his nationality and become Swiss. The deed had been done as soon as he had reached adulthood. Worse: For many years thereafter, he had been an outspoken pacifist. Either that or his change of nationality would have been enough to make him contemptible to a man like Förster. But worse still: After much soul-searching, Einstein had renounced pacifism to speak publicly against Hitler and Nazism—the man and the system that had given Förster his pride and position. And worst of all, Einstein was, of course, Jewish—an *untermensch,* subhuman. For Albert Förster, that explained everything about Albert Einstein.

Great Peconic Bay covers thirty-five square miles or so in the middle of Long Island. Shelter Island protects it from the Atlantic swell and makes it a wonderful place for leisurely sailing, which was why Einstein had gone there for his vacation from Princeton University; he loved sailing, and at Nassau Point he could also practice the violin in peace. But this afternoon, instead of sailing or playing, he was sitting, pensive and worried, on the veranda of his holiday home. He and his companion, Leo Szilard, had been friends for many years; in 1921, in Berlin, they had jointly invented and patented a refrigerator. The two scientists were strikingly different in appearance. On one side of a small slatted table, Szilard, a stocky, heavy-looking man, was upright, neat and trim, clean-shaven, with short dark hair, wearing a long-sleeved shirt with collar and tie; as a concession to the weather he had at least taken his jacket off. Opposite him, leaning forward, Einstein sat in short sleeves, with his collar open, and puffed on a very long-stemmed pipe; the smoke circled his lined face, his wild white hair, and wooly mustache. With his elbow on his thigh, resting his head on his fist, he gazed at the papers in Szilard's hand, at the bottle of ink, the pen, and the other papers scattered on the table.

Just four miles away across Great Peconic, easily visible from Nassau Point, was Conscience Point. It was an apt name for the scene. Over the past few years, through experiments in England, France, Denmark, Germany, and Italy, the international scientific community had learned how to split atoms and had found that doing so released astoundingly large bursts of energy. Hungarian-born Szilard had been the first to suggest that a chain reaction might occur, and, early in 1939, working with the Italian Enrico Fermi at Columbia University, he had come close to an experimental proof. He and Fermi were both refugees from the politics of Europe; Fermi's wife was Jewish, and in September 1938 anti-Semitic laws had been introduced in Italy. Now both men had realized that the work they had left behind could be developed by the dictatorships they had fled. Perhaps it was only an outside possibility . . . but the Fascists might succeed in building an atomic bomb.

An odd sequence of events had first brought Szilard to Nassau Point. Like Albert Einstein, Queen Elizabeth, the Queen Mother of Belgium, loved the violin. Because of that shared love, they had become firm friends. At Columbia, Szilard and Fermi had conducted their experiments with uranium, since its atoms contained the heaviest and most highly charged nuclei known;

by chance, most of the world's uranium ore came from the
Belgian Congo. Szilard had begun his mission to Nassau Point
in the hope that Einstein would agree to find out if, somehow,
the Queen Mother could prevent Nazi Germany from buying
ore from the Congo.

It seemed an unlikely chain, but the chance of a chain reaction
of uranium nuclei had seemed unlikely, too. Nevertheless,
Szilard was profoundly worried. The stakes were inestimably
high. The idea of Hitler as master of a nuclear bomb was an
unthinkable nightmare. To rely on Einstein's friendship with the
Belgian Queen Mother was too weak a defense, and Szilard had
thought of another approach, more certain of success. Einstein
should write directly to President Roosevelt and warn him of
what might happen.

This was what they were discussing as they sat on the shady
veranda together, and it had placed Einstein in a serious ethical
dilemma. What, he wondered, could the President do? He could
hardly prevent any German experiments; at best he could autho-
rize a research program that might beat the Germans to the goal.
And if so, what kind of a goal was this for a humane pacifist to
recommend? It would create a danger that no one had ever
conceived. On the other hand, could Einstein, understanding
the kind of power that success could give to the Nazis, ignore
Szilard, pat him on the back with a regretful refusal, send him
away, and sail peacefully over the bay? Conscience Point had
come to Nassau.

At last, Einstein agreed to Szilard's request, and together they
drafted the letter, to be sent to the President over Einstein's
signature: "Some recent work by E. Fermi and L. Szilard, which
has been communicated to me in manuscript, leads me to expect
that the element uranium may be turned into a new and important source of energy in the immediate future. Certain aspects of
the situation seem to call for watchfulness and, if necessary,
quick action on the part of the Administration."

Nothing but Einstein's conviction that Nazism was more evil
than war itself could have persuaded him to write this letter. In it,
he explained the sense of duty that impelled him, and warned

that "extremely powerful bombs of a new type" might be constructed: "A single bomb of this type, carried by boat or exploded in a port, might very well destroy the whole port together with some of the surrounding territory." And he added, "I understand that Germany has actually stopped the sale of uranium from the Czechoslavakian mines which she has taken over. That she should have taken such early action might perhaps be understood on the ground that the son of the German Under-Secretary of State, von Weizsäcker, is attached to the Kaiser Wilhelm Institute in Berlin, where some of the American work on uranium is now being repeated."

The letter was signed, the ink blotted; the two scientists shook hands, and, just before he left, Szilard, satisfied and much happier than when he had arrived, reassured Einstein: He had undoubtedly done the right thing. But when Szilard was gone, he seemed to have left some of his first fear and doubt behind him. Heavyhearted, Einstein stared out over the water. It had grown too dark to see Conscience Point. Night must come, even to Great Peconic Bay, and now it was too late for any sailing. He turned sadly indoors and picked up his violin.

2

The earth's a good place

Early in the morning of Thursday, August 3, Kit Dennis's parents clambered into their Austin 16 and set off on their regular excursion to the Corn Exchange in Plymouth. Most of the farmers of the county would gather there once a week to do business, buying and selling produce and livestock; and, while their wives met for tea, the menfolk bargained, with a look at the teeth and an experienced hand on the ribs and legs and backsides of cattle and pigs and horses. Later, as the men settled a deal over a pint in the pub, they talked of crops and workmen and mutual acquaintances: who had died, who was getting married, how the land would be joined or divided; who was doing well and who badly, who might have to sell and who might be able to buy; the cost of feed and, with gasoline at ninepence (17½ cents) a gallon, the cost of cars. They did not gossip — that was for the women — but they did enjoy a businesslike chat.

About the same time, Kapitanleutnant Fresdorf, first staff officer of the U-boat department of Germany's Naval High Command, completed a paper for Kapitän zur See Karl Dönitz. Fresdorf — in the U.S. Navy or the British Royal Navy, he would have been a lieutenant commander — was confident that Captain Dönitz would endorse the paper's analysis of their department's needs. Working closely together, the two officers knew each other's thinking well. Captain Dönitz, forty-seven years old, had been in charge of the U-boat arm of the Reich navy for almost exactly four years. His superiors described him as "an excellent officer of iron will, goal-oriented certainty, and unwearying toughness." Tall, slim, eagle-nosed, with eyes at once alert and wary, Dönitz was a charismatic leader. With unbounded confidence in his boats and their crews, he deliberately fostered in the officers and men the sense of being an elite; and they responded

with fierce loyalty. Under his leadership, the U-boat arm had
grown rapidly, and he was committed to its continued growth —
hence Fresdorf's confidence that his own paper would be welcome. In January, Hitler had approved an ambitious naval staff
plan, the Z Plan, which included a target figure of 249 U-boats
to be built by 1947. After exercises in the spring aimed at
theoretical British supply lines across the Atlantic, Dönitz had
raised that number to 300. Just a month ago, at the beginning of
July, he had introduced a proposal for large "workshop ships" to
be on permanent foreign stations, so that damaged U-boats
could be repaired without having to return to Germany. His
proposal had emphasized that "an essential part of the war
against England will fall to the U-boats in the commerce war,"
and now Fresdorf had taken the analysis further. Fast long-range
boats should be placed off the American coast to follow convoys
as they sailed; attack boats would wait in the eastern Atlantic.
Milk-cow boats, acting as underwater tankers, would replenish
fuel and food stocks, while smaller boats would operate in the
Baltic and the North Sea. The total U-boat fleet required would
be around 500. Such a program would need much money and
time; but, since Dönitz had taken control of the U-boat arm,
money for its development had always been forthcoming, and
there was plenty of time — through Admiral Raeder, Commander-in-Chief of the Navy, Dönitz had received Hitler's personal assurance that war with Britain, if it came at all, would not
come soon. "Do not believe the Führer would bring us into such
a desperate position," Raeder had said after an inspection only
twelve days ago, "for a war with England would mean *Finis
Germania!*" They were naval officers, not politicians; they
accepted the Führer's word without question and happily, for it
meant that they could continue as they were, training, building,
planning. At the moment, Dönitz was away on leave, so Fresdorf
reread the grand proposal and, with a glow of satisfaction, placed
it in the captain's file to await his return.

★　★　★

About half past eleven in the morning, a small, slightly built man arrived at Charing Cross railway station in London. Walking briskly down the Strand and across Trafalgar Square, he soon came to Horse Guards' Road — a pleasant approach to work, running as it did next to Saint James's Park. Few people passing him in the street would have recognized him or paid much attention to him; with his neat mustache, sober suit, rolled umbrella, and soft trilby hat (which he preferred to a bowler), he looked the epitome of a pleasant, undistinguished City business-man. But, under the soft hat, taken off as he entered his office building at 11:40, was the high intelligent forehead of his aristo-cratic background; and in this building, Sir Alexander Cadogan — youngest son of the fifth Earl Cadogan, ex-Eton, ex-Balliol, and thirty-one years in the diplomatic service — was in charge. This was the Foreign Office, and Cadogan was its Perma-nent Under-Secretary of State.

Breaking a holiday at High Corner, his newly bought cottage in East Sussex, he had come up to town in torrential rain ("a very good day to go to London," he said wryly) simply to check on the progress of events. His own Private Secretary had already briefed him on the substance of the talk between Hitler and Lord Kemsley. *Seems to me,* Cadogan had thought when he heard it, *as harmless, and as useless, as most such.*

There is quite a lot that can be said in favor of things that are harmless, even if they are useless; but there is even more in favor of things that are harmless and useful. Teaching the children, serving in shops, simply growing vegetables or delivering the post — these are hardly world-shattering occupations, yet their very innocence makes the world worthwhile. Cadogan had put it well early in April: With spring in the air, the daffodils were out, "and most primroses," he had written in his diary at that time. "Country beginning to look very nice. The earth's a good place, if only Hitler weren't on it!"

* * *

Living with her widowed mother in the Welsh village of Tonna,
Dorothy Williams was a teacher at Cadoxton school, working
with the little ones from four to six years old. She did not actually
like it very much. Before, she had taught drama and art, which
she enjoyed, in another school, which she had liked, to older
girls, whom she had found more rewarding. The sole reason for
the change to Cadoxton was that it was only twenty minutes' walk
down the valley from her mother's home, and her mother —
overweight, with a heart condition and a chronic cough from
bronchial pneumonia — had to be looked after. So it was back to
the three R's. That was tolerable, even satisfying in its way; what
made life so difficult were her colleagues in the staff room. She
tried to fit in but couldn't seem to. Little things: She hated
smoking, but in the breaks everyone else puffed away happily,
expecting to share each other's packs of cigarettes, so, rather than
seem mean or supercilious, she did the same. By itself that was
nothing much; but, all through the summer term, there had been
arguments in the staff room about the prospects of war or
peace — and in those she always ended up isolated. Everyone else
seemed to accept the promise of Munich without reservation —
because, she said, they wanted to. They didn't want it to go wrong,
so they would not let in the idea that it might. Keeping the peace
by incantation, she called it. Of course she wanted peace as much
as anyone, but she thought it was wise to prepare for the worst;
and then they would call her a scaremonger and would laugh,
which made them feel better and her feel foolish. *Dorothy, dear, I
think we'd better just call you Dotty, hadn't we?*

She still flushed at the memory. She had kept back the retort
that sprang to her lips: *You're just like the Monkey People in the*
Jungle Book: *"We all say so, so we must be right."* Instead she had
answered, simply but finally, "Well, I'm sticking to my ideas."
There was no point in being rude in return, and it seemed all
were thankful to drop the subject.

In the village, a few of the older people who had lived through
the Great War believed another would come and that it would be
very different. She had listened to them, and when she was asked
if and how she would help "in the event of war," the phrase had

both frightened and excited her. And there was one thing that she could do very well that might be useful: She could speak Welsh. Perhaps it was going a bit far to imagine a German invasion, but perhaps not. That was a chilling thought. Yet if an invasion came, there would be a resistance, and whatever the Germans spoke, it was not likely to be Welsh. "In the event of war," then, Dorothy had a job: to take messages in a language an invader could not understand.

She could not imagine what it might be like, and in her more confident moments it did sound almost childishly cloak-and-dagger. But at least she knew that, in the direst of emergencies, she could help a little and that she was ready. By itself, that calmed her, and, when the term ended, she embarked on the holidays with a lighter heart. Though she would not be going away, there was much to do that she enjoyed – blackberrying, making jam, perhaps picnicking on the beach at Aberavon, dancing at the Empire Ballroom in Neath . . . Except when she met someone of like mind, when suddenly she would be overtaken by apprehension, her thoughts of war receded. There might be no man in her life just yet, but there were many friends; she was never lonely, and August was a happy month.

So it was for Molly McAndrew as well, and not least because of Ernie Brown. She was just twenty-one, he was almost twenty-three; for two years they had been engaged to be married, and sometime very soon they would decide on a date. Molly had been a late and only child, born when her mother, now a widow, was already forty-seven. Like the Williamses in Wales, the McAndrews in Newcastle lived together, but without the sense of duty; it was simply convenient for everyone, until Molly and Ernie finally got married. Then the newlyweds would have a fine modern council flat, for Ernie's work as a pattern maker brought good money – three guineas ($14.27) a week. Between them, Molly and her mother had less than two guineas a week coming in: Molly earned one ($4.75) for her work at Woolworth's store, while her mother had fifteen shillings ($3.51) 'from her widow's pension and another five shillings ($1.17)' from her work as a washerwoman in a Chinese laundry.

The hours at Woolworth's were long — from 9:00 in the morning until 7:00 P.M. Monday to Thursday and until 8:00 P.M. on Friday and 9:00 P.M. on Saturday — but Molly enjoyed the bustle. She was a strikingly beautiful young woman, and the red zip-up uniform set off her dark hair well. She was proud of that uniform, with its motto "FWW — I'm one of Woolworth's girls," and her appearance and liveliness made her popular with the customers. The store, Ernie and his boat — a converted lifeboat called the *Monarch* — her mother and their cramped little tenement flat: These made up the major part of her life, and she was happy with them all. The world beyond Newcastle hardly intruded. Mrs. Blair, who lived in the ground-floor tenement below the McAndrews, had a wireless and would sometimes come breathlessly up, summoning them to hear some news; very occasionally, if they could afford it, they bought a newspaper. On those days, or if someone else bought a paper, it would be passed from house to house up and down the streets — no point in everyone buying their own when its news would soon be old. Otherwise, all Molly knew of world events came from newsreels in the cinema, and they did not worry her at all. All that about the Germans taking over Austria last year — it was far away, unreal. They had done the same last March with Czechoslovakia. What a name! She could barely get her tongue round it, and, though she had seen the maps, she still did not really know where it was and did not especially want to know. When she did think about it, she felt quite safe, because one thing she knew for certain was that Britain was an island. But still she could pretend to be frightened, sometimes, just for fun; then, knowing perfectly well it was only an excuse to cuddle her, Ernie would tell her not to worry: He would go out in the *Monarch* and drive the Germans off, if ever they dared approach the coast. And she would say how brave he was, and they would ignore the goose-stepping soldiers on the screen.

It was all a matter of how much you wanted to know, how much or how little you cared — or dared — to imagine. In Bressay, far away in the Shetlands, the Anderson family was better informed of events than was Molly in urban Newcastle. Despite its imposing name, suggesting the sprawling one-time residence of a church minister, the Old Manse was a simple croft, a tiny farmhouse typical of the islands: two rooms "but and ben" (one at the front and one at the back of the house) with two attic bedrooms for guests. Normally Lollie, the island postman, his brothers Tommy and Willie, and their father were on their own there, but just now the place was full to bursting; five of the family were visiting, on holiday from the isle of Foula. There was Lizzie, one of Tommy and Lollie's sisters; her husband, Willie Smith; and their three daughters, Stella, Nanette, and Jessamine. Those were good names — uncommon, quickly remembered, and distinguished. Often, because so many Christian names and surnames were alike and so many of the Shetlanders were related, one way or another, it became easiest to have nicknames. Three men, for example, living within 200 yards of each other and all named Alec, were better known as Muckle Alec, Peerie Alec (his adult son), and Square Alec, unrelated to the others, very muscular, and as wide as he was high. Likewise, Lollie's brother Tommy was named after their father; and always, when someone got married, some of the new relatives' names would match those of the existing family. Lizzie's man, Willie, for instance when they wed, there was already another Anderson brother called Willie. This brother, at least, was away fishing just now, which was as well, considering the numbers crammed into the house.

All, Andersons and Smiths, were true islanders: The "mainland" for them was Shetland's major island; anywhere else in Great Britain was simply "south." Foula, four miles long and a mile wide, was the most westerly of the island group; after its precipitous western face, the 1,200-foot vertical cliff called the Kame, there was nothing except Atlantic Ocean all the way to America. It was remote even by Shetland standards, and, when the Smiths made their annual trek back to Bressay, they were always greeted with "Well, my dears, and are you come ashore again?"

In terms of money, they were no better off than the McAndrews in their Newcastle slum. But at the Old Manse they

were able to dig their own peat for fuel, they could raise vegetables, and they had two cows that gave good milk. It was all much
smaller and far poorer than Kit Dennis's farm in Devon, but it left
a little money over, so they had a wireless, which the McAndrews
had not, and they bought the *Shetland News* regularly. Above all,
they were voracious readers, people of inquiring minds, curious
about the world and its goings on. Everything they heard and
read about the world that summer, however, was utterly depressing. Lollie and Tommy talked of the future, and, as their four-
teen-year-old niece Stella listened, she found it sinister and
disturbing. "This'll be the end of everything," they said, and she
believed them literally. Armageddon was coming, the end of the
world. But she was a stoic and sensible girl; privately refusing to
let her fear show, she decided that, with her mother's help, she
would have time to finish the dress she was making.

★   ★   ★

Cadogan's appointment with the Foreign Secretary, Lord
Halifax, had produced little. They had met at noon, when
Cadogan heard again details of Lord Kemsley's interview with
Hitler. Herr Hitler was asking once more for British requirements to be put down on paper; the Foreign Secretary and
Under-Secretary agreed that he, not they, should be the one to
put something in writing first and that Kemsley could act as go-
between again with Otto Dietrich, the German Press Bureau
chief. Halifax was also much exercised about the Far East, where,
for the past two years, Japanese forces had been waging
undeclared war on China. Since the end of 1938, they had
occupied most of northern and central China and would have
gone further but for British and American aid to China's recognized ruler, Chiang Kai-shek. Six months ago they had occupied
Hainan Island, only 250 miles from Hong Kong; less than three
weeks ago they had begun blockading the British Concession in
Tientsin. The Concession — there was another in Canton — was
an area leased in perpetuity to the British Government for trade.
Around 600 Britons lived there and were now more or less

captive; the few who were allowed out had been humiliated by being stripped and searched in public. Two Royal Navy escort vessels sent to the area had had little effect, and Chamberlain had come very close to a de facto recognition of Japanese rule in China.

"We can probably go quite a long way on police, the neutrality of the Concessions, and so on," said Halifax to Cadogan. "What about currency and silver, though? What do we do when we get on to them?"

"Stall," Cadogan answered at once. "We shall have to. And in the end, we can't give way."

"I agree. I'll talk to the P.M. about it again. Meanwhile, there's Russia. Yes, I know — there always is," said Halifax as Cadogan grimaced. "We may neither of us like the idea, but it's becoming clear that a pact of some sort will have to take place; and at least Neville has stopped saying he'll resign rather than be Russia's ally. So the next step is to get the military talks going alongside the political — three men each for our mission and the French, and whoever the Russians want to put up for themselves."

Cadogan knew the three British officers selected. "Drax, Burnett, and Heywood," he murmured — an admiral, an air marshall, and a major general. "Drax is . . . unstimulating, really. Burnett certainly knows air strategy, and Heywood speaks French and German. It's a pity we don't have more people who speak Russian."

"Can't be helped. Anyway, it may be helpful — so much the easier to take the conversations slowly. As for their transport, they obviously can't go by rail, since that would mean going through Germany. They could fly, but there is no suitable aircraft available. The Admiralty doesn't want to give up a cruiser, although it might impress our Bolshevik friends, so," Halifax concluded, "they've decided to charter a liner — *City of Exeter,* I believe. Maximum speed twelve knots."

"That means it's bound to take them the better part of a week to get there."

The Foreign Secretary nodded, and Cadogan noticed how tired he looked. Knowing there was nothing more to talk of in foreign affairs, he changed the subject: "Will you be having a holiday? You could do with one."

"Well . . ." Halifax sighed, "I don't anticipate a real break."

"No, you *must* have one. In fact, if I were your doctor, I'd order you to. I can't tell you how well a bit of time off has set me up again."

"I don't doubt it." Halifax sighed again. "Yorkshire, Yorkshire — of course it's tempting. Well, we shall see."

★ ★ ★

Vyacheslav Molotov, the Soviet People's Commissar for Foreign Affairs, was just then busy extending an unexpectedly warm welcome to Count Friedrich von der Schulenburg. The German ambassador to Moscow was gratified and encouraged: When he had asked to visit Molotov the day before, he had been refused — Comrade Molotov was attending the Soviet Agricultural Exhibition. It was a splendid show, covering 350 acres and dominated by two enormous statues. One, on a tower at the entrance, showed a tractor driver and a peasant woman holding on high an immense sheaf of corn; the other, in pink stone — the nearest natural color to red — was of Stalin. Appropriately, it was even larger than the statue honoring the workers.

However, it was not because of any good mood engendered by the heavily symbolic celebration that Molotov felt ready to welcome von der Schulenburg; the Commissar was not a man to be swayed by moods. With a round head, thick black mustache, slightly receding hair, and, behind spectacles, eyes that seemed to understand everything and everyone he saw, he looked like the genial doctor who should have sent Halifax on holiday. He was skilled in speech, imperturbable in behavior — and completely ruthless. All were qualities essential for survival and success under Stalin's rule. Less than three months earlier, Maxim Litvinov — Molotov's predecessor in office — had been dismissed ("sacked like a maid caught stealing," Litvinov said bitterly, "without so much as a day's notice"). Molotov considered that Litvinov and his wife Ivy had been fortunate only to be relegated to the status of "unpersons"; it was more usual for high officials suddenly out of favor to be equally suddenly dead. The new Commissar understood perfectly the reasons for that dismissal: Litvinov, a Jew married to an Englishwoman, was too much in favor of Britain, too much opposed to Germany, to deal in a detached manner with either. For his own part, Molotov knew that any such personal feelings were to be quashed; they could damage the interests of the Party and the Motherland. Today, therefore, he would be cordial toward the Count.

★   ★   ★

While Lord Halifax thought wistfully of taking time off in Yorkshire, Dr. Claud Kennerley was there, doing exactly that. Thursday afternoons were his one half-day off each week from the constant duty of attending to people's coughs, colds, and broken bones. He was a man with a pronounced sense of duty — sometimes, thought his wife Eleanor, too pronounced. Of course, most general practitioners faced the same kind of draining work that Claud did: available twice daily in the office, morning and evening; visits to patients' homes throughout the afternoon; and any kind of emergency from childbirth to car crashes at any time, day or night. But to that, because of his sense of duty, he added his work in the Territorial Army, as Medical Officer for the Fifth Battalion of the York and Lancasters. He was a major now; he had joined in 1934, before they had married. "Just felt I ought to be able to contribute a bit more," he had said to her, almost apologetically. "I mean, one never knows, of course, but one hears these things from Germany . . ." It was the year after Hitler had come to power. "The thing is, if I'm ever needed, it would obviously be better if I had some training, at least. You do see, don't you?" She did, but she agreed with him fervently when he added, "Of course, one hopes I'll never be needed in that way at all." Once, recently, when he had been particularly tired and still had another evening at the drill hall to go through before what would probably be a broken night, she had asked him if he ever thought about giving up. "Think about it?" he had said with a wry smile, standing in front of the mirror as she brushed his uniform jacket. "Only about five times a week." She glanced at him with a sudden small hope, then he added vaguely, "But one couldn't, really — not yet, anyway . . ."

Understanding him perfectly, Eleanor knew she had not truly expected any other answer and that she would not ask him again; so, straightening his already straight tie, she kissed him and let him go.

She helped him and protected him in many ways. Before they married, she had trained to be a dispenser (passing her exams, as she liked to tell people, when she was coming down with chicken pox and going to a royal garden party the same day — happily, she had never heard of any of the royal family falling ill afterward). Now their house on the outskirts of Rotherham was also their workplace, a square dwelling designed by one of her uncles, an architect, to fit their needs exactly. At 8:30 each morning, the front two rooms, waiting room and office, were open, and the patients began arriving — farmers, miners, children, steelworkers; people who contributed to a panel fund, a simple form of insurance; unemployed people on parish relief, their medicines paid for from local funds; the poor employed, who might have to spread payment of their bill over several months at a few pence a week. They were the ones she felt sorriest for. She did not feel sorry for the private patients, the solicitors and company directors, and certainly not for their wives. Those who lived in the large houses with big gardens in Moorgate — "the Devil's mile" — had quite frightened her at first. Somehow they seemed especially fierce and powerful, all gunning for each other, competitive and ambitious. The class divisions of the community were plain and deep. Sometimes, outside Mason's, the main jewelers in Rotherham, she would see the distinctive Rolls Royce, black and yellow with wickerwork doors, that belonged to Lord Fitzwilliam's family. She did not begrudge them the beautiful vehicle; but, ever since she had been with Claud to visit a miner with pneumonia, she had wondered sadly at the gulf. That visit had taken place in winter, and the man had lain visibly steaming in bed — his fever was so high, his blankets so sodden with sweat, and his house so icy cold.

Even if Eleanor and Claud went out to a film of an evening, he might still be called out from the cinema, so they had quickly determined that Thursday afternoons must be sacred: absolutely no calls — instead, golf. It might, of course, be gardening or paying social visits, but Claud was as good at golf as at doctoring.

By 4:00 British time, the discussion in Moscow between the Count and the Commissar had ended. In London, Sir Horace Wilson — head of His Majesty's Civil Service and one of the few men whose advice Chamberlain had sought during the Munich crisis — was just beginning an equally secret conversation with Ambassador Herbert von Dirksen. Claud Kennerley and his old friend and regular partner Bill Elmhurst were waiting at the seventh green on the Thrybergh course, hoping that a rather slow pair ahead of them might let them play through. And, at the same time, in Haus Wahnfried, Wagner's old home in Bayreuth, two other old friends were meeting for only the second time in thirty years: August Kubizek and Adolf Hitler.

Kubizek was escorted by an SS officer. When he saw them, Hitler came forward, took Kubizek's hand in both of his, and said with real pleasure, "Gustl!" It was the nickname he had invented in 1905. "I am happy we have met once more on this spot — it was always the most venerable place for us both." They had first met in their teens, when a shared passion for opera had drawn them together. August was a talented musician, then hoping to make his living through music; Adolf ("a pale, skinny youth," August remembered) had read him his poetry and confessed his wish to be an artist. Now one was Führer of the Third Reich; the other was town clerk of Eferding. Kubizek was so overcome with emotion, he could scarcely say a word. Very shyly, he produced some postcards depicting Hitler: Would the Führer consent to sign them, for friends at home in Austria? Of course he would! Pausing only to check that no photographers were present, Hitler donned his reading glasses, sat down, and on card after card scrawled his angular autograph.

3

The keys of peace and war

At thirty-six years of age, Galeazzo Ciano, Count of Cortellazzo, found it easy to turn women's heads. He was vain enough to believe himself very handsome and confident enough with the opposite sex to exploit every opportunity that arose, especially outside Italy—in spite of having been married for six years. A well-built body, brooding eyes, and a sensual mouth helped him in his conquests, as did his association with power. His wife Edda was the daughter of Italy's national leader, the Duce Benito Mussolini, and since 1933 Count Ciano had been his Foreign Minister. From America came the sarcastic comment: "The son-in-law also rises."

Mussolini had taken power in Italy in 1922, the year he now spoke of as the first of the Fascist era. Adolf Hitler—then regarded as little more than the rabble-rousing leader of a minority political party—had admired the Duce's aims and methods and had sought to imitate them in Germany. The attempt had landed him in jail. But, since 1933, when National Socialism legally and legitimately had become Germany's ruling creed—and still more since 1934, when Hitler, again legally and legitimately, had become Führer, Reich Chancellor, and supreme commander of the three armed forces of Germany—it had become more and more clear which of the two would be the senior partner, so to speak, in a Fascist Europe.

Time was, just after Hitler had come to power, when Mussolini's gorgeous uniform and confident bearing contrasted embarrassingly with the Führer's uncertainty and shabby, ill-kempt appearance. Time was, too, when Mussolini publicly denounced Hitler as leader of a country of murderers and pederasts, declaring that, despite their superficial similarities, Italian Fascism and German Nazism could not be compared.

Fascism, he had said in 1934, was rooted in the Italian people's cultural tradition, recognizing religion, family, and the rights of the individual. "National Socialism, on the other hand, is savage barbarism: In common with barbarian hordes, it allows no rights to the individual; the chieftain is lord over life and death of his people. Murder and killing, loot and pillage and blackmail are all it can produce."

By the spring of 1939, however, that kind of rhetoric was only a memory. True, Italian forces had occupied Albania that March and Abyssinia two years earlier. The Albanian occupation had been relatively straightforward, but the Abyssinian had involved long hard fighting and much bloodshed, even though the only opposition had come from Emperor Haile Selassie's small, poorly armed, and ill-trained army. Italians admitted privately that it had not been the smooth, spectacular display of might for which they had hoped. In contrast, the Rhineland border area between France and Germany, demilitarized by the Versailles Treaty, had been occupied by German troops; Austria had been incorporated into the Reich; Czechoslovakia had been dismembered when its German-speaking area, the Sudetenland, had been taken over, and all those acquisitions had been gained without fighting. The Duce could only remark resentfully, "Every time Hitler occupies a country, he sends me a message."

At the beginning of August 1939, Mussolini still hoped that he might play a crucial role in the immediate future of Europe. War might not be avoided indefinitely, but it had to be staved off for at least three years if Italy was to be ready; so the Duce, who had figured in the Munich agreement between Hitler and Chamberlain, proposed a world peace conference. At the same time, Ciano began to think that perhaps he should have another meeting with Joachim von Ribbentrop, Hitler's Foreign Minister, to try and find out exactly what was going on. Late in May, they had signed an agreement with a resounding title — the Pact of Steel — which said, among other things, that each would inform the other in advance of any international events that might endanger the other's national interests. Since then there had been a stream of insistent messages from the Italian ambassador in Berlin to the effect that Hitler was planning something drastic for August 15. But not a word had come from von Ribbentrop, and Ciano cheerfully reckoned that "either the ambassador has lost his head, or he sees and knows something that has completely escaped us. Appearances are in favor of the first alternative."

By Friday, August 4, however, the glamorous young count was starting to feel much less optimistic: "The situation seems obscure to me . . . . The moment has come when we must really know how matters stand."

★   ★   ★

Sixteen years previously, in 1923, the then king of Great Britain, George V, had paid a state visit to the Italian king, Victor Emmanuel III. King George had taken this opportunity to create Signor Mussolini a Knight Grand Cross of the Order of the Bath, Britain's second highest order of knighthood. During the same year, the Duke of York, King George's second son, had married Lady Elizabeth Bowes-Lyon. Now no longer Lady Elizabeth or Duchess of York, she would never forget the trauma of 1936: the death of the old king, the accession of his eldest son as Edward VIII, the crisis when Edward would not give up his decision to marry an American divorcée. No monarch could marry a divorced person. The only alternative, an extraordinarily painful and shocking experience for everyone, was Edward's abdication, and so—unexpectedly, unwillingly, but unavoidably—the Duke and Duchess of York had become Their Majesties King George VI and Queen Elizabeth.

That alone had made history, and in the summer of 1939 the royal couple had been the center of another historic event: During June they had visited the United States, the first king and queen of Great Britain ever to do so. At the beginning of the year, when the dates of the visit had been announced, the writer H.G. Wells had dismissed it as "of very small importance" and had been equally offhand about the "young people": "I believe, a very charming couple, constantly smiling and bowing, but they mean absolutely nothing in the problems of today." On both counts, he was wrong. When the king had decided to go, Prime Minister Neville Chamberlain was still trying to cope through appeasement with the difficulties being created by Germany, buying the Führer off with one agreement after another. Yet, in the face of those same difficulties, one of the king's principal motives in visiting the States had been to strengthen the relationship between Britain and America. Hardly the behavior of an out-of-touch young man; and the visit had been a terrific success. Of course, many Americans had felt suspicious — they could hardly have felt otherwise when their ancestors had fought for liberty against an English king — but few of them could refuse their national instinct for being hospitable or resist the queen's equally instinctive charm. "You've been here about four minutes," Mayor La Guardia's secretary told her, "and all New York is in love with you." And as they had driven through the city, surrounded by cheering crowds estimated at three and a half million people, the mayor had reckoned that their coming had done more good than sending a dozen ambassadors or swapping fifty diplomatic notes. "In fact," he had said to the king in delight, "you've negotiated a treaty of friendship that will take many years to revoke."

"Very kind of you to say so," His Majesty had replied — an understated answer, for he was deeply pleased.

At home, George and Elizabeth were becoming a very public king and queen, setting a new pattern for British royalty; but even they had their days of privacy, and August 4 was one of them. On that Friday, as Galeazzo Ciano thought uneasily about Ribbentrop, the British royal family — father, mother, and their two daughters, Princesses Elizabeth and Margaret, aged thirteen and ten — were on holiday in the peaceful seclusion of Balmoral Castle. Above the castle to the south, Balmoral Forest's dark shades rose up the slopes of the Grampians. Below it to the north ran the river Dee, and beyond the river the Cairngorm Mountains began their climb 4,000 feet and more into the Highland sky. Before the war was over, Princess Elizabeth would be serving as a mechanic and truck driver in the Auxiliary Transport Service. Today, however, she and her little sister had something far more important to think about: It was their mother's thirty-ninth birthday.

* * *

In London, Parliament adjourned at 4:00, and ministers and members dispersed. At the same time, Nicholas Winton began considering again the likely fate of several hundred people much younger and less publicly prominent than the queen or any politician. With the business of the day done, he had gone directly from his office in the City of London to another in Bloomsbury. The making of money was over for the week; work was not. Each evening — and it had been going on like this for the past eight months — he stopped only when he was too tired to make any more sense.

His background was as unusual as his unpaid evening work. His family had originally come from Germany and until only a year ago had been called Wertheim — a very obviously Jewish name. But they were thoroughly British: His grandfather had become a naturalized British citizen, had converted to Christianity, and had served as British Consul in Moscow before the revolution. Nevertheless, during the Great War they had often been ostracized in England — by Jews because they had abandoned the faith, by Christians because they were converts, and by Britons generally because of the German ring to their name. Their decision to change their name to the more English-sounding Winton had been a direct result of Chamberlain's peace mission to Munich. There had been an upside-down kind of logic to it: Had he returned with a message of war, they would have stayed Wertheim and put up with the same suspicion they had endured in 1914–18; they were not cowards. But all of them — especially Nicky, who worked on the Stock Exchange as a specialist in South African trade — were tired of the worn-out old jokes about Jews, and before the prime minister had left for Germany, they had decided that, if he brought back a promise of peace, it would be as good a time as any to leave the past behind.

No one could say, then, that they had done it because they were afraid.

Nor, indeed, could anyone say truthfully that Nicky Winton's present work sprang from his Jewish ancestry. Certainly, in Germany he would have been classified Jewish by race, and 85 percent of the names on the list he was reading were Jewish, but his motive was simply humanitarian: to help in the evacuation of threatened children from Nazi-occupied Czechoslovakia.

Late one Tuesday evening just before Christmas 1938, he had arrived in Prague, bewildered, not knowing what to expect: He should have been skiing in Switzerland. He had canceled that trip at the last minute after a phone call from a friend, Martin Blake, who had merely said he was on a most interesting assignment and needed Nicky's help. Since then, the "assignment" had developed into a job filling every spare hour.

Together, Martin and Nicky had seen for themselves the crowds of refugees — Communists, Jews, gypsies, intellectuals, and many who were simply frightened — who had come from Germany, Austria, and the Sudetenland. Organizations already existed for the evacuation of adults — Martin worked for one, the British Committee for Refugees from Czechoslovakia. But no system had been established to bring children to safety. Martin had asked Nicky to set one up, and he had accepted.

Ever since, he had been dazed by the size of the task he had taken on. In Prague, the worst moments — and they had occurred every day — were when he had to explain to distraught parents that safety for their children meant separation, with no guarantee of when or even if they would be reunited. Trying to solve their awful plight had been so absorbing that, until there had been only four days of his "holiday" left, he had forgotten he must go back. Thereupon he had written to his firm, asking for an extension; now, in August, he still had the senior partner's reply, dated January 9.

"Dear Winton," it had said, "I have just returned today to the City after a nice holiday at my new Villa in the South of France. There is very little doing in the Kaffir market, but I would sooner you were taking a rest here, rather than doing heroic work for thousands of poor devils who are suffering through no fault of their own . . . . I still think Western Holdings will go lower — probably West Wits and Western Reef also. There is so much new capital required, both in South and West Africa, that there is little chance of good markets while all this fresh money has to be found." And it had ended: "We hope you may be able to get back to the office here by next Monday. With best wishes for the New Year, and may it be more profitable than the last."

The letter still infuriated him. When he felt charitable, he could say the man simply had no imagination; he had not seen, as Nicky had in Prague, the endless queues of desperate families. He had not seen the map predicting the rise of Greater Germany from 1938 to 1948, detailing step by step the projected acquisition of Austria, Czechoslovakia, Hungary, Poland, Yugoslavia, Rumania, northern France and the Low Countries, eastern Russia, and at last the whole continent of Europe, including Britain. He had not read the printed letter from the commandant of the concentration camp at Weimar-Buchenwald — "The date when the detainee will be released has not yet been determined. Visits to the camp are forbidden. Inquiries are useless" — or seen the letters postmarked with the swastika and the message *Wir sind frei* — We are free.

Perhaps it was only that: Perhaps the man had no imagination at all. But, in his more critical moments, Nicky Winton suspected that the truth was that his employer just did not care in the least; there was no money to be made in evacuating children.

Nevertheless, more than 500 had been brought out now, some to Sweden, most to England; some to caring guarantors, some to homes that offered little more than a roof over their heads; children of all ages, from three to eighteen, the older ones knowing they might never see their natural parents again; all still frightened, confused, and lonely — but all, at least, safe. Whatever happened to them in their foster homes, it was certainly better than the alternative, the concentration camps. Yet God only knew how many more there might be waiting to come out, how many might follow, or how much time might remain . . . Well, at any rate the weekend was beginning, and, on Bank Holiday Monday,

the Stock Exchange would be closed. He could work in Bloomsbury House for three full days.

*   *   *

"A quarter of a century ago today, we were closing our first day of
war." On Saturday, August 5, the leading article in the *South
Wales Evening Post* was meditative and defiant. Victory had been
won in the Great War, but "all in vain, it seems: Embattled as
never before, the nations march and countermarch under a sky
dark and sultry with thunderclouds and lit by summer lightning.
Halifax may be guarded, Inskip" — the chairman of the Committee of Imperial Defense — "may be optimistic, but the British
common man has long determined that there is but one man
who holds the keys of peace and war, and that is Adolf Hitler,
who can keep his own secrets." Recalling the Munich crisis —
"that dire week in last September, when a sense of horror
surcharged the air and there was a public instinct that we had
been caught unarmoured" — the article ended uncom-
promisingly: "No more surrender; our backs are to the wall in
European issues, and our strength is mobilized, yet far from its
summit."

What a load of nonsense, thought Tom Elliott. To him, a seven-
teen-year-old tinplate worker, the promise of Munich seemed
perfectly secure. Turning the pages of the newspaper's lunchtime
edition he snorted at the photograph of "youth's example in ARP
work" — Swansea Boy Scouts helping to box gas masks for delivery to householders. "Look at this, Da," he said to his father.
"Make you look like a real monster, those do. And the ones for
the kiddies, with the Mickey Mouse ears, they're even worse.
Wouldn't be seen dead in one myself."

"Might be seen dead without it, boy," his father replied.
"When we get issued with them, you'll carry yours like everyone
else, and like it."

Tom grunted disdainfully and continued flicking through the
paper. Three dead, five injured in holiday train smash in Salt-
coats. And where was that? Somewhere in Scotland — long way

off. Inside prospects for the Denbigh National Eisteddfod: a vintage year for poetry expected. So it should be; Wales always led the world in poetry. Jazz band concert and fete this afternoon, given by the British Legion in the castle grounds at Oystermouth . . . Ah — the Castle cinema: "Boris Karloff is back in *The Mystery of Mr. Wong.*"

He closed the paper. "Right, Da, I'm off out. Going to the pictures."

"Call in at the Town Hall on your way, if you can," his father said. "You might pick up a few gas masks while you're passing."

* * *

At 2:13 P.M. British Summer Time, a 23½-ton Caribou flying boat belonging to Imperial Airways took off from Southampton Water, curved westward, and roared over the Solent. Inside were bags of parcels and letters. If it succeeded in its 3,500-mile flight, it would be the first-ever British transatlantic air-mail service. In Europe, less than one hour later, Albert Förster, Gauleiter of Danzig, arrived at the Berghof and was in conference with Hitler; and, in Danzig itself, Marjan Chodacki was coming to the end of one of the most trying weeks of his life.

Danzig's positions, geographical and political, were curious in the extreme. The area designated as the "Free City" was about thirty miles west to east, about twenty-five north to south. Its eastern border divided it from the German province of East Prussia; its western border divided it from Poland — or at least from territory that, since the end of the Great War, had been Polish: the contentious Corridor. Yet only twenty-five miles further west was the Corridor's border with the rest of Germany. The narrow slice of land was Poland's only direct outlet to the sea; the port of Gdynia, where the Olszolwskis lived, ten miles up the coast from Danzig, was newly built for the express purpose of channeling Polish exports and imports to and from the rest of the world. Ruled by a senate under the guardianship of the League of Nations, Danzig itself — or Gdansk — was legally neither Polish nor German. Both nations therefore maintained customs officials on their borders with the city and diplomatic representatives in it. Marjan Chodacki was Poland's representative, but in the Free City he often felt himself to be a minority of one. Ninety percent of its population of 400,000 were German; most, led by Albert Förster, were members of the Nazi party; the senate, not surprisingly, was dominated by Nazis; and, since the beginning of the week, they had been exchanging angry notes with Chodacki on the subject of customs barriers.

Here was the crux of all the rising European tensions of the year. Danzig was German in virtually every way except geographically, and that was an artificial separation, only twenty years old. Should it now remain a Free City, or should it be reincorporated into the Reich? In Germany and the Danzig senate the answer was, naturally and emphatically, yes to the latter; in Poland, equally emphatically, no — and equally naturally, for, in practical terms, Danzig's free status was inseparable from Poland's independence.

Before Hitler's annexation of the Sudetenland had taken place, the same arguments had applied for the Czechoslovakians and the Germans. The reincorporation of the German-populated Sudetenland had seemed common sense in Berlin; in Prague, it had promised the destruction of the nation, which, like Poland, had only been independent for twenty years. The country's independence had been guaranteed by France and Britain if the country became the subject of unprovoked aggression; when German troops had taken over the Sudetenland on March 15, war between the guarantors and Germany had only been avoided because both France and Britain had chosen to accept that the annexation — and the immediate loss of independence for the rest of Czechoslovakia — had resulted from a legal Czechoslovak request. But the takeover had also made absolutely plain to Chamberlain and to Édouard Daladier, the French Prime Minister, that Hitler could not be trusted one inch; for, in spirit if not in letter, he had shattered their agreement at Munich.

Had he waited, Czechoslovakia would have become German territory anyway. But, though he had not used force, he had used the threat of force, thoroughly and effectively, to bully the Czech leadership into submission, and thus the time of appeasement had abruptly ended. British and French guarantees of independence were issued to Poland, and this time everyone accepted that they would be honored. Everyone, that is, except Hitler.

Under other circumstances, the customs dispute in Danzig would have seemed ridiculous. When the House of Commons was debating its own adjournment, Arthur Greenwood, deputy leader of the Labour party, had remarked, "No one is going to pretend that Danzig at the present time is a pleasant seaside holiday resort." In fact, to outward appearances, it was swarming with tourists — at least 6,000 had arrived in the past few weeks. But, oddly enough, they were all men, they were all German, and none of them was leaving. This was because they were all stormtroopers. Theoretically, the Free City was demilitarized, but arms, ammunition, and military vehicles from Germany were pouring in virtually unchecked; the "tourists" were physically preventing the Polish customs officials from carrying out their work.

In protest, Chodacki had told the senate that, if harassment did not stop, his customs officers would cease clearing the city's duty-free exports of margarine and herrings to Poland — a more potent threat than it sounded, for those two products accounted for one-sixth of Danzig's revenue. The senate had replied that, in that case, on Sunday morning they would open the border to East Prussia and stop the Polish officials from checking anything at all; whereupon Chodacki had responded that, if they did not withdraw that order before Saturday evening, the Polish Government would commence immediate reprisals.

The senate could work out the consequences. During Parliament's adjournment debate, Arthur Greenwood had stressed Danzig's delicate balance. If "one of the great personages of Europe" (and everyone knew whom he meant) happened to be suffering from a bad liver and heard that half a dozen German subjects in the Free City had been shot, "it only needs such a situation for the world to be at war within twenty-four hours."

On Saturday afternoon, in the grounds of Balmoral Castle, King George and Queen Elizabeth were giving a tea party for

200 boys from the King's Annual Boys' Camp. Each year the queen noticed how even the shyest of the boys relaxed when confronted with a table of orange squash, cake, and sandwiches. While the children were happily tucking in, the Danzig senate (with extremely bad grace) canceled its order, telling Chodacki that he must have misunderstood, that a joke had been played on him. He knew then that, with a mixture of bluff and bravery, he had won a round. But he knew, too, perhaps better than anyone else, that Arthur Greenwood's remark was correct: The world had been within a day of war. If that was the senate's idea of a joke, Chodacki could only say that they had a very German sense of humor.

4

Holiday time, ladies and gentlemen!

Sunday, the sixth of August: the Feast of the Transfiguration. It was a warm dry morning in England, the sky overcast. In the church of Saint Philip Neri's, in Mansfield, Oscar Baker and his elder sister Theresa sat in reverent silence and listened to the first reading—chapter one of the second epistle general of Saint Peter. *"Carissimi: non doctas fabulas secuti fecimus vobis Domini nostri Jesu Christi . . ."*

High Mass, sung in Latin, was the most satisfying of all the services, and especially so on a day like today, marking one of the most important events in the life of Christ. There was also a practical reason for Oscar and Theresa to be glad of the rest and restoration they found in the church: This morning, as they did each Sunday, brother and sister had walked five miles from their home village of Rainsworth to be there. Even with the best will in the world—and particularly on such a warm morning—they found it tiring. As the reading continued, Oscar let his mind drift peacefully. He liked Saint Philip Neri's; its services, like any in the Roman Catholic church, gave him a sense of stability, continuity; he felt in touch with the earliest roots of Christendom, hearing the ancient words that generation on generation had spoken and sung before him. And the physical church itself, the building in which he sat, embodied the lasting strength of that tradition, for it was virtually brand new. Modeled on an Italian church, its design had won a special papal award; now it was only thirteen years old. It occurred to Oscar that the building was just a year younger than he was—which made it all the more *his* church, spiritual and temporal.

"Cui bene facitis attendentes . . ." The end of the reading came like a gentle rebuke—"you do well to attend"—followed imme-

diately by a comfort: "as to a light that shineth in a dark place, until the day dawn and the day star arise in your heart."

Theresa was already on her feet for the response to the Graduale; today it was Psalm 44. Oscar stood up hastily and cleared his throat. Behind him there was a muted rumble, a heavy shuffling—of course; he'd forgotten the soldiers. For the past four or five weeks they'd been turning up regularly from a camp or garrison close by. There were usually a couple of dozen, always filling the two back pews. Being closer to the front, he found it easy to forget them, but there were two things he liked about them. One (he could hear it now) was how their deep male voices added beautifully to the singing, and the other was that they always left their weapons in the vestibule—a respectful thing to do, he thought.

* * *

The steamship *City of Exeter* proceeded at a sedate pace across an almost calm North Sea. Ivan Maisky, Soviet ambassador in London, had come down to Tilbury to see the combined Anglo-French delegation on its way. It occurred to Admiral Drax that it was almost as if Maisky wanted to make sure they were actually going.

Their route to Russia went near Drax's old stomping ground—they passed the sites of the 1914 battle of the Dogger Bank; the battle of Heligoland Bight, a year later; and Jutland, the Great War's greatest sea battle. He had always respected the German Navy, and had a suspicion that nowadays he should do so even more. Air Marshal Burnett certainly respected the Luftwaffe; and both agreed with Major-General Heywood that the task ahead of them would not be easy. Their instructions included the discouraging observation that "the Russian is suspicious by nature, and a hard bargainer"; and they were disturbed to find that, while they had been told to make the slowest possible progress in the talks, their French colleagues had been told not to return without a pact.

Certainly in *City of Exeter* the British contingent's part was being fulfilled: They never traveled at more than twelve knots.

That at least gave them all, French and English, plenty of time to work out a common approach, which they did in twice daily sessions in a most incongruous setting. In the small liner there was only one room large enough for the combined delegations to meet in any comfort—the children's playroom.

★   ★   ★

In London, even close to Victoria Station, the streets were quiet. Inside Westminster Cathedral, less than a quarter of a mile from the station, the air was heavy with the sultry smell of incense. As the echoes of the choir's alleluia died away, the second reading of the High Mass of the day began—Matthew, chapter seventeen, verses one to nine: "In that time Jesus taketh unto him Peter, and James, and John his brother, and bringeth them up into a high mountain apart; and he was transfigured before them. And his face did shine as the sun, and his raiment was white as the snow." In every Catholic community in the country, after the text had been read in Latin, the same elegant rhythms of the Douai translation were being spoken. Although Francis Vanek knew it almost by heart, he followed the service in his missal eagerly; this was one of his favorite passages: "And as he was yet speaking, behold, a bright cloud overshadowed them, and lo, a voice came out of the cloud, saying, This is my beloved Son, in whom I am well pleased; hear ye him." Exactly the sound of a proud father, Francis reflected. Even a person of no faith—and his own was very strong—would recognize that. And the rest of the reading was particularly apt that day for him and the sixteen friends with him: "Jesus came and touched them, and said, Arise, and fear not. And they, lifting up their eyes, saw no one but only Jesus."

Parked outside the cathedral were seventeen bicycles with saddlebags and knapsacks. As soon as the service was over, the Saint Christopher's Cycling Club would go over to Victoria and board the boat train for Newhaven and Dieppe, the first stage in a 600-mile pilgrimage to Lourdes. "As they came down from the mountain, Jesus charged them, saying, Tell the vision to no man, until the Son of man be risen again from the dead." Then, with a glorious burst of music, the choir stood to sing the Credo.

At the same time, in Rome itself, Count Ciano had his mind on a different sort of glory. "Thank you, Duce," he said. "Of course I shall be most honored, and I am deeply grateful for your help." His voice was grave. Mussolini nodded, still not entirely convinced that he had made the right decision, and Ciano tried hard to conceal his pleasure. The Collar of the Order of the Annunziata! The king had recently expressed his intention of awarding it to him. Anyone wearing the Collar was deemed an honorary cousin of the king, but His Majesty had wanted Mussolini's advice, and the Duce had been doubtful. "It might lead to compromises," he had said, "that it would be better not to make." However, now he seemed to be persuaded that Ciano should have it, and he had promised to write to the king tomorrow saying so. It was a good moment to change the subject, and Ciano cleared his throat. "As for the Germans," he began, "we must find some way out."

★ ★ ★

On the seafront at Tynemouth, Bill Hardcastle and John Landells, cub reporters for the *Shields Evening News*, were beginning to despair of finding anything to write about—Bank Holiday Mondays were generally a dead loss for news. Usually it had to be something exciting, and there was very little going on in Tynemouth that could be called exciting, nothing but holiday-makers enjoying themselves. However, more news than they could dream of was being shaped that holiday weekend: preparations in all secrecy for the making, the avoiding, and the near-breaking of pacts, treaties, and alliances that, soon and suddenly, would alter the face of Europe and the world. Drax and his colleagues, English and French, working toward agreement on a common approach in Moscow, hoped reluctantly that they might achieve a military agreement with their Russian counterparts. Ambassador von der Schulenburg hoped earnestly that he had moved a step closer to achieving the same thing, and more, for

Germany. Yet, though Commissar Molotov had behaved toward him in a much less reserved and more friendly manner than usual, von der Schulenburg remained pessimistic; it had been embarrassing, for example, trying to support his assertion that the Anti-Comintern Pact was not aimed at Russia. Neither Mussolini nor Count Ciano knew anything of the exploratory talks between Berlin and Moscow. Indeed, they decided that the next occasion Hitler and the Duce met should be, in Ciano's words, "at some other time, when the Anglo-French-Russian negotiations have been concluded." Moreover, they agreed that, in spite of the Pact of Steel — only eleven weeks old — it would be essential to renege on its obligations if those meant following Germany into a war. And in London, Ambassador von Dirksen meditated on his conversation with Chamberlain's chief adviser, Sir Horace Wilson.

This conversation had been an extension of earlier secret discussions, making it clear that the time for negotiating was not over. Britain was prepared to increase trade with Germany, talk constructively about Germany's need for colonies, take a helpful view of Germany's need for expansion in southeast Europe, announce jointly a cooperative program to help improve the world economic situation, look seriously at the possibility of limiting armaments (including a possible loan to Germany to offset the financial difficulties such limitation would bring), and finally, agree not to intervene in matters concerning the Greater Reich, which would include Danzig. Anyone outside the diplomatic world — and many people inside it — would have been staggered at the list of possible concessions. There was only one precondition: that Germany and Britain should sign a treaty of nonaggression, in which both sides would renounce unilateral aggressive action as a policy method. Von Dirksen concluded that "the dominant feeling was that, compared with an effective adjustment with Germany, the ties that had been formed in the last few months with other powers were only a subsidiary means, which would cease to be operative as soon as agreement with Germany, the all-important objective worth striving for, had been really attained."

Intrigue, conspiracy, secret international jockeying for favor, position, power; and everyone, with one exception, trying to work for peace at almost any price, even national humiliation or unnatural alliance. Yet not even those most closely involved could know precisely what was going on behind closed doors, or tell what the next few days and weeks would bring.

At 2:27 A.M., British Summer Time, on that Monday, August 7 (9:27 Sunday evening, New York time) the Imperial Airways Caribou had landed at Manhasset Bay, one of the innermost sections of Long Island Sound. Droning in over Einstein's retreat at Nassau, it had taken more than thirty-six hours to complete its flight from England, fighting headwinds and blinding rainstorms the whole way. That evening in southern England, however, the sunset was calm and bright. At his country cottage in Sussex, Sir Alexander Cadogan wrote in his diary for August 7: "A good omen, I hope. The view at sunset was so peaceful and lovely: I hope it bodes that we may spend some days here in peace. Back to London tomorrow."

And while Francis Vanek and his sixteen fellow pilgrims cycled innocently southward from Rouen over the great plain of the Beauce, yellow with grain, and sighted from far away the spires of Chartres Cathedral — their first objective — Sir Alexander thanked God for his holiday and prayed for strength to face the future.

★ ★ ★

Not all flights were as successful as the Caribou's arduous transatlantic effort: On Tuesday, August 8, a woman walking on Beachy Head was killed when an RAF bomber crashed 300 yards inland, ploughed through her, and plunged over the 575-foot cliff into the English Channel; its crew of three men were killed as well. Meanwhile, at Fishguard, in the far west of Wales, a close watch was being maintained for IRA suspects attempting to enter or leave the country; from the beginning of the year there had been sporadic bombings in British stores and cities. In Scotland, the royal family's holiday continued, with the two princesses carrying on with their Girl Guide training. Princess Elizabeth was pursuing nature studies, adding new specimens to her collection of native British wildflowers and plants, identifying each and recording them meticulously.

Three hundred and seventy-three Jewish refugees arrived that day in Haifa; and from Paris, German mobilization was reported as being nearly complete. Claude Viviers, writing in the newspaper *Ordre,* foretold a second September crisis; press propaganda for the return of Danzig to the Reich, accentuated by moves of the German Army, made the twentieth seem to him the likeliest date for the next critical increase in international tension. "The danger of war is as real as ever. At any rate, even if Germany has realized that she cannot yet risk a war, one can be convinced that she will risk a large-scale bluff."

★ ★ ★

This is the time to fight — to speak — to attack! So Churchill had advised his despondent supporters when Parliament had prepared to adjourn, and now he set the example, with a fifteen-minute radio broadcast to the United States.

"Holiday time, ladies and gentlemen! Holiday time, my friends across the Atlantic!" Taking time off from Chartwell, where he was working on his *History of the English-Speaking Peoples,* he sounded breezy and ebullient at first. But in a few moments his tone changed. Only twenty-five years had passed since the outbreak of the Great War — the war to end wars, in which more than 8½ million military people had died. In the past few days, the first week of August 1939, the anniversaries had gone by: Germany's declaration of war against France on the third, Britain's declaration against Germany on the fourth. Twenty-five years — just enough time for a new generation of soldiers, sailors, and airmen to come to maturity. The radio speech was bitter, heavily ironic, and very powerful.

"Let me look back — let me see. How did we spend our summer holidays twenty-five years ago? Why, those were the very days when the German advance guards were breaking into

Belgium and trampling down its people on their march towards Paris!"

Skillfully he drew his listeners in: ". . . Listen! No, listen carefully; I think I hear something—yes, there it was quite clear. Don't you hear it? It is the tramp of armies crunching the gravel of the parade grounds, splashing through rain-soaked fields, the tramp of 2 million German soldiers and more than a million Italians—'going on maneuvers'—yes, only on maneuvers!"

America had counted 126,000 dead in the Great War. To those who had survived, his images were horribly clear, his mockery of Hitler and Mussolini simultaneously compelling and un-nerving:

"Of *course* it's only maneuvers—just like last year. After all, the dictators must train their soldiers. They could scarcely do less in common prudence, when the Danes, the Dutch, the Swiss, the Albanians—and of course the Jews—may leap out upon them at any moment and rob them of their living-space . . . Besides, these German and Italian armies may have another work of liberation to perform. It was only last year they liberated Austria from the horrors of self-government. It was only in March they freed the Czechoslovak Republic from the misery of indepen-dent existence. It is only two years ago that Signor Mussolini gave the ancient kingdom of Abyssinia its Magna Charta. It is only two months ago that little Albania got its writ of Habeas Corpus . . . No wonder the armies are tramping on when there is so much work of liberation to be done."

But, he reminded his invisible audience, "the hush of sus-pense . . . the hush of fear" that lay over the world was broken in one place: From China, distant, muffled, but immediately dis-tinguishable, came the dull echo of Japanese bombs, continuing to fall after two years of undeclared war.

As Churchill made his broadcast, Count Ciano received a message from the Italian embassy in Berlin. Written in "a rather soothing tone," he noted, the message said that the ambassador "does not foresee any immediate aggressive intentions on the part of Germany, even though the Danzig situation is grave and dangerous." If Churchill had been sent the same message at the same moment, he would have simply snorted and continued with his broadcast; it would have taken much more than an optimistic note from an Italian diplomat to soothe him. No one could truly say whether the conflicts and threats of conflict could be contained. So — while the Chinese fought to defend their homeland and the neighbors of Italy and Germany tried to read the future — Churchill's voice came crackling out of American radios; and with a grim warning, he urged Americans to "give them a cheer across the ocean — no one knows whose turn it may be next. If this habit of military dictatorships breaking into other people's lands with bomb and shell and bullet, stealing the property and killing the proprietors, spreads too widely, we may none of us be able to think of summer holidays for quite a while."

THE SECOND WEEK

August 9–17, 1939

5

Different worlds

On the morning of Wednesday, August 9, at precisely 8:00, the sailors of 133 warships of the British Reserve Fleet began to dress ship. At 9:55, having traveled overnight in the royal train from Scotland, King George arrived in Weymouth, on the English south coast, to inspect them. Like the ships, the streets of the town were gaily decorated with flags to greet His Majesty. In fourteen lines, each four miles long, the vessels stretched rank on rank across the wide bay, from Portland breakwater nearly to the cliffs of Redcliff Point.

As an inspection rather than a review, it was not just a show for the benefit of civilians: It was a fully naval occasion. Everywhere there were flag officers and commodores either accompanying the King or waiting in their ships for his arrival, and, as a courtesy to the national ally, Fleet Admiral Jean Darlan, Chief of the French Naval Staff, was to be presented to His Majesty. For the journalists present, the serried gray shapes on the glittering water made "a striking picture of grace and power in the brilliant early morning sunshine," but — unfortunately for the sailors lining the sides of the ships — when the time came for His Majesty to begin the inspection, a light rain was falling. The men had no option but to remain at attention and get wet.

The royal yacht *Victoria and Albert* was in attendance. From twenty-one designated naval guns, a salute crashed out, reverberating across the bay. As all other boat traffic ceased, the royal barge bearing the King sped among the warships. At one — the aircraft carrier *Courageous,* originally built in 1917 as a light battle cruiser and converted nine years ago — the barge stopped. Wearing the undress uniform of an Admiral of the Fleet, His Majesty transshipped to the carrier and remained on board for forty minutes, inspecting her forty-eight aircraft and 1,500 crewmen.

He would visit three more ships personally that morning, and in the afternoon would be taken in the royal barge past every other vessel in the fleet.

Watching from the shore, at least one journalist did not grasp the fine distinction between an inspection and a review. Nevertheless, his report was accurate enough: For the Reserve Fleet, this was the greatest occasion since "the War."

★   ★   ★

Ambassador Herbert von Dirksen was ready to go home on leave from London. Before departure, he went to say good-bye to the Foreign Secretary, Lord Halifax, expecting a short interview. It developed otherwise.

Without preamble, Halifax asked him directly, "Have you any explanation, Ambassador, for the present sharp tone of the press concerning Danzig? Sharp, I may say, on both sides."

Von Dirksen was not surprised at the question — only a little at the Foreign Secretary's bluntness. He was ready with an answer: It was the fault of the Polish paper *Czas,* which had published a statement saying that, if there was any attempt to incorporate Danzig into the Reich, Polish troops would open fire on the Free City.

"Moreover," he added, "the Polish Commissioner-General, Chodacki, has told Karl Burckhardt, the League of Nations Commissioner, that opening the customs frontier between Danzig and East Prussia would mean war. This further confirms our fear that, at any moment, the local Polish authorities might jeopardize peace."

"You may be sure," replied Halifax, "that I and the British Government will do all we can to incline the Poles to moderation. And I am certain that neither Foreign Minister Beck nor Marshal Smigly-Rydz desire a conflict with Germany."

"Poland's great weakness has always been giving out many different political declarations," von Dirksen retorted. "Such is the case now."

"Nevertheless," said Halifax, "it would be highly desirable for both sides to display moderation, as I am sure you will agree.

Tranquility might then be achieved, and then perhaps agreement by negotiation."

But von Dirksen was not to be put off. *"We* have amply manifested calm and moderation. The danger is exactly that means of negotiations have been blocked on all sides. Not only the attitude of Poland and the false information put out in the world's press; Mr. Chamberlain's declarations, too, make the Danzig question practically unamenable to negotiations. We hear disquieting news of military commissions going from Britain to Poland or Moscow, news that Germany's potential adversaries are being strengthened financially by Britain. jIt goes without saying that we watch these things closely — and draw our own conclusions."

In Bressay, the Smith family's holiday was ending. Stella's dress had taken longer to finish than she had expected — cutting out patterns from old newspapers, she always tended to get engrossed in the bits of news she had missed. But now it was done, four flared pieces with a short waist top, all of good-quality cotton, green and blue on a white background. She put it on and twirled around, to the approval of the adults; while outside, Nanette, a tomboy at heart, who liked to ride the cows bareback in Foula, set off with their grandfather on the two-mile walk to the peat bank.

The diplomatic conversation in London continued. "You must understand, Ambassador, how things have changed since Munich," said Halifax, carefully keeping impatience from his voice. "Then I thought we were embarking on fifty years of world peace. If I may, perhaps I could repeat my understanding as it was at that time."

Von Dirksen inclined his head. "Please."

"Very well. Germany would have been the dominant power on the continent, with predominant rights in southeastern Europe, especially in commercial policy, where Britain would engage only in moderate trade. Lines of fortifications on both sides would protect Britain and France from conflicts with Germany. We would have had friendship with America and Portugal; Spain, for several years at least, would have been an indefinite factor; Russia would have remained an out-of-the-way, vast, scarcely surveyable territory; and we would have safeguarded our Mediterranean communications with the dominions."

"Admirably put."

Halifax lifted a hand. "Ah—but then came the march into Prague. That changed everything. Above all, it destroyed the idea that world stability had been attained and created doubt as to where Germany would stop, if at all."

★　★　★

In the heart of France, the cycling pilgrims had an easy day's journey: sixty miles from Tours almost directly south to Poitiers, crossing the Loire and the Indre, along the right bank of the Vienne as far as Châtellerault. Although the whole thing had been Paddy Murray's idea—and he had organized it—Francis Vanek spoke the best French among the seventeen cyclists and had been elected interpreter for the group. By now, the third full day in France, he was getting accustomed to a seemingly standard question, wherever they stopped: "Monsieur, do you believe there will be a war?" The first time, he had been taken aback and had simply answered truthfully that he did not. But that did not appear to be enough.

"Really, Paddy," he said impatiently, "they seem to think I know something they don't, just because I'm English."

"So tell them what you think," Paddy answered easily. "A man like you can dream up something, that's for sure."

When they stopped for lunch at Châtellerault, it came again; after orders for food and drink had been given, it seemed to be the only other question in anyone's mind. But this time, Francis felt certain he had a better reply and said with confidence, "No, monsieur, absolutely not." Pausing for effect, he then continued, "And if you would like to know why, it is for two reasons—first, would we be here if we thought a war was coming? Of course not; we would be safe at home across the Channel. Second, it would be illogical for a war to begin; if France and Britain stand together, no one will dare attack us."

The double appeal to logic and mutual patriotism was, he felt, clear and convincing, so he was surprised when the waiter said pensively, *"Eh bien, monsieur,* let us hope you are right."

It was not until they were leaving the town that Francis noticed a large building on the opposite side of the river, apparently with its own wharf. It was the national arms factory.

★   ★   ★

"Naturally," von Dirksen answered Lord Halifax, "these things look entirely different from the German aspect. I will not repeat how often our confidence has been deceived, nor what sad experiences have compelled us to rely on our own swift decisions, instead of negotiations. I understand your view of British policy, but you must put yourself in the mental position of a German statesman. Then you will understand that all we see is an ever bigger coalition being formed against Germany and, as far as we are concerned, the war potential constantly growing in our disfavor. At best, it is as if you had thrown a net over our heads — you tell us that if we keep quiet, nothing will happen to us, but if we move, we will suffer. So it is not surprising, surely, if Germany is rather skeptical when British statesmen say they are willing to consider German demands voluntarily and by negotiation . . . . On the English side, especially in view of the democratic system and the untutored behavior of the press, the premises for a peaceful settlement do not exist."

Nodding, Halifax said, "I have to agree with you that, at present, public opinion in this country is" — he paused — "highly excited and distrustful of negotiations with Germany; and indeed the difficulties you mention are, for the time being, insoluble."

He must bring the interview to a close. It was not going as he had hoped; von Dirksen was being quite intransigent, and it was made no easier by the fact that he, Halifax, could understand at least part of the German's attitude. Odd how it was sometimes actually simpler to deal with diplomats one thoroughly disliked — such as von Dirksen's predecessor, Ribbentrop, who liked to use the noble prefix "von" as well, although he was almost certainly not entitled to it. Dreadful, pretentious man, best summed up by that embarrassing episode, just three years ago, when, in presenting his credentials to the king, he had given His Majesty a Nazi salute. Ever since, he had been remembered as Brickendrop.

Time for one last effort, however, before letting von Dirksen depart. Rising to his feet, Halifax said firmly, "Ambassador, I am *certain* that a period of calm will enable us here to pacify public opinion. Then, undoubtedly, it will be possible to discuss appeasement questions. I repeat, the British Government keenly desire that this should come about and would be prepared to go very far for the achievement of that aim."

For the first time in the interview, von Dirksen was surprised. The Foreign Secretary had actually used the word *appeasement* — virtually a dirty word since the Reich had acquired Czechoslovakia. Perhaps it was only a slip of the tongue; perhaps not — politicians like Halifax were not prone to slips of the tongue. Perhaps Chamberlain believed he could persuade the British public that a return to his old discredited policy was for the best, after all. But, as impeccably discreet as ever, the ambassador merely rose to his feet, bowed and, shaking hands, said, "Thank you, *Herr Aussenminister.*"

★ ★ ★

"We may none of us be able to think of summer holidays for quite a while." Barkley Goodrich had not heard Churchill's speech, and, even if he had, it would not have concerned him much. Coming out of the wooden two-holer outhouse that served as a toilet, he had nothing whatever to think of except summer holiday, and he loved it: He was in Vacationland. The car license plates said so, but he didn't need to be told; he had lived all his fifteen and a half years in the state of Maine and was certain that there was no better place in the world to be at any time of year. A few weeks back his father, a dentist, had closed up his office as he did every summer and taken Mrs. Goodrich and

Barkley, their only child, away from the city of Auburn, forty miles northeast to the family cottage at East Pond. Now his parents had returned to Auburn, their holiday over, but, with an aunt and uncle, Barkley was still free at the cottage.

Deep, clear, and unpolluted, East Pond was the smallest of the chain of five that made up the Belgrade Lakes in southcentral Maine. With lunchtime approaching, Barkley had already made his first trip of the day to the family farm, half a mile away: The tenant farmer supplied them with milk, quarts of heavy cream so thick it had to be spooned from the bottle, and water; although they had electricity and electric lights, there was no running water in the cottage.

It was a large, single-story building set up on posts, the only private dwelling on the cove. Its central room was big—thirty feet by forty feet—with a brick fireplace. Off to one side were three bedrooms, with two more and the kitchen on the other side; right across the front, facing the lake, was a broad screened porch. That was where Barkley preferred to sleep, snuggled deep in a feather bed. Sometimes at night, thunder would sweep across the lake; then the adults would rush out and put down big wooden shutters, racing to beat the storm, and he would snuggle deeper, loving the warmth of the bed, the sudden freshness in the air, and the sound of the rain drumming on the tin roof.

Pausing on his way to the shore, he absently picked and ate some blueberries. "Barkley!" His aunt's voice came from the cottage, and he ran down. The kitchen was full of the smell of baking.

"Uh-huh?"

"Barkley, are you busy?"

"I was thinking of going fishing again. Maybe catch some hornpout."

"Mm-hmm—as long as you're the one to clean it. They're fine to eat, but I just cannot abide the sight of those ugly things until they're in the pan. But right now, I've got two cakes in, and I'm about to start the pastry. What kind of a pie do you want today?"

"Blackberries aren't quite ready yet. We had raspberries yesterday. The blueberries should be good."

His aunt was a stern lady, even dictatorial at times. Straightening up, she looked at him. "Should be? Barkley Goodrich, I think you know that for a fact — unless that's a bruise all around your mouth." He blushed and wiped the blue juice away. But then she smiled and relented. "All right, blueberries it is. And pick a few peaches while you're out there — but just a few, mind — and then you can go fishing all you want."

★   ★   ★

Colonel Josef Beck, Poland's Foreign Minister, was resting at a country retreat outside Warsaw when a report reached him from Prince Lubomirski, his Chargé d'Affaires in Berlin. What he read astonished and angered him. Lubomirski had been summoned to an interview with Ernst von Weizsäcker, the Reich Secretary of State, and there — to put it simply — he and Poland had been directly threatened. Evidently acting on instructions from Ribbentrop and refusing to let Lubomirski speak, von Weizsäcker had announced that any repetition of the Polish demands on Danzig, amounting to an ultimatum, would aggravate relations with Germany and lead to consequences that would be Poland's responsibility.

The semifarcical customs dispute could have been contained and kept in its proper proportion, and would have been, but details of the affair had been officially released to the Polish press, picked up by French and British newspapers, and made to appear as a victory for Beck over the senate in Danzig. That, in turn, had led to a wave of mutual recriminations in German and Polish papers; von Dirksen's remark to Lord Halifax about press interference had been substantially correct. But what the ambassador had omitted to say was that Hitler, reacting furiously to the international publicity and the insufferable humiliation of the Nazi senate, had himself ordered the German papers' anti-Polish campaign.

Colonel Beck was not the kind of man to spend time wishing away the past. If Herr Hitler did not care for demeaning publicity, that was his own business, but relations between the Free

City and the Polish Government emphatically were not his business, and at once Beck sent a reply to Berlin saying just that. "Now," he observed grimly, "it begins."

★　★　★

At 6:00 P.M., the royal train left Weymouth. An hour later the fleet began to disperse, and at sunset — 7:36 P.M. — the sailors began to undress ship. The inspection was complete; the British Reserve Fleet was now formally mobilized. Less than half an hour after that — 11:00 P.M. Moscow time — *City of Exeter* came cautiously into Leningrad harbor. André Beaufre, a member of the French delegation, reflected that it had really been an agreeable voyage. After three days of discussions in the liner's playroom, a common policy had been established and its written text approved by every delegate, French and British. Essentially it proposed that France, Britain, and Russia should agree to provide assistance to either Poland or Rumania, or both, as soon as requested; and, as Admiral Drax had said, "We've agreed; you've agreed; now all we need is for the Russians to agree as well." It showed, thought Beaufre, that, between *des hommes de bonne volonté,* men of good will, there need be no insoluble problems. All very satisfactory so far. Between working sessions, there had been games of deck tennis, which the English admiral had always won. Beaufre's only personal regret now was that there would be no more of those excellent curries, heaped high by turbaned Indian stewards, that had made such pleasant interludes in the daily discussions. In business of any sort, he believed, one could tell a lot from the level of hospitality offered: A good meal and some good wine generated good humor; it made visitors affable and showed that their hosts were serious. And, of course, the opposite was true, too: If the only offering was a poor meal, poor wine, or even — he shivered — no wine at all, one might as well go home at once, for one could be sure that any agreement would be unsatisfactory, reached (if at all) only with reluctance. It would be interesting to see what the Russian table was like.

Despite the late hour, it was still light. Eager for an early look at Russia, Beaufre decided to leave his cabin and go up on deck.

From there, what he could see of the port was not very prepossessing — merely a port, much like any other: quays, warehouses, office buildings — so he climbed higher, to the bridge, for a better view. And there, standing beside Admiral Drax, he was suddenly struck by the sight. No one appeared to be taking any great interest in the liner as it slowly drew alongside the quay. The men busily warping the ship in were not dockyard workers, but *City of Exeter's* own Indian crew; and apart from a small group of soldiers in green caps, with a very few shabbily dressed bystanders, there was scarcely a Russian to be seen.

★   ★   ★

The bombers came in over England that night. With fighter support, there were 500 machines sweeping in from points east. People heard them first as a dull distant throbbing in the southern skies, growing steadily to a roar as they searched for targets across the country. Only five major cities were blacked out — Birmingham, Rochester, Bedford, Brighton, and Derby — but around them all air bases were on maximum alert, and 800 aircraft were rapidly in the air, ready to challenge the attackers.

Only challenges were necessary. It was the largest air war exercise the RAF had ever mounted, and, on the morning of Thursday, August 10, the authorities declared it broadly successful: Had it been real, the "Westland" forces would have fought off the "Eastland" forces, and bombers approaching London had had particular difficulty because of the balloon barrage above the capital.

Sir Kingsley Wood, Secretary of State for Air, visited Biggin Hill Airfield in Kent to watch fighter exercises that day. As a member of the Air Defense Research Committee (and, incidentally, as a local resident — the airfield was only five miles from Chartwell), Churchill accompanied him. There was a heavy drizzle, and the cloud base, at 800 feet, was low.

"Well, Winston, what do you think?" Wood asked.

Pondering the final paper he would write for the committee, Churchill saw in his mind's eye the sky darkened with relays of

enemy aircraft crossing the sea, hour after hour, and wondered
aloud what toll could be extracted from them. "One-fifth
knocked out each go will soon bring the raids to an end," he
remarked. It seemed a high target in the gray dismal light. He
was confident, however, that it could be done; and afterward, he
predicted, the danger would alter. Heavy enemy casualties would
force a change of tactic: With daylight raiding too expensive,
random night bombing of towns and cities would probably
begin. These were gloomy thoughts, but, staring across the rainy
airfield, he added with grim reassurance, "It is not child's play to
come and attack England."

★ ★ ★

With bags packed, Ginger the cat safely in a box, and the
budgerigar safely in its cage, the Smiths made their way from the
Old Manse to the island's little pier and boarded the tiny ferry.
By themselves they filled half of its single cabin. As their parents
stowed the luggage under the narrow wooden benches,
Jessamine ignored Stella's reprimand ("Set dee *doon,* Jessamine,
du'll fall o'er") and knelt on the bench to wave to Uncle Lollie
and their grandfather; Uncle Tommy was working on the roads
and had already said his good-byes.

"Never leet, lass," said their father. "She'll no' fall very far, if
she does." Twelve-year-old Nanette stayed in the boat's open
cockpit, glad she was old enough to do so. It gave her a chance for
a last look at the island, a chance to set in her memory all the
things she loved about the Old Manse: the spinning wheel and
the upright chair her grandmother used to use; the big American
clock on the wall; the green and red parakeet, from somewhere
in South America — it could say "pretty Polly" but little else, and,
whenever it was in a bad temper (sometimes she would tease it
on purpose), it would bend right over and squawk, *"Waikeet!"*
She had also learned from experience that, short as the trip was
across the water to Lerwick, it was better done in the fresh air,
even if it was raining; if the fumes from *Brenda's* thudding diesel
engine seeped into the cabin, she was sick at once.

With a jerk, the ferry started from the pier. Caught in the middle of waving, Jessamine fell over and began to cry.

★   ★   ★

The Red Arrow Express left Leningrad for Moscow at midnight, too soon for the French and English delegations on the night of their arrival. Thus they slept on the *City of Exeter,* and next day, August 10, since they had finished their joint preparation and had nothing better to do, they spent the whole day sightseeing — escorted, naturally, by courteous Russians. It was a fascinating excursion, full of history and grandeur, visible culture and echoed brutality. Apart from containing upward of 700 bridges crossing its many rivers and canals, Leningrad was the scene of the 1917 revolution, and, in a setting of squares, parks, wide avenues, and neoclassical baroque buildings, pastel-painted with gilt spires and domes, the tourists saw Nevsky Prospekt and the Peter and Paul Fortress; the home of the Kirov Ballet, founded in 1735; and, not least, the Winter Palace of the czars. It was a worthwhile tour by almost any standards — except, perhaps, those of immediate political need. For, as Admiral Drax, the French General Doumenc, and their colleagues admired their surroundings, Georgi Astakhov and Julius Schnurre, 900 miles away in Berlin, were talking serious business.

Astakhov was Chargé d'Affaires at the Russian embassy in Berlin; Schnurre was a member of the German Foreign Ministry's Economic Department. Just over two weeks previously, in a discreet and exclusive Berlin restaurant, their first discussion had begun on economics before slipping swiftly and permanently to politics. Schnurre was completely open — so much so that Astakhov, being both Russian and a diplomat, could hardly believe what he was hearing: a proposal that their two countries should abandon their ancient rivalry and dislike of each other, and work together as friends and partners to rechart the continent of Europe.

At first Astakhov demurred, pointing out that such a radical shift in German policy toward the Soviet Union would be scarcely credible in Moscow and that moves were afoot to forge a link with Britain. "What could Britain offer Russia?" Schnurre asked bluntly, and answered his own question: "At best, participation in a European war and the hostility of Germany — hardly a desirable end for Russia." On the other hand, a link with Germany could offer neutrality, no Russian involvement in a European war, "and, if Moscow wished, a German-Russian understanding which . . . would work out to the advantage of both sides." He added specifically that German policy was now directed against Britain and that, from the Black Sea to the Baltic, it should be possible to make a "new arrangement" beneficial to Germany and Russia alike.

It was this extraordinary suggestion that had prompted the talk between Molotov and Ambassador von der Schulenburg on August 3, one week ago. The Count had come away from that ninety-minute meeting with mixed feelings: Molotov had been less reserved than usual but was plainly distrustful, insisting on proofs of honest German intentions. Two days later, however, Schnurre had learned Molotov's own view of the session: positive, urgent, and serious. So, once again, Schnurre and Astakhov met, and, while the French and British delegations toured Leningrad, Schnurre spoke to Astakhov of the megalomaniac Poles, the likelihood that a serious conflict would break out any day, and the benefits to Russia of an early agreement with Germany. Astakhov promised to inform Moscow at once.

★   ★   ★

"Heat, and more heat every day from the blazing sun." Niusia Zamecka was one of those millions, not important enough to be noticed individually, whose lives — slowly, almost invisibly — were drifting out of control. For diplomats and statesmen, it was more abstract, lines on a map, changed or maintained by equations of military power and political agreement. But, if a map is enlarged again and again and again, eventually it matches reality, inch for inch, and people fill it. In Julius Schnurre's scale of things, Niusia was one of the megalomaniac Poles. In her own scale, she was a ten-year-old girl holidaying on her grandfather's smallholding outside Warsaw, sweltering in midsummer heat. "The grass is brown," she scribbled in her diary, "the flowers are drooping, there's not much water in the well." Thirty-eight degrees centigrade, 100 Fahrenheit — it was enough to make anyone do strange things. But, Niusia followed the example of her pet dog Pempela and took a long afternoon nap.

For Nanette Smith, sleep would have been an unbelievable blessing. A hired car had carried the family across the Mainland to the village of Walls. There they had clambered along a shingle and boulder dike jutting out into the sea and had embarked in the Foula mailboat *Advance*. Although the thirty-foot boat was completely open — only the engine was covered against the spray — Nanette's father, Willie, always enjoyed the three-hour crossing, especially when the weather was fine, as it was today: cool, overcast, refreshed by an occasional shower and a light southerly wind. But he was an experienced sailor. For the others, it was simply an endurance test, and one that Nanette always failed. With an uninterrupted fetch of 3,000 miles, the Atlantic swell was high even on the best of days. As the bow of the vessel began its rise and fall, nothing seemed to work: Looking at the far horizon did not help; looking at something inside the boat was worse. She knew the sequence of signs all too well — first feeling hotter and hotter, then a dryness in her mouth, then the rising sourness. Within minutes she was leaning out, head down over the gunwale, watching with a glazed, distant fascination as the water changed from green to iron gray and the bubbles sped past, a foot below her face.

"Feedin' the fishes again, lass?" asked her father, as he always did.

"Wheesht, Willie," said her mother's voice. "Let the bairn be." Someone's hand — she did not know whose — was placed protectively, affectionately, on her shoulder, yet it seemed so far away it could scarcely touch her.

At the same time in Wales, there was scandal and celebration. The conveners of the Eisteddfod had expected a vintage year for poetry; now it was announced, to "groans from the huge crowd," that neither the chair nor the crown could be awarded — the standard had been altogether too low. On the other hand, eleven-year-old David Price from Pontardawe won the solo soprano for boys under sixteen. "We have had a great deal of experience of competitions of this kind," said one of the judges, "but we do not remember having heard anything so satisfying, perfect, and sweet as the performance given by this boy." And, in Germany, Hitler's interpreter Paul Schmidt was flying from one end of the Reich to the other. Recalled early from leave, just as he had feared, neither he nor the pilot had known where they were going until the time of takeoff.

★   ★   ★

At midnight on August 10, Drax, Doumenc, and their colleagues left Leningrad in the Red Arrow Express for Moscow. That night in Britain the blackout was repeated and extended, covering half of England, and it was generally a dismal failure. London, in particular, was as visible from the night sky as a blazing wreck at sea. In one sense, it did not matter: Finding weaknesses was part of the point of the exercise. But, on the following morning, Friday, August 11, as the Anglo-French delegations finally arrived in Moscow, Lord Halifax in London learned that, by the fifteenth, Germany would be in a state of complete military readiness.

★   ★   ★

"Wach' auf, so rufet uns die Stimme!" In the beautiful, ancient university town of Tübingen, a thin man of late middle age was awakened by the sound of singing. It was an appropriate hymn for the morning — "Wake up, a voice is calling us!" — and he listened with pleasure. Outside his window, drenched in brilliant sunshine, was the market square with the old Rathaus — the Council Chambers — and the fountain around which, every year, people would gather to celebrate May Day. The sight gladdened his heart, softening his usual careworn, lined expression, and he

decided to climb up to the castle that dominated the heights above the river Neckar.

His name was Ulrich von Hassell. He was fifty-nine years old, a native of Hanover, an ex-soldier, ex-diplomat, and confirmed opponent of the Nazi regime. As a young man he had studied languages in England and Switzerland. Before the Great War he had been Vice-consul in Genoa. In the army, he had been badly wounded at the battle of the Marne. With the return of peace, he had rejoined the diplomatic service, finally becoming Germany's ambassador in Rome. He was sacked from that post in 1937 — he would not support the Anti-Comintern Pact — and since then, while lecturing on the economic situation in Europe, had become firmly anti-Nazi. It was a strange half-shadowed life, growing steadily more dangerous, with a constant uncertainty about whom he could trust; yet there were many like him. Some he knew, most he did not; there was as yet no organized resistance to Hitler's rule. But one day he would join the conspiracy to kill Hitler and would hang when the conspiracy failed.

That, however, was five years in the future. On August 11, 1939, Ulrich von Hassell gazed from the ramparts of the castle across the countryside. The Neckar lay in its full splendor at his feet, the bells of the college chapel below seemed to him to ring out comfort and peace, and he could see people hurrying toward it. *This picture,* he thought with sad affection, *represents the real German character.*

Meanwhile, Gauleiter Förster had returned to Danzig from his conference with the Führer. The message he relayed to his colleagues was simple: "We know what is coming. We know we will return to the Reich, but we do not know when. The important thing is that we should prepare ourselves." From Danzig, summoned to a private meeting at the Berghof, League of Nations' Commissioner Karl Burckhardt flew south in Hitler's personal Condor plane. For Oscar Baker in Nottinghamshire, it was a day much like any other, although it was his fifteenth birthday; his family did not mark birthdays particularly, but, since it turned out to be warm and sunny, he spent his time quite happily in his father's orchard, mowing the grass and trimming the hedges. Francis Vanek, Paddy Murray, and the fifteen other cycling pilgrims were having another easy day's ride toward their goal, covering the fifty miles from Bergerac to Agen; and in Schloss Fuschl, close to Salzburg, the Italian Foreign Minister Count Ciano was listening with disgust and incredulity as von Ribbentrop (Ciano credited him with the noble prefix) said icily, "The decision to fight is implacable."

Ciano had come to Schloss Fuschl — a castle in theory rented, in practice commandeered, by Ribbentrop — with Mussolini's blessing: "The Duce is more than ever convinced of the necessity of delaying the conflict." Mussolini himself had drafted a paper for the meeting, telling Ciano he absolutely must get the Germans to understand that a conflict with Poland should be avoided. "It would be impossible to localize it, and a general war would be disastrous for everybody." Ciano agreed wholeheartedly but, even before he left Italy, had been doubtful about the outcome; and now that he was inside the Reich, his doubts grew every moment. The conversation was very tense; neither man trusted the other. Ciano, speaking with what he considered to be "brutal frankness," found Ribbentrop completely unmoved, and began to realize that Italy counted for next to nothing in German opinion. For a long time, Ribbentrop would not give a direct answer to any direct question of national policy toward Poland. *He has lied too many times,* Ciano thought contemptuously, *not to feel uneasy now about what he must tell me.* Eventually, in exasperation, the Italian asked as plainly as possible: What precisely did Germany want of Poland — the Corridor, or Danzig?

"Not that anymore," Ribbentrop replied. "We want war." From the way he said it and the way he looked, Ciano instantly realized that, for once, the German was probably telling the truth.

★   ★   ★

Tadeusz Orlicki was so tired he could not even curse anymore. On Fridays he always went out to see his parents, and was very proud of his new Fiat; in it, the journey was only half an hour.

His father thought little of the car; the family horse, Samson, was a much better value in his view. "He gives what he takes," he had said when Tadeusz first showed off the car. "At the end of each day there is enough manure to grow a sack of potatoes. And what do you hope to get from your Fiat?" Today the answer was nothing but sore feet. The car had broken down irrevocably, leaving Tadeusz with an hour's walk. "Well," his father pointed out, "it's silly to expect too much from a mere motorcar."

"Uncle Tadeusz revived at once," Niusia wrote in her diary, "and said something really naughty. I can't say what he said because I don't know how to spell it." But, to Tadeusz's annoyance and his father's amusement, the only thing to do was to take Samson out and pull the car home.

At that moment, in his private teahouse far above the Berghof, Adolf Hitler was talking to Commissioner Burckhardt about just such people — or shouting, rather. *He looks much older and whiter,* Burckhardt thought, remembering the last time he had seen the Führer. Now there seemed a considerable change. *An impression of fear,* the commissioner thought. *Nervous, pathetic . . . almost shaken at times.*

Nevertheless, Hitler's views came across loud and clear: "If the slightest incident happens," he bellowed furiously, "I shall crush the Poles without warning in such a way that no trace of Poland can be found afterward." Ignoring the spectacular views across the mountains, he faced Burckhardt: *"Do you understand me?"*

"Very well, Chancellor," Burckhardt answered, with extraordinary self-control. "I quite realize that means a general war."

Hitler glared at him. "If I have to wage war, I would rather do it today than tomorrow." Since his fiftieth birthday in April, he had said the same thing often and would say it again: He did not know how long he would live, and Germany would never be better led than by him; therefore, if there was no alternative to war, the sooner it came the better it would be for the Reich.

Around the same time, Admiral Drax, General Doumenc, and their respective colleagues paid a courtesy call on Commissar Molotov and Marshal Kliment Voroshilov, the Commissar for

Defense. Their welcome was considerate: The visitors must be tired after such a long slow journey. Would it not be better to begin the talks tomorrow? All could have a pleasant evening beforehand. The Western delegates accepted and were entertained with a banquet and a concert in a thoroughly cordial atmosphere. Only Drax felt uneasy — *Iron hand in a velvet glove,* he thought.

As the French, British, and Russians wooed each other toward an alliance, dinner in Schloss Fuschl was an altogether more frigid affair. Ciano and Ribbentrop were, of course, allies already, yet, during their meal, the two Foreign Ministers did not speak a single word to each other. Though he was host, Ribbentrop made no attempt to break the icy silence. As for Ciano, he had made up his mind. Later that evening, he wrote down what he thought about Ribbentrop in particular and Germany in general: "He rejects any solution that might give satisfaction to Germany and avoid the struggle. I am certain that, even if the Germans were given more than they ask for, they would attack just the same, because they are possessed by the demon of destruction."

6

Can the Red Army march across Poland?

For 500 years, the city of Bradford had grown on the backs of sheep from the West Riding of Yorkshire into a center for woolen and worsted manufacturing. It was a place composed of mills and factories where, like a Muslim priest calling the faithful to prayer, sirens would blare out twice daily to call the men and women to work, while smoke poured constantly from the tall chimneys. Wool was the very fiber of Bradford's muscle, smoke its breath, thunderous noise its heartbeat; but, on Saturday, August 12, the whole city lay silent, and Elsie Harmes rejoiced. It was the first day of Bradford's annual holiday week, the one day in the year when the mills were quiet and the chimneys ceased. Then the wind blew the smoke away, and for that day alone, high above the city, the moors were visible — wild, empty, and beguiling — visible as they had been to her only fifteen times in her short life. But it was not only the peace that made the girl rejoice; the following day would be her sixteenth birthday. Then, her parents had agreed, she could officially change her name from Elsie to Elspeth; and for the first time she would go away from Bradford on holiday, traveling with two girls from work. Even though Hilda and Margaret had been to posh grammar schools and she had not, they were all close friends. Together, they would travel eighty miles by train to Silverdale on the coast of Lancashire where they would see *the* sea — strange and mysterious, a thing only dreamed of or read about in Elsie's many books of poetry. Jumping from the tram a stop early, she walked through Ivegate, a narrow street leading to Westgate, short and steep — Bradford was full of hills — and started the climb toward her work in the ribbon and lace department of Lingard's clothing and hosiery store. It was a tiring walk, guaranteed to leave you breathless; but,

with her head full of the sea, Elsie was happy, for she had saved
another penny toward the journey.

Far away across the invisible water, USS *Tuscaloosa* was being
prepared for a distinguished passenger. One of the perks — and
there often seemed to be few — of being president of the United
States was the chance of vacationing on board an American
warship. It was perhaps not everyone's idea of the perfect cruise
ship, but it offered virtually complete security, and, like his
distant cousin Teddy, president before the Great War, Franklin
Delano Roosevelt was particularly fond of the sea and the U.S.
Navy. Both Roosevelts had been assistant secretary of the navy
before reaching the presidency, and both knew well the U.S.
Navy League's formula for world peace. Only two things needed
to be done — "Abolish: Kings, Oligarchs, Race Antipathies,
Unfair Competition, Land Grabbing, Injustice, and Sin. Establish: The Rule of the People, A Satisfactory World Tribunal,
Justice, Charity, and A Changed Human Nature." And in case of
difficulty in achieving those goals — "Ad Interim: MAINTAIN A
STRONG NAVY." Teddy had seen the transition from an anti-
quated navy of sail and wood to a completely modern one of
steam and steel and had dreamed up the world cruise of the
Great White Fleet; Franklin (who one day would be asked by a
general to stop referring to the navy as "we" and the army as
"they") would oversee the American navy's transformation into
the largest maritime fighting force in history. But today, he was
simply weary, very weary; "I think," he wrote to his wife Eleanor,
"I shall spend most of the first few days sleeping."

"I look at the papers anxiously," she wrote back, "but hope
you get the whole of your cruise, not just for your sake but for the
sake of the poor people in Europe."

Curiously enough, her sympathetic thoughts would have
seemed kind but unnecessary to some of those poor people. In
Northern Ireland, David Howarth felt just then that he was
living in a pretty good approximation of paradise; and certainly
his situation was one that Elsie Harmes or even President Roosevelt might well have envied. His weekly work as director of talks
for BBC radio was more stimulating than Elsie's job on the shop

floor at Lingard's and infinitely simpler than Roosevelt's in the White House. Sometimes it was helpful in a practical way to the ordinary folk; the series given by a housewife and a doctor on feeding a family with a healthy diet on one shilling per person per week had been a splendid example. There was a certain frisson in the private knowledge that the doctor was reputed to be a chief in the IRA. Once Howarth had had lunch with the IRA doctor, followed by dinner with Lord Craigavon, the British Governor of the province — an odd but interesting contrast. Never once, though, did he feel any fear or threat from such strange combinations; it seemed that he was accepted by both sides as a friendly neutral, although he suspected that this was only because they all wanted to get their points across. Now, with the week's work done, he turned again, as he always did, to the peace and solitude of Strangford Lough, half a mile from his rented cottage, the Porter Lodge, outside Killinchy. There was nothing left of the big house. That, when he thought about it, was somewhat spooky: Next to the lodge was a pair of large gates, leading to a long drive, leading to nothing — the IRA had burned the house down. On the sea-lough, however, there were no politics. One of the first things he had done after moving to Ireland from London was to rent a boat, twenty two feet long, with a small cabin and two berths. After a few sails, he was glad he had not actually bought her — she was dead rotten, falling apart. Nevertheless, within the almost landlocked lough, she was safe enough, even for someone whose sailing experience was confined to the Norfolk Broads, the wide, placid network of pools near England's east coast.

David Howarth had come to the conclusion that he was not cut out to be a city dweller. The whole of the Irish north coast, especially the counties of Antrim and Donegal, was his idea of a good coast — to the northwest, the extraordinary Giant's Causeway and the mountains of Antrim reaching almost to the sea; to the northeast, the Derryveagh and Blue Stack Mountains, the rocky bays and inlets with their evocative names: Sheep Haven, Bloody Foreland, Inishfree Bay. He could, and would, walk or drive for miles without seeing a living soul, hearing nothing but wind, larks, sea, and gulls; or, as he was doing this weekend, he would range where he chose across the seventy-five square miles of Strangford Lough, learning by trial and error how to work the boat best with wind and water. Sometime, sooner or later, he would find a suitable anchorage for the night; and then, with a hurricane lamp, some simple food, a book, and a flask of gin, he would find a depth of peace that he would not have exchanged for worlds.

Yet one important link with the city remained: Richard Dimbleby, his closest friend in broadcasting. Both young men were prone to wild enthusiasms, and, when Richard was around, life was always exciting; he bubbled with new ideas, and David, a physics graduate, worked out how to put them into practice, even if the BBC hierarchy disapproved. Together, three years ago, they had covered the burning down of the Crystal Palace in a live outside broadcast—something no one had ever done before. They had reported from the tarmac when Chamberlain returned from Munich; they had gone to Germany together when the Sudetenland was annexed. Around the time David left for Ireland, Richard was informed that, should war come, he could be the world's first radio war correspondent—an offer that he accepted eagerly, with the request that David should be allowed to go with him. The BBC agreed. On the quiet waters of Strangford Lough, David Howarth knew at the back of his mind that one day a call would come from London, and that he would respond.

★   ★   ★

In the grandeur of the Spiridonyevka Palace, Admiral Drax was deeply embarrassed. On the other side of the large round table, Marshal Voroshilov waited. Beside him was an impressive array of senior officers: the Chief of the General Staff of the Red Army, the Commissar for the Navy, the Chief of the Air Force and the Deputy Chief of the General Staff. All were full of expectation. Close by, General Doumenc let a flicker of uneasiness cross his face: Surely the British admiral was not so ill-prepared? This first session had begun with an amiable talk on procedures, after which Voroshilov, rising from his seat, had ceremoniously produced a paper giving him authority to conduct and conclude military negotiations. General Doumenc, in turn, had provided his credentials, which were examined and pronounced satisfactory; yet now, though some such authorization to negotiate was obviously essential, it seemed that Admiral Drax had none.

In fact, he did have a document giving him the appropriate power; but, by an absurd oversight in London, it formed part of his instructions — and they were secret. He could not show one without revealing the other. Caught off guard at the outset, angry with himself for not having noticed the flaw, and mentally cursing whoever was responsible, Drax did the best he could and explained that full plenipotentiary powers had never before been granted to a British military delegation. Knowing that it was hardly a sufficient explanation, he could sense the surprise and exasperation of all those around the table. Everything else and everyone else was ready, but the negotiations could not proceed. The only thing to do — and he did it at once — was to send a telegram to London requesting written credentials, and wait. It was not a good start.

Count Ciano was not enjoying himself very much either. He was in the Berghof with Adolf Hitler. *Very cordial*, Ciano noted mentally, *but he, too, is impassive and implacable in his decision*. Stretching from side to side of the large drawing room, there was an enormous picture window with a terrace beyond. Visitors usually gasped at the view outside and gasped again when the Führer demonstrated how a concealed mechanism could lower the entire window silently right down into the floor. It was an enviable gadget; today, however, Hitler was not showing off his house but his war plans. A wide table was covered with maps. With them he explained to Ciano just how powerful Germany had become under his rule, impressing the Count with his profound military knowledge. Ciano was not sure if it was a pretense or if Hitler was saying what he believed to be the truth. Interpreting between them, Paul Schmidt decided that Ciano had considerable debating power: He was decisive, he was cool, he was statesmanlike. Nevertheless, he could not dent Hitler. Several times Ciano tried to persuade him that a war with Poland could not be localized, but, though he listened, the German leader shook his head. "I personally," he declared, "am absolutely convinced that in the last resort the Western democracies will recoil from unleashing a general war," and he added that the war must be fought while he and the Duce were still young. Privately considering this an exceedingly selfish reason for such a course, Ciano took this opportunity to point out how badly a war would affect the Italian people. Hitler's reaction was, if anything, even more disconcerting than before; he paid attention, but a faraway look came into his eyes — quite clearly he was not interested at all.

★   ★   ★

"Hitler has decreed *Spannung* for the 15th," wrote Sir Alexander Cadogan. By that date, only three days away, Germany would be fully ready for war. *Spannung* means "tension" or "suspense"; in his diary, Cadogan translated the word as "the opening of the 'battle of nerves,'" adding, "Hope mine will be all right!"

In Poland, ten-year-old Niusia Zamecka was quick enough to have grasped that Germany posed a real threat to her country — her parents spoke often of it, and at school she had learned how to wear a gas mask — yet she was trusting enough to believe her teachers: "I don't think the Germans have a chance. One can buy a lot of bullets for one zloty, and if everybody saves, then we can give Hitler a proper thrashing." But that afternoon she had forgotten such things; she was sitting on a blanket in the shade of a cedar tree, learning to crochet. Her mother had a windup gramophone, and, as they crocheted, they listened to all their favorite records — the tango "Jealousy," songs by Jan Kiepura, and the Charleston, which her mother adored. Niusia had to choose a good sharp needle for that one, and she clapped with glee as her mother danced. "I've never seen you do it so well!" she cried, and then asked what it was her mother was making — a tiny white lacy garment.

"Well—" Her mother paused, clearing her throat, and Niusia guessed at once. Their maid, Irka, was "with child." Niusia had heard it from her brothers, and now she told her mother so. "Mama's eyes nearly popped out of their sockets . . . . I thought it best," she concluded innocently, "not to ask Mama whether Irka was getting her baby from a stork or from under the gooseberry bush."

★ ★ ★

Cycling through France, the pilgrims were making excellent progress; from Agen that morning, they had passed through Auch and were on their way to Tarbes, capital of the Hautes-Pyrénées. Eleven hundred years earlier it had been occupied by the Saracens, and for the past 100 years English and Arab bloodstock had given it an international reputation in the horse-breeding world. But, more important for the pilgrims, it was barely fifteen miles from Lourdes, their target. They would get there easily next day, with a full forty-eight hours in hand before the Feast of the Assumption of the Blessed Virgin Mary.

They were a happy group, young, fit, and full of faith. A glance ahead showed the Pyrenees, a high blue and brown line in the distance. But, while they were pedaling cheerfully south along the rising N21, Count Ciano, with deep unease, was watching one of the most sinister sights he had seen: Adolf Hitler in a state of joy.

Moments before, a message from Julius Schnurre had been delivered to the Führer. It contained galvanizing news. As he had promised, Georgi Astakhov had reported to Moscow, and his new instructions were that Russia was ready to talk. All issues outstanding between Germany and the Soviet Union could be discussed—in particular, the Polish problem. Hitler's piercing blue eyes glittering with delight, he told Ciano that Danzig must be settled "one way or another before the end of August." After that the weather would be too bad; the autumn rains always turned Poland into a colossal quagmire. And he revealed one further reason for his confidence that his move could be made soon. Would Russia, Ciano inquired, intervene on behalf of Poland? Hitler's reply was triumphant: "Probably never."

Ciano realized that there was nothing more he could do. "He has decided to strike, and strike he will," he wrote that evening. "As far as the Germans are concerned, an alliance with us means only that the enemy will be obliged to keep a certain number of divisions facing us . . . They care for nothing else. The fate that might befall us does not interest them in the least."

★ ★ ★

"Everything," wrote Neville Chamberlain on Sunday, August 13, "is going wrong here from the fishing point of view . . . I am sending you a salmon (not caught by me) and will be glad if you will distribute such of it as you don't want yourself to any of the staff who are on duty." Cecil Syers, the Prime Minister's Principal Private Secretary, could not avoid a wry smile at the last part of the patrician letter: "The cook or the kitchen maid at No. 10 will cut up the fish." Whatever his faults, the P.M. was a considerate, kindly man, and meant well.

It was, of course, an appropriate day to arrive in Lourdes. After early Mass before breakfast in Tarbes, Francis Vanek, Paddy Murray, and their fifteen friends rode the last few miles of their pilgrimage at a leisurely pace but with a sense of mounting excitement. Bernadette Soubirous — the girl whose visions of the Virgin Mary in 1858 had focused worldwide Catholic attention on the town — had been declared a saint only six years ago, and, for most of the cyclists, including Francis, this was a first visit to the holy place.

They were not disappointed. Lourdes is set in a fine Pyrenean landscape on both sides of the river Gave de Pau. Passing through the old town, they could see, on the east bank, the ramparts of Château Fort, the medieval fortress that once — for more than forty years, at the end of the fourteenth century — had been held by the English, but it hardly interested them. Parallel to the Rue Bernadette Soubirous ran the Boulevard of the Grotto, and along that they rode directly to the river bridge. With the year's main religious festival only two days off, the streets were packed with other pilgrims, but, in spite of the crowds, they decided it would be quite safe—and more suitable—if they dismounted and left their bicycles. The last half-mile to the grotto with its sacred spring should be traveled on foot, with reverence.

Simultaneously, after a second, briefer talk with Hitler, Galeazzo Ciano was returning by plane to Rome. During the talk, the interpreter Paul Schmidt had been astonished to see how Ciano had transformed overnight: *Folded up like a jackknife,* Schmidt thought. The Count had not seemed to care anymore what happened, telling Hitler wearily that, for all he knew, Hitler was the one who saw things most clearly: "You have been proved right so often before, when we others held the opposite view." But in his diary the Count confided his true feelings: "Completely disgusted with the Germans, with their leader, with their way of doing things," he wrote. "They have betrayed us and lied to us. Now they are dragging us into an adventure that we do not want." And he decided on the advice he would give to Mussolini: "I think that our hands are free, and I propose that we act accordingly, declaring that we have no intention of participating in a war which we have neither wanted nor provoked." For Italy's safety and survival, he was determined to break the Pact of Steel.

★ ★ ★

The following day, Monday, August 14, was a busy one for Ulrich von Hassell. Back in Berlin after his visit to Tübingen, from 10:00 in the morning until late at night, he had meetings with other Germans who felt as he did. First, Carl Goerdeler, in his lodgings on Askanischer Platz. In the two years before Hitler came to power, Goerdeler had been the Reich's Price Control Commissioner—a hard and thankless task as depression took root after the nightmare inflation of the 1920s. Subsequently he had been mayor of Leipzig, but had resigned, sickened by the Nazi government's measures against the Jews. Von Hassell found him "fresh, clear-headed, active . . . . One hears generally that he is imprudent and is being closely watched." No doubt—any form of protest, even simple resignation, could well be called imprudent. *It is a relief, though, to speak with a man who wants to act rather than grumble.* Von Hassell found his company a tonic, for Goerdeler was sure that resistance, albeit scattered and disorganized, was growing again in Germany and that world war would be no solution. Heartened by their shared confidences and agreeing to use whatever influence they could for peace, they parted warmly.

Goerdeler, too, would be arrested in 1944, after the plot on Hitler's life failed, and, after protracted torture, he would die in Plötzensee Prison.

But he and von Hassell met again, unexpectedly, on that Monday in 1939 in the Hotel Adlon. Goerdeler was accompanied by Hans Gisevius. *No doubt intelligent, informed, and active,* von Hassell thought with faint suspicion, *but I don't quite make him out.* It was only sensible to be cautious: Gisevius had joined the Gestapo in 1933, then the army, and was now attached to the legation in Switzerland. They decided to go for lunch together on the Esplanade, and there encountered what von Hassell called "a veritable stock exchange," including the president of the Deutsche Bank and Herbert von Dirksen, who had arrived from London that morning. From one of the "stock exchange" came the somber affirmation that at best Germany had only six weeks' supply of the raw materials needed for war. Greeting von Dirksen as an old colleague from diplomatic days, von Hassell inquired whether he was on holiday or had been summoned back. Von Dirksen snorted derisively—"Ha! Of course I was summoned!"—before explaining that, try as he might, he, the ambassador to Great Britain, could get no appointment with either Hitler or von Ribbentrop.

Von Ribbentrop's name came up again later that afternoon, when von Hassell had tea with Baron Ernst von Weizsäcker and his wife. Their house, "next to the verdant garden of the Krupp building," was new and beautiful, but the baron—Secretary of the Foreign Office—was too worn out to enjoy it. Von Ribbentrop's behavior was worrying him greatly; the Foreign Minister would tell him hardly anything about what had happened with Count Ciano. "What do you suppose the Italians will do," he asked von Hassell, "now that they have been turned down?"

"As a matter of fact," came the dry response, "they are no longer free to choose."

For Ulrich von Hassell, that Monday ended with a private dinner with Ludwig Beck, "a most cultured, attractive, and intelligent man." Not only that, he was also a Colonel-General and until 1938 had been Chief of the General Staff of the Army. Like Goerdeler, he had resigned his post — in Beck's case, because of Hitler's policies during the Sudetenland crisis. "Unfortunately," von Hassell noted in his diary, "he has a very low opinion of the leading people in the Army. For that reason he could see no place where we could gain a foothold." Nevertheless, the ex-diplomat and the ex-soldier were in absolute agreement on one matter: Both were "firmly convinced of the vicious character of the policies of the Third Reich."

That was the reason why, in 1944, when Hitler survived the plot against his life, Colonel-General Ludwig Beck committed suicide.

♦   ♦   ♦

Meanwhile, Monday, August 14, 1939, was the third day of the military discussions in the Spiridonyevka Palace. Marshal Voroshilov came to the meeting that day knowing that he would find out exactly how influential, how prepared, and how committed the French and British delegates — and by extension, their governments — really were. To do so, he had to ask only three questions. Yesterday he had indicated what they would be when he had pointed out an elementary fact of geography: The Soviet Union did not have a common border either with Britain or with France. How, then, he had inquired, did the British and French missions imagine there could be joint action against an aggressor? Today, chairing the session, he wanted to know the answer.

If Russia was to fight in Europe on behalf of Britain and France, Russian troops would have to cross over either Poland or

Rumania; even a schoolchild could see that, merely by looking at an atlas. It was no trap or trick on Voroshilov's part; the question was obvious and legitimate, the reply critical. Yet, on that very question, both the French and British governments had just crossed their fingers and hoped it would not arise. The ideal offer, from their point of view, would have been a promise of a steady supply of military hardware manufactured in the Soviet Union. There was very little likelihood — indeed, virtually no chance at all — that the Polish or Rumanian authorities would allow tens of thousands of Russian soldiers to cross over their territory. So, seeing no easy solution to the problem, neither London nor Paris had made any preparation for it, and neither Drax nor Doumenc knew what to say.

Voroshilov put his questions clearly. First, if Poland was attacked, would Russian land forces be allowed in to help with its defense? Second, would the Red Army be allowed passage over Poland in order to make contact with the enemy and fight him in the south? Third, if Rumania was attacked, was it proposed to allow Soviet troops across Rumanian territory? "These," he finished simply, "are the three questions which interest us most."

For a long time, Doumenc and Drax whispered together. Being military men themselves made the situation even more embarrassing and difficult for them; they understood Voroshilov's point and privately agreed with it. Hardware was all very well, but it would not be enough. Yet they were not authorized to say that kind of thing. Doumenc, doing his best to avoid the question, gave the first reply. Agreeing that Voroshilov had indicated the right areas of Soviet troop concentration, he remarked that their distribution would be at the marshal's discretion. "I think the weak points of the Polish-Rumanian front are their flanks and point of junction," he concluded. "We shall speak of the left flank when we deal with the question of communications."

Voroshilov was not to be diverted. "I want you to reply to my direct question. I said nothing about Soviet troop concentrations. I asked whether the British and French General Staffs envisage passage of our troops toward East Prussia or other points to fight the common enemy."

Doumenc's next words sounded disarming and candid: "I think Poland and Rumania will implore you, Marshal, to come to their assistance."

"And perhaps they will not," Voroshilov snorted. "It is not evident so far."

Drax and General Heywood conferred at length. Eventually the admiral spoke: "If Poland and Rumania do not ask for Soviet help, they will soon become German provinces . . ." The listeners around the table stiffened; everyone knew he was speaking the military truth. "Then," he continued, "the USSR will decide how to act. If, on the other hand, the USSR, France, and Britain are in alliance, then the question of whether or not Rumania and Poland ask for help becomes quite clear."

As far as Voroshilov was concerned, it was not at all so. Once again he pressed for a plain response, and this time Drax gave the pathetic political truth. In his own view, Poland and Rumania were almost certain to ask for help; but, he acknowledged, that was only his personal opinion. "To obtain a precise and satisfactory answer, it is necessary to approach Poland."

So there it was, just as Voroshilov had suspected and feared. The Soviet marshal stared heavily across the table; his voice was stern. "I regret that the Military Missions of Great Britain and France have not considered this question and have not brought an exact answer." *How*, he wondered silently, *could they have been sent to the conference table so ill-prepared at such a critical time?* The only conclusion seemed to be that their governments were not trying seriously to negotiate. "Without an exact and unequivocal answer to these questions," he declared, "further conversations will not have any real meaning."

There was no getting around it—he was right in every way. Shortly afterward, the meeting adjourned, and the French and British delegates walked despondently through the palace gardens together. "At least he's agreed to carry on until we get replies," said Admiral Drax. "But quite frankly, I think our mission is finished." As André Beaufre noted, everyone felt the same, and had they known the instructions Count Friedrich von der Schulenburg had just received, their suspicions would have become certainty. Von der Schulenburg was to tell Commissar Molotov that Hitler's Foreign Minister, Joachim von Ribbentrop, wished to come in person to Moscow at the earliest opportunity.

The authorities had been quick enough to provide a plane to bring Paul Schmidt down to the discussions with Ciano, but to his disgust he was not given one to take him back. After a long slow journey, he had just arrived back in his beloved Norderney, "only too thankful that Ribbentrop let me continue my leave."

In Italy, hymns were being sung. Walking on the seashore with the Polish ambassador, Count Ciano could hear them and noticed that the churches were full. Word had come from the Italian counselor in Warsaw that the Poles would fight to the last man, and Ciano, speaking in roundabout terms, was trying to advise moderation. The words of one of the hymns drifted out to him: "Oh God, help us save our country . . ." *These people will be massacred by German steel tomorrow,* he thought with anger and compassion. *They are innocent. My heart is with them.*

7

This is no time for half-measures

On Tuesday, August 15, having nothing better to do, Herbert von Dirksen decided to pay a call on Bernardo Attolico, Italy's ambassador in Berlin. Both had served their respective countries years before in Moscow and had become close friends, so von Dirksen did not feel any appointment would be necessary; and, sure enough, Attolico was delighted by the visit. With profuse and exuberant apologies, he explained that he did have another visitor at the moment but that this visitor was about to leave, after which there would be plenty of time for the two old friends to chat. Attolico had not altered, and von Dirksen, amused, settled himself down to wait.

While he was waiting, the telephone rang, and he could see Attolico becoming highly excited and disturbed at the conversation. Then, slamming down the receiver, the Italian rushed through.

"My dear friend—I am so sorry—I have to go to Rome—at once! Oh, I am so sorry! Now, listen to me—I must talk to you immediately, man to man, friend to friend. There are times, I think, when this must be done. It is Ciano. You know of his discussions with Herr von Ribbentrop? Yes, of course, of course. Well, it seems there have been decisions made that might easily result in war, namely with Poland. And what is more, much more, those decisions are based on the notion that England will not join in!"

"Wait—wait." Von Dirksen raised a calming hand. "I have just returned from England. What are you saying? That we are going to war with Poland? And that the Foreign Minister believes England will not fight?"

"Precisely. But they will. And so I must go to Rome this instant and present my report."

"No, this cannot be right. I, too, am on the brink of presenting my reports and I assure you, my friend, I know the English mind well now, and I know that full account will have been taken of the possibility they will fight."

Attolico refused to accept it, saying that von Dirksen must do his duty and change the opinion of the leading German authorities. Their whole conversation lasted less than five minutes; with Attolico as hurried as he was excited, von Dirksen was only able to throw in a few brief remarks before, in a shower of hasty apologies, the Italian ambassador ushered him to the door.

Once outside, von Dirksen frowned thoughtfully. It was difficult to conduct diplomacy, even between friends, at such speed. But at least he had conveyed his own view. He had felt instinctively that it was important to challenge Attolico's double assertion—that war with Poland was inevitable and that Germany had not taken the British factor into account. If only von Ribbentrop would consent to see him! Hoping, not very optimistically, that Attolico had registered his comments, von Dirksen decided it might be as well if he put them on record.

For their part, Tadeusz and Zofja Olszolwski had decided it might be as well if their two small boys, Stefan and Andrew, were taken from Gdynia to the family estate of Moniaki, 300 miles away. Deep in Poland, it was the safest place they knew, and, in the large, bustling household, the children would be surrounded by relatives—Zofja's father and two of her aunts; her sister Ann, Ann's husband, who ran the 8,000-acre estate, and their three children, as well as the cook, the maids, and the housekeeper. Their silver and the carpets from the Villa Sadyba in Gdynia could go for safekeeping to Tadeusz's parents in Warsaw. These were not easy decisions; Tadeusz and Zofja knew they would miss the children but also that it was a sensible precaution. As for the precious objects: "There doesn't seem to be much point in owning such things," said Zofja, "if we can't use them, and the villa will look very dull and empty."

"Better to lose the use for a while than perhaps lose them all for good," Tadeusz reminded her. And then, to her delight, he told her he had a little surprise for her. With the demands of his work, he felt they had not been seeing enough of each other. "So I thought we'd take two or three days together, just by ourselves, and go to Copenhagen. What d'you say?"

Putting her arms round his neck, she smiled. "I say: I love you, Tadeusz. You're such a kind and thoughtful man. The boys are very lucky to have you for a father — and I'm very lucky to have you for a husband." Kissing him, she added, "But I do hope we can all be back together very soon."

★ ★ ★

"Entschuldigen Sie, bitte, Herr Kapitän — ein Ferngespräch aus Berlin für Sie."

Captain Karl Dönitz, head of the U-boat arm of the Reich Navy, nodded his acknowledgment and followed the receptionist through to the hotel's front desk. The deferential Austrian handed him the telephone receiver and busied himself with some papers. If he had hoped to overhear any news, he was disappointed; punctuated with short pauses, the conversation was brief and one-sided.

"Hier Dönitz. Ja, guten Morgen. Ja . . . also, wann? Heute? Ja, natürlich; ich bin jederzeit bereit — und auch seeklar. Sie auch, nicht? Gut. Also, danke schön; auf Wiederhören. Heil Hitler!"

Handing the telephone back to the receptionist, Dönitz informed him that, regrettably, he would have to cut short his holiday and leave the hotel today. Could his bill please be made up at once?

Climbing the stairs to his bedroom, Dönitz's regret was genuine: for the past few years, since he had learned to ski, he had usually taken his holidays in the South Tyrol and liked it as much in summer as in winter. Bad Gastein, his chosen resort this year, was particularly attractive. The hot springs that gave it its name ran at a constant temperature of nearly 120 degrees Fahrenheit — blissfully comfortable. The town was small, with a population of only about 5,000. Lying on the northern slopes of the Austrian Alps, it was tucked between the Hohe Tauern and Niedere Tauern mountain ranges. Against a backdrop of steep

evergreen forests, its pretty, color-washed buildings were divided
by a river. Dönitz could see it from his window and could hear
the roar of the great waterfall that cascaded under the stone
bridge in the very heart of the town. Yes, he would be sorry to
leave.

As it happened, Bad Gastein was only forty miles south of
Hitler's fortified mansion, the Berghof. Not that Dönitz needed
to be close to the Führer to have him constantly in the back of his
mind. They had met only once so far, nearly five years ago, but
on that occasion Hitler had seemed to Dönitz "brave and
worthy," and nothing had happened since to make him change
his opinion. True, the recall to duty in Kiel was sudden, pre-
maturely ending his scheduled six weeks' leave, but not entirely
unexpected; and, as he had said, he was always ready.

That was virtually all the receptionist had been able to overhear — that and the words "and ready for sea, too." It was tan-
talizingly little, but, while adding up the neat columns of figures
in Dönitz's account, he reflected that it was more than anyone
else in the hotel knew. When the captain had gone, it would be
interesting to gossip about it and speculate on what it might
mean.

Neither the humble receptionist nor even Karl Dönitz could
guess, but his early recall was intimately connected with events
taking place that Tuesday, August 15, in Moscow. In one part of
the Russian capital, the Anglo-French delegates faced Marshal
Voroshilov again; in another part, Commissar Molotov and
Ambassador von der Schulenburg were deep in discussion,
unknown to the French and Britons. The timing of Hitler's next
move depended on the outcome of these separate, rival talks, and,
whatever happened, he intended to have his forces ready in all
respects.

The previous evening, under Voroshilov's threat of suspending
the military talks, the chief foreign delegates and their respective
ambassadors had held an emergency meeting and sent urgent
telegrams to London and Paris. Sir William Seeds, the British
ambassador, had sent one already: "All indications so far show
that Soviet military negotiators are really out for business," he

had said, stressing that, unless Admiral Drax was given much greater freedom of action, the Russians would conclude that there was no serious British intent to reach agreement. But that telegram had been sent on the twelfth, three days ago, and there was still no reply. Today, in a state of nervous tension, the delegates could only wait, hoping for a rapid and suitable response, and listen to Voroshilov expounding at length on Soviet military power and plans.

Molotov's session with von der Schulenburg was of an altogether different character. Where there had been suspicion, there was now a growing candor, and, before nightfall, the German ambassador was able to send to Berlin a telegram with staggering implications. Although Commissar Molotov was hesitant about the idea of von Ribbentrop coming in person to Moscow and supervening the normal channels of diplomacy, the Russian stated that he was now confident of Germany's good faith and wondered what the German Government might say to three proposals: First, would a nonaggression pact be of interest? Second, could Germany offer assistance in Russo-Japanese relations? Third, might it be possible for Germany and Russia jointly to guarantee the frontiers of the Baltic states? As he drafted the telegram, von der Schulenburg shook his head in pleased surprise: Molotov had gone further than he would have imagined possible, actually explaining the benefits that Russia would gain if agreement on those three points could be reached. It all came down to one word: security. When — not if — Poland was attacked, a Russo-German nonaggression pact would leave Russia in peace. Russia's long-running dispute with Japan concerning the border with Manchuria could, with German influence, be solved, and the safety of Russia's Baltic borders could be ensured by Germany to a degree that was simply impossible for either France or Britain.

Signing his name with a flourish, von der Schulenburg half-wished he could be with von Ribbentrop and the Führer when they received the message. Perhaps the progress was not quite as swift as they would have liked — Molotov's seeming unwillingness to receive von Ribbentrop was coupled with a desire to conclude economic agreements before political ones — but it was certainly promising. The ambassador felt a professional satisfaction.

Five years later, he, too, would be one of those involved in the conspiracy against Hitler's life; he, too, would be executed when it failed.

★　★　★

Never in his life had Francis Vanek seen such a huge crowd of people — tens, scores of thousands, maybe more — he could not begin to estimate the numbers. The day before, feeling the need of another long ride, he had cycled out thirty-five miles from his lodgings in Lourdes to Gavarnie, nearly 4,500 feet up in the Pyrenees and only five miles from the border with Spain. It had proved one of the most tiring stretches he had done so far, but worth it if only for the exhilarating return trip down the mountains. He had slept soundly that night and, quite early on the morning of August 15, the Feast of the Assumption of the Blessed Virgin Mary, he went with his friends toward the Esplanade des Processions, the wide avenue leading arrow-straight to the Church of the Rosary and the grotto where Saint Bernadette's visions had taken place. There was a spring there that had arisen miraculously when, on the directions of the Holy Mother, Bernadette had scratched the dry ground. This was literally the fount of holiness, the place where all the pilgrims most wanted to be, for its waters could cure. Not everyone who drank them was so blessed, but, in the eighty-one years since it had first begun to flow, more than 200 people whom doctors had declared incurable had been restored to full health. Francis himself was exceedingly fit and healthy, for which he thanked God; and, as he approached the bridge across the Gave de Pau, he thanked God, too, for giving him the sense to have visited the grotto already; there would be precious little chance of doing so today.

Even before they reached the bridge they could hear the people. More and more were coming from each direction, from the Quai Saint Jean, the Rue Bernadette Soubirous, and the boulevard itself, all congregating on the bottleneck of the Pont Saint Michel. As they made their way slowly over, they could see ahead the somber Breton Calvary, a forty-foot granite crucifix from Brittany, towering over the heads of those in front. The 500-yard Esplanade was filling steadily. Many of the people were blind or crippled, hobbling on crutches, trundling in wheelchairs, even being pushed in wheeled beds, their faces shaded from the climbing sun; and all were praying. Some were silent — an old lady moving only her lips as fingers distorted by arthritis struggled to move the beads of her rosary; a young man crossing himself with his left hand as his right dangled limp and withered beside him. Others were crying out loud, in English, French, and languages Francis did not understand: *Dear Lord, restore my sight . . . Oh God, let me walk again . . .*

Instinctively crossing himself, overwhelmed by the enormous demonstration of faith, Francis closed his eyes in prayer.

Elsewhere in France, a pilgrimage of entirely secular purpose was beginning: Winston Churchill had come as a guest of General Joseph Georges, Commander-in-Chief of the armies in France, to see for himself the Rhine sector of the Maginot Line, the main French land defensive barrier against Germany. Begun ten years previously and named after the then War Minister, André Maginot, it had been fabulously expensive and was very well equipped indeed. Telephone exchanges, power stations, ammunition dumps, miniature railways, underground barracks, cookhouses and hospitals, ammunition hoists and drainage systems, a garrison of 300,000 men, and gun emplacements elaborately planned to cover every square foot of ground ahead — everything was there.

Their tour lasted three days. Starting from Lauterbourg, the northeasternmost corner of France, where the border with Germany made an acute angle, they continued south for 100 miles up the Rhine to the Swiss border. The first thing that struck Churchill was the harsh contrast in atmosphere with England. He wrote of it later, in his usual lucid, dramatic fashion. At home, he knew, there were families holidaying on the sands, contented and carefree. But here — any temporary bridges across the river had been moved to one bank or the other; all permanent bridges were under heavy guard on both sides and, at least on the French side, were mined as well; they could be blown up at the touch of a button. French riflemen crouched in pits; Germans shoveled earthworks. Any person or vehicle crossing, and there were very few, was subjected to close scrutiny on both sides, though the border posts might be only 100 yards apart. Between such posts there was absolutely no contact, and along lengthy stretches of the river, no civilians were allowed to walk. *Yet,* he thought, *Europe is at peace. There is no dispute between Germany and France.*

Perturbing though it was, he admired what he saw; still, it had flaws, and he saw them, too. "The French Front cannot be surprised," he reported to the British Secretary of State for War. "The flanks of this front, however, rest upon two small neutral States" — to the north, Belgium; to the south, Switzerland. Since 1815, no nation had threatened Switzerland's neutrality, and — although Hitler had once remarked that, after conquering Europe, he would take Switzerland with the Berlin fire brigade — in Churchill's judgment, the French were safe from that side. Nevertheless, their defenses there were as strong as on any part of the Rhine, whereas along the Belgian frontier, from Montmédy to the sea 170 miles away, there were only occasional pillboxes; and it had been through Belgium, neutral in 1914 as in 1939, that Germany had invaded France.

For the Englishman inspecting the defenses of France, however, the single most remarkable effect of the Maginot Line was its psychological influence on the French — "the complete acceptance of the defensive which dominated my most responsible French hosts and imposed itself irresistibly on me . . . . France had no longer the life-thrust to mount a great offensive. She would fight for her existence — *Voilà tout!*"

In Lourdes, a prayer went up from every French-speaking mouth: *"Dieu nous donne la paix!"* Many of the French pilgrims had come especially to offer that prayer, and Francis Vanek echoed it, although he still believed it unnecessary. At his side, Paddy Murray nudged him.

"What was that they said, Francis?"

"They said, 'God give us peace.' They really are frightened."

Paddy crossed himself. "Amen to that. God give us peace."

★ ★ ★

At 5:00 P.M. English time on August 15, the Foreign Secretary, Lord Halifax, and the Minister for the Co-Ordination of Defense, Admiral of the Fleet Lord Chatfield, approved for dispatch a draft telegram written by the Deputy Chiefs of Staff in reply to Sir William Seeds. The chance of an alliance with Russia, which for so long had seemed undesirable and awkward, began to seem more and more attractive as the possibility of losing it increased. Released from their previous political constraints, the Deputy Chiefs wrote their response eagerly. Accepting in full Seeds's urgent recommendation that Admiral Drax should be given a looser rein, it authorized him to bring the military discussions to a satisfactory conclusion as quickly as possible.

As soon as the telegram was sent, the second plea arrived from Moscow. Its tone was emphatic: Voroshilov appeared sincere, but the question of Russian passage rights over Poland *must* be resolved, or all might fall through. Around the same time, the French version of this telegram arrived in Paris, and for once, in both capitals, a condition of extreme urgency was immediately recognized. For their own good, the Poles and Rumanians had to be brought with the utmost speed to the same recognition: They must be persuaded to allow the Russians through.

Tuesday, August 15, the Feast of the Assumption, ended in Lourdes as it always did. From the Basilica, a nineteenth-century building in the style of the thirteenth century, came a torch-lit procession of pilgrims of many nations. Above them in the darkening sky rose the Basilica's 230-foot bell tower. Turning right, they commenced the winding march past the Stations of the Cross, climbing half a mile to the top of Mount Calvary.

Such processions, lit by flickering brands in gathering darkness, always have an instinctive and powerful effect on those who see them or those who take part. Adolf Hitler, an instinctive man in many ways, understood this, which was why he preferred such processions, above all others, as a conclusion to any Nazi rally. There, too, the cheers would ring out — *Heil Hitler! Sieg heil!* Hail Hitler! Hail victory! *Ein Volk, ein Reich, ein Führer!* One people, one empire, one leader! — and the daunting, rousing anthem, *"Deutschland, Deutschland, über alles . . ."*

In torch-lit Lourdes, the pilgrims sang hymns of Christian faith. They sang with hope and with fearful defiance; and their power was greater than they knew.

⋆ ⋆ ⋆

By noon on August 16, Marshal Voroshilov was thoroughly annoyed. The talks had been in progress for four days, and he still had not seen or heard anything that could be called proof of firm intention from either the French or British delegates. He was also losing interest. After his own account of Russia's plans and forces the previous day, General Doumenc had followed with an outline of Western naval plans and, this morning, was continuing with an account of Western air strength. The general was making some play of the idea that this was all very secret information, trying thereby to convince the marshal of good intentions. Instead, Voroshilov merely felt insulted — secret? What rubbish! He wondered if the general thought him a simpleton, or a schoolboy. There was no intelligence service that did not know all this supposedly secret information already. Moreover, the British and French kept on asking for agreed principles, when all he was interested in were physical realities — the totals of men, ships, guns, planes, and tanks that all three nations together would put into action, and when, where, and how it would be done. And central to it all remained the unanswered question of passage rights across Poland and Rumania.

At last he had had enough. Abruptly, saying it was a waste of time, he called the session to a halt and repeated his earlier warning: Firm answers must come, and soon, or the entire idea would have to be abandoned.

In the British Foreign Office, Cadogan was very worried about how much of this to let out to the press. Publicizing the progress, or lack of it, and all the difficulties surrounding the talks could easily make everything even worse; yet there was no escaping the fact that people were eager, desperately and naturally eager, for news, and, if nothing was said, they would go by guesswork, which could have just as bad an effect. Among the many millions around the world who found the skimpy newspaper reports of the Moscow talks a subject of consuming interest were John Neville Scott, a rebellious English teenager, and Charles King, an idealistic Australian. Their roots and circumstances had little in common: Nineteen-year-old Scott was a brewing research chemist; forty-one-year-old King was an unemployed teacher, the father of three daughters. King's own father, long dead, had been a womanizer and a heavy drinker, while Scott's father, recently retired from work as a supply manager, was a man of stately appearance and strict moral rectitude. The young Englishman and the middle-aged Australian had never met and never would meet, but, in direct reaction to their very different backgrounds, both were firm, paid-up supporters of the Communist party.

As it happened, within a year neither would belong to the Party any more. King, the unpaid editor of its monthly publication, *World Peace,* was expelled in 1940 for writing a leading article that savagely criticized Russia's invasion of Finland. Scott had communism knocked out of him by his wartime service: His parents had learned not to ask where he had been when he came home late in the evenings — if they did ask, a bitter political argument usually followed — but real working-class people, in destroyers and the Fleet Air Arm, saw through him. They did not mind that he had been given his middle name in honor of the Prime Minister, and he, helping illiterate seamen to write their loveletters, was honest enough to realize that distributing the *Daily Worker* and going to smoky, conspiratorial meetings was little more than an intellectual game.

Nevertheless, in August 1939, both John Scott and Charles King were certain that peace in Europe could only be maintained by an alliance among France, Britain, and Russia, united against Fascism. As Communists, it was much easier for them than for many others, mistrustful of Bolsheviks, to accept the idea; and, since nothing definite was published to the contrary, they assumed that progress was satisfactory. Actually — although they would never have admitted to panic — the professional diplomats of Britain and France were frantically trying to stave off a complete collapse.

The first pressure on the Poles came from Paris. The Polish ambassador to France was urged to recommend cooperation with the Russians; the Polish Foreign Ministry was given the same strong advice from its French counterpart; and a French delegate from Moscow was sent to Warsaw with the same message for the Polish General Staff. Meanwhile, in Britain, the deputy Chiefs of Staff were writing a passionate second report to Whitehall: "This is no time for half-measures . . . every effort should be made to persuade Poland and Rumania to agree to the use of their territory by Russian forces. . . . It is perfectly clear that, without early and effective Russian assistance, the Poles cannot hope to stand up to a German attack on land or in the air for more than a limited time. . . . We suggest it is now necessary to present this unpalatable truth with absolute frankness both to the Poles and to the Rumanians."

This was plain speaking from men who had until now been held back from expressing their full opinion — the same men who, in the event of a war, would be responsible for Britain's strategy. "To the Poles especially," the Deputy Chiefs continued, "it ought to be pointed out that they have obligations to us as well as we to them; and that it is unreasonable for them to expect us blindly to implement our guarantee to them if, at the same time, they will not cooperate in measures designed for a common purpose."

A Polish soldier was shot dead by a Danzig frontier guard that day. During the course of the afternoon, Francis Vanek relaxed in the unaccustomed luxury of a train ride from Lourdes to Paris. Winston Churchill gazed in amazement at German and French propaganda posters facing each other across the Rhine. Galeazzo

Ciano, trying to avert disaster for Italy, attempted to persuade Mussolini to renege on the Pact of Steel; and Captain Dönitz arrived in Kiel. Taking over from his Chief of Staff, he began to implement Hitler's instructions for *Fall Weiss*, Case White — preparations for an assault on Poland; and Joachim von Ribbentrop sent an urgent telegram to Ambassador Count von der Schulenburg in Moscow, telling him that Commissar Molotov's three proposals were all acceptable and could all be met at once.

8

In order to escape

At 4:47 A.M. on Thursday, August 17, the sun rose over the North Sea. Looking out from his cabin under the trawler's bridge, Lionel Tomlinson had again that feeling of confidence he could never quite explain, even to himself. The forecast was good, and as the stars dimmed he could see, as he had sensed all night, that the sea was smooth and the wind almost nonexistent. Under his feet the 115-foot *Evelina* vibrated rhythmically with the regular thump of her triple-expansion steam engine. He had had her command for only a month — his first job as a skipper, although he had got his master's ticket more than a year ago, when he was twenty-two. He knew that everything about her was in perfect condition; with the different members of the crew, he had checked it all himself the previous morning before leaving Tynemouth. But since then, they had been steaming for twenty hours, including two sessions of shooting the nets, with no result. Weather, ship, and men could all be perfect, but sometimes the fish just would not come. Today, however, he was sure they would. He could not say why; he simply felt it.

A bowler hat bobbed past his window, and a moment later the third deckhand stuck his head in the door. "Mornin', Skipper — just checking you're up. Chuck's about to mash a brew."

"Morning, Darky — looks like a good one. I'll be with you in a moment."

The half-caste nodded. "See you in the wheelhouse."

As the door closed, Tomlinson smiled: Darky Coates was a rum one, all right, what with that bowler, which he always wore — never wanted a sou'wester, even if it was pouring rain — and was it his pa or his grandpa who had been a black man? Tomlinson could never remember, but, whichever it was, it didn't matter a jot. No one ever thought of calling him anything other than Darky, and no offense was meant or taken. Born and bred in Sunderland, Darky Coates was pretty well as much a Tynesider as Tomlinson himself and a good deckhand — those were the important things.

When he came into the wheelhouse, Chuck the cook was already there, handing out big mugs of tea. He was a little man, thin but wiry, always lively. "Here's yours, skipper," he chirped. "Strong and sweet, just like me."

Tomlinson took it gratefully. "Good and hot, too. That's grand." Even on the best mornings, and this was definitely one of them, it was always cold on the water first thing. "Hot?" said the cook. "In India we'd've called that cold. That's the thing about tea — if you're cold it warms you, if you're hot it cools you down. No, in India it was hot enough to — "

"To cook a canary?"

India and canaries were almost Chuck's sole topics of conversation. He'd been with the army in India ("How long did you say, Chuck? Two years?" "Huh! I was under chloroform for longer than that!"), and he was mad about canaries, with a whole room of his house set aside for their breeding. Now he looked pained.

"Not a nice thing to say, with all the work I do for you. Anyway," he added with comic dignity, "you'd only get a mouthful from a whole canary."

The chief engineer came in, his flannel shirt damp with sweat. "Mornin', skipper. Mornin', all. Got a cuppa there, Chuck? Ta." He drank thirstily; whatever the weather, the engine room was always hot, and, with only one assistant and the need to keep steam up constantly, his job was five hours on and five hours off. "No problems below, skipper, everything sweet as a bell. I'm off to get my head down now."

"Right, Chief. See you later. I think we'll be busy."

As Tomlinson checked their course on the pelorus, flicked on the Marconi echo sounder, and turned to the chart, the man at the wheel glanced briefly at him. "Reckon we'll be lucky today then, skipper?"

"I do. Don't ask me why. I just feel we're going to get a big haul."

"Certainly could do with it—just as long as it's not one of them bloody German mines again."

Although the war had been over for twenty years, fishing boats still netted ancient mines from time to time. It had happened twice to Lionel Tomlinson. The first time, he had been excited, just to begin with—born in 1915, he had never seen a real mine before. But he had learned quickly that it was no laughing matter. The thing could not be cut free to drift, and it was too dangerous to try and blow it up at sea, so it had to be towed very gingerly all the way back to the coast, until some official boat with trained people could come out, take it over, and explode it safely. Then, briefly, the fishermen were local heroes and would have their picture in the paper, with a picture of the explosion alongside. But that was all; there was no reward or anything, so, at best, netting a mine was a waste of time and money for the skipper and crew concerned. And, at worst, they could all be killed. It had happened before, and no doubt would happen again.

"That'd make things go with a bang, that would," said Chuck, gathering up the empty mugs. For a moment Tomlinson went cold inside; he could imagine it all too clearly. "Mind you," the cook continued, "in India, if we wanted things to go with a real bang, we'd have a good hot curry. That'd clear you out, and no mistake. That's the thing about curry—"

"Chuck—" He was glad to hear the cook chattering on, but there was business to be done. "Get out of it, will you, and cook us all some breakfast. It's fish we're after, and I think there's going to be a lot of them."

"Aye aye, Captain." With mock formality, Chuck saluted. At that, Tomlinson smiled; he was a member of the Royal Naval Reserve, and Chuck's salute was an army one, as incongruous at sea as Darky's bowler hat.

★ ★ ★

Commanded by Heinrich Himler, the Nazi police force—the *Schutzstaffel*—was best known by its insignia, a pair of twin bolts of lightning that depicted its initials: SS. One branch of the SS was the SD, the *Sicherheitsdienst* or security service.

One thing Adolf Hitler liked about General Reinhard Heydrich was his appearance — tall, blond, blue-eyed, muscular, handsome: the perfect Aryan, emblem of the perfect German. Another agreeable attribute was his character — devious, unscrupulous, and utterly ruthless: the perfect chief of the SD. On August 17, he had a proposal for the Führer that Hitler could only admire as typical of the man.

It was a solution, simple but effective, to the problem of how to justify — at least in German eyes — an assault on Poland. The old-fashioned phrase was agent provocateur: If the enemy would not oblige with a timely offense, an offense would be provided and made to look like enemy action. In this case, Heydrich suggested, it would be very suitable if Polish soldiers launched an attack on German soldiers near the border. Even better if they targeted, say, a radio station such as the one at Gleiwitz, took it over, and broadcast insults against Germany. No doubt some of the attackers would die in the process. So, if Admiral Canaris, the head of the *Abwehr* — the intelligence service — could obtain 250 Polish army uniforms, a corresponding number of Polish weapons with appropriate ammunition, and suitable identifying Polish military documents, he, Heydrich, would arrange the rest. Just call it a "special SS operation" — there was no need for Canaris to know any more than that. Soldiers from the SS, trained to obey Polish commands, would play the active part. But there was a passive part as well. It could not be merely a set of reported episodes. "Physical evidence," said Heydrich, "is essential for the foreign press and for German propaganda purposes." That evidence would be provided by the corpses of some of the "attackers" — bodies taken from a concentration camp (there were more than enough) and dressed up in Polish uniform.

There was only one little thing that worried Hitler in what was otherwise an excellent plan. One could not refer in orders to the use of dead bodies; presumably General Heydrich had thought of that? Indeed he had; in any written orders, the corpses would be described as "canned goods." Cynical but suitable, and, without further hesitation, the Führer approved the plan in every detail.

Less than three years later, on June 4, 1942, when he was Reich
Protector of Czechoslovakia, General Heydrich ("a man with an
iron heart," said Himmler) was blown up and killed by Czech
resistance fighters. Admiral Wilhelm Canaris lived a little longer;
as another of those who plotted against Hitler's life, he was
arrested by the Gestapo in 1944 and, in 1945, was executed in the
Flossenburg concentration camp.

★   ★   ★

From the Foreign Office in London, the report of the Deputy
Chiefs of Staff was telegrammed almost word for word to Sir
Howard Kennard, Britain's ambassador in Warsaw. He should
ignore the government of Rumania, at least for the time being;
the Polish authorities posed the critical problem. In order to
persuade them, he should support his French colleague Léon
Noël and do everything he could to convince the Polish Foreign
Minister, Colonel Josef Beck, that Soviet troops must be allowed
free passage across Poland. Kennard was empowered to point out
to Colonel Beck that, if he did not agree, responsibility for any
breakdown of talks in Moscow would be on his shoulders.

A dramatic sideshow took place at the same time in Harland
and Wolff's shipyard in Belfast: At noon, a brand-new aircraft
carrier, HMS *Formidable,* launched herself. "Sir Kingsley Wood,
the Air Minister, and Lady Wood had just arrived on the launching platform," newspapers reported, "when pieces of timber
were seen to be breaking away from the cradle supporting the
vessel on the slips, and, to the consternation of everybody, the
vessel began to move. Shipwrights, hundreds of whom were
below the vessel ready to play their parts in the launch, ran for
their lives, while pieces of timber from the broken cradle crashed
around them . . . . Iron nuts and bolts were flung into the air,
and some of them fell among the thousands of spectators . . . .
Tugs had been standing by to take charge of the *Formidable* after
the launch, and, when they saw the ship entering the water, they
had to proceed at full speed ahead in order to escape."

As the tugs sounded their warning sirens, in a scene of great
excitement, Lady Wood showed astonishing presence of mind

and, despite everything, managed not only to call out the name of the new ship but also to crack a bottle of champagne across *Formidable*'s bow. But, in the drama, nineteen people were injured, and one, a woman called Mrs. Isobel Kirk, was killed.

* * *

In Moscow, the annual Soviet air exhibition was taking place. Not far away from it, the foreign delegates in the Spiridonyevka Palace were aware that they were only spinning things out; nothing had been heard yet from London, Paris, or Warsaw. Even so, at the end of the morning session, they were not expecting Marshal Voroshilov to say what he did.

"The Soviet Mission," he announced, "considers that we shall have to end the work of our conference until we get a reply to our questions." Pausing, he added smoothly, "Until receipt of their reply, I recommend our dear guests to rest, see the sights of Moscow, visit the Exhibition, and make themselves at home."

Under the circumstances, a dispassionate observer might well have said this was a sensible and reasonable thing to do. Certainly Voroshilov considered it so: As things stood, the conference was getting nowhere, and, until there was a chance of progress, it was a waste of time to talk for the sake of talking. But the decision hit Admiral Drax and General Doumenc like a hammer blow. True, they had not been able to offer — yet — the confirmation wanted by the Russians, but neither had Voroshilov accepted their own desire for agreements in principle. Unless they could keep the Soviet delegation at the conference table or at least leave with a firm commitment to meet again at a definite date, both the Frenchman and the Englishman felt they would lose even the limited control they had on events. Joining in a strong protest, they could not change Voroshilov's mind; until something was received from abroad, he saw absolutely no point in carrying on. At length, though, and with reluctance, he agreed that there should be a specific date for the end of the adjournment. The conference could begin again in four days, on August 21.

Otherwise, he was adamant, and eventually Drax and Doumenc accepted that they could move him no further. Doumenc was angry and concerned, but Drax was furious. The episode inflamed all his latent distrust of Russians. "Something devilish is going on behind the scenes, I'm sure of it," he fumed to his colleagues in private. "Some kind of intrigue of which we know nothing. Just what the hell d'you think they're up to?"

Of course no one could give any definite answer, and the admiral took everyone aback with his next remark: "Be blowed to diplomacy. I'll tell you what I'm going to do, next time we see them—I'm going to ask them straight to explain exactly what they're playing at. *Then* we'll see what happens."

That precipitated a welter of argument. Finally, acknowledging that he might feel calmer by the twenty-first, Drax was persuaded to await developments. He still grumbled in dissatisfaction. But he would have been even more disturbed if, instead of being in Moscow, he had been in Washington, D.C., for then he might have learned how well-founded his suspicions were.

★ ★ ★

By that time Lionel Tomlinson was six feet of pure concentration. The routine for shooting the nets was long established and familiar to all on board, but the skipper could not afford to miss a beat: Ship and men were, in the end, his responsibility—his own life, their lives, the livelihoods of all were on his shoulders—and, though accidents were rare, if they happened, they were bad. Poisoned fingers, pierced by wire or fish bones, were commonplace, taken as a risk of the job, and a man—especially a family man—would continue to work in spite of the pain; but there could be clumsiness, and sheer bad luck could never be ruled out. Quite recently, in another vessel belonging to the Tomlinsons, one man had been standing in the wrong place when a huge bag of fish was being lifted. The masthead block swivel had broken under the strain, and, though the fish were inboard, the block had caught the man on his wrist and broken it. He would be off work for months—possibly might never work at sea again. Tomlinson wanted to do all he could to prevent such an accident while he was skipper of *Evelina*.

The men were good. Even so, from his decision to shoot, it always took half an hour to get the lashings off the nets. Then warps were run out from the heavy-duty steam winch on deck. They were connected to the trawl doors, two weighty metal contraptions designed to move to each side as the water flowed through them, opening the mouth of the net. Normally they were stowed between the gallows and the rail, but, once over the rail, they were hung on a preventer hook until the time came to let them go. Then came the bobbins, each fourteen inches high, fixed on the ground range at every two feet, to keep the line rolling sweetly over the seabed.

From amidships, the net was streamed to windward, with the ship going to leeward. Over went the bobbins. Now all was hanging by two fifty-fathom ground cables. In rapid response to his orders, the ship turned to bring the net off her quarter, then stopped before the wind. Now the net was pulling heavy astern, taking out the rest of the fifty-fathom line. Over the tops of the gallows, the patent clips to the trawl doors were unclipped — lower away the fore door — amidships — lower away the aft door — slow ahead. Everyone knew what to do, but the orders were essential: Only one man was in charge; the others moved at his bidding. Full ahead — the warps, leading off the sides, began to pay out. Their final length would be three-and-a-half times the depth of water. Judging that was the mate's job, and his alone. Every twenty-five fathoms, the steel warps, two-and-a-half inches thick, had rope markers spliced into them. When there was a sufficient length out, the mate gathered the two warps and locked them together with a block of heavy steel. From there they spread out in a V, and *Evelina* began to trawl. If the V closed and the warps drew together astern, it could mean a good bag of fish. It could also mean they had netted a rock. It could also — and there was that shadow again — it could also mean they had netted a mine.

* * *

Since the spring, the Roosevelt administration had known far more than anyone in Britain about the political relationship between Nazi Germany and Communist Russia. For fear of compromising their source, the Americans hitherto had passed hints but nothing more to the British. The hints, however, had not been enough, and today in the State Department it was decided the time had come to sound a clear alarm. The British ambassador, Sir Ronald Lindsay, heard it in the elegant setting of the office of Sumner Welles, the under secretary of state.

Welles's message was unequivocal; he gave Lindsay a complete rundown of the conversation, only two days earlier, between Molotov and von der Schulenburg: the German suggestion that von Ribbentrop should come to Moscow very soon; the Russian proposals of a nonaggression pact, help with Soviet-Japanese relations, and guarantees for the Baltic frontiers — everything. In the assessment of the U.S. State Department, Welles explained, a Russo-German pact was imminent, which, freeing Hitler from any fear of attack from the east, would immediately bring about war.

At the end of his tour of the Maginot Line, Winston Churchill gratefully checked into the Ritz Hotel in Paris. About the same time, Francis Vanek and his friends, spiritually fulfilled by their visit to the shrine of Lourdes, were going shopping in the French capital; Francis needed new cycle clips for his trousers, and, to his delight, the others bought a bottle of champagne. The group shared it, all seventeen of them, in honor of their achievement. As they did so, Count Ciano, in Rome, was struggling through another day of Mussolini's changing moods. After his experiences in the Reich, Ciano was positive that, come what may, Italy must avoid the commitments implied by the Pact of Steel, but the Duce dithered, caught between his own sense of military honor and Ciano's blunt practicality. Since Ciano's return from the visits to von Ribbentrop and Hitler, Mussolini had (as Ciano noted in his diary) "refused to act independently of the Germans," then become "convinced we must not march blindly with Germany," then thought it might be "a good idea to reaffirm his determination of going along with the Germans." That, Count Ciano thought, would be "a mad venture, carried out against the unanimous will of the Italian people." They might not yet know quite how things stood, but, after "a sniff of the truth," said the Count, they had had "a sudden fit of rage against the Germans." By August 17, in spite of everything, old scruples of loyalty were returning to Mussolini: Now he felt, after all, that, if the democracies threw themselves into the furnace of war, Italy should join with Germany. All day long, Ciano fought against the idea. Believing in the end that he had prevailed, he conducted individual interviews with other ambassadors, ending with Sir Percy Loraine, from Britain.

"I tell him that Europe needs a great deal of common sense if it is to avoid the crisis," the Italian wrote in his diary. "He answers that the common sense is there, but that Europe will not tolerate the periodical diktat of Hitler. If the crisis comes, England will fight. Personally, he would like to participate in such a fight. He regrets only one thing: that for the first time in our history, our two countries may be at war with each other." Ciano did not reply to that, yet he felt sure that Loraine understood that he did not wish for such a thing to happen.

That evening in Moscow, Commissar Molotov and Count von der Schulenburg met once again. *A strange meeting,* thought von der Schulenburg. The Commissar, comparing the high political status of Germany's proffered visitor adversely to the British delegate, was positively jaunty, yet still he seemed to have misunderstood the speed at which Germany was willing to proceed and spoke of the need for trade agreements and credit agreements. But he did also mention the desirability of each government drafting a nonaggression pact, and, in that context, he brought up the idea of a secret protocol, "defining the interests of the contracting parties in this or that question of foreign policy." Ambassador von der Schulenburg reported it all dutifully; von Ribbentrop could make of it what he would.

★   ★   ★

Evelina's decks were covered with blood and silver. Somehow, the crew had found the shoal — a dream shoal, net after net. Shooting and hauling were continuous as Lionel Tomlinson, with the master's prerogative, stood at the wheel and gently coaxed the vessel in the direction he thought the fish were going. It was not all magic — the echo sounder, bouncing back from apparently unnaturally shallow depths, revealed them — but there was an essential element of feel in it, the touch that came only with experience. And, as Tomlinson would have been the first to admit, there was an element of luck, too. Once they seemed to have lost the shoal; he searched for half an hour before the telltale trace showed on the echo sounder again, and during that time he had had no real idea where to go — not that he said so to anyone. By then their haul was already big enough to have justified the journey, but still he was glad when the fish were relocated. This time, he knew the only limit to their catch would be *Evelina*'s capacity or their own physical endurance.

Each time the fishermen hauled in the net it took fifteen minutes; with everything prepared, the shortest shoot and haul took between twenty-five minutes and half an hour, with a good haul being fifty baskets of fish at eighty-four pounds each. As soon as the fish were inboard, still flapping and flipping, the men began gutting them, sorting them by size and type, passing the clammy corpses below, where they were stacked on shelves between layers of ice. From time to time someone would sluice water across the quivering deck, washing livers and stomachs and small tubular joining bits through the scuppers and over the sides for the gulls and the other fish still swimming below. Silver and blood, blood and silver — and every fresh-iced fish a payment toward the coal, the ice, the oil, the carbide, the food, and the welfare of the men and their families. But what precise payment no one could tell, until after the catch was landed and auctioned next day.

★   ★   ★

There had been public signs of a possible Russo-German reconciliation since April, when a defector known as Krivitsky had announced to American newspapers that, in 1934, Stalin had tried to negotiate with Hitler along such lines. It was also in

April that Hitler's speeches had lost their previous powerfully anti-Soviet tone. But, though Krivitsky's information was later found to be correct, in the summer of 1939 British intelligence, having nothing with which to corroborate it, still treated it with caution and some skepticism. The Americans, with good reason, did not; from members of the German embassy in Moscow, the U.S. ambassador to Russia was receiving a steady supply of completely reliable material and had been doing so since before the Munich agreement.

In Washington, summarizing the whole, Welles pointed out to the shocked and excited British ambassador that, when he reported to London, there must be no mention in any telegram of the source. Lindsay gave his promise on that, agreeing that no cipher could be guaranteed to be completely secure; he would only put the identity of the source in the diplomatic bag.

On August 17, at 9:00 in the evening Washington time, he sent to London his ciphered telegram, containing the most reliable and accurate information on Russo-German negotiations yet seen by British eyes. Hoping that it might enable his colleagues to preempt any deal between Molotov and von Ribbentrop, Lindsay remarked, "It should be there first thing tomorrow morning, their time." It was, but it sat there, undeciphered, for four crucial days.

THE THIRD WEEK

August 18–25, 1939

9

The present unusual situation

It may have been accidental. In these weeks of crisis, unusually large numbers of telegrams were flowing into the Foreign Office. Extra staff had been taken on to try and cope with them, but the volume of traffic and the inexperience of many of the clerks meant that serious delays were occurring all the time. Moreover, first attention was being given to messages from Europe, and Lindsay had not attached any special priority marking to his telegram. But its deciphering and final delivery may also have been held up, at that critical time, on purpose: For some years past, the Foreign Office had suspected that at least one of its members had been leaking classified information. Early in the coming September, on new evidence, Sir Alexander Cadogan noted in his diary a positive "fear that someone in the office is compromised." Soon after, an investigation produced an "awful" discovery: Captain John King, one of those who handled the Communication Department's cipher traffic, was actively spying for Russia. On September 27, he was arrested; three weeks later, he was sentenced to ten years in jail.

It was not revealed whether King was personally responsible for the particular delay of Lindsay's telegram or whether, as one of the Foreign Office's senior officials said regretfully, it was simply "a bad oversight." By the time King was convicted, this was, of course, an academic question — by design or by default, the damage had been done, and Europe was at war.

While that telegram arrived in the Foreign Office on Friday, August 18, and became buried in someone's in-tray, Cadogan received something that also required early attention — a salmon from the Prime Minister. Chamberlain seemed to be sending them to everyone. *Hope he's having good sport,* Cadogan thought a trifle enviously. With the P.M. in the north of Scotland and Lord

Halifax in Yorkshire, he was having what he called "a rather complicated time" in London. However, one item of news that day caused him to reflect that, if it was complicated trying to stave off a war, it seemed to be just as complicated, in unexpected ways, for someone trying to start one. The head of the Secret Intelligence Service, Admiral Quex Sinclair (whom Cadogan always discreetly referred to only as "C"), told him from a very good source that, two days previously, Hitler had had an interview with a worried man—the chief of the Reich railways. Orders were out already for the mobilization of 25,000 men. Hearing rumors of further mobilization and knowing that a Nazi rally was scheduled for September 2, the railway boss had wanted to find out which he should prepare for. "He could arrange transport for Party Rally or for mobilization," Cadogan learned with amusement, "but not for both!"

Nevertheless, good as the source was, it seemed that, even though arranging for the physical transport of troops was a basic requirement of mobilization, no one yet knew for certain what Hitler's reply to the railway chief had been. It was reported that he had chosen the rally, but Cadogan noted soberly that this was "unconfirmed."

The Reich navy's U-boat arm contained at that time a total of fifty-six boats. In Kiel, Captain Dönitz found that, much as he had expected, twenty-one were undergoing various repairs and periodical maintenance work, while thirty-five were fully *seeklar,* ready for sea in all respects. At once he began dispatching them to their positions, planned long before. Eighteen would go to the eastern Atlantic, scattered from the Straits of Gibraltar (where three boats—U-39, U-40, and U-41—patrolled up to 1,000 miles out into the ocean) all the way to the northwest of Ireland, where U-53, U-27, and U-30 were stationed. These eighteen boats could work an enormous area: approximately 1.5 million square miles of sea. The other seventeen were all destined for the Baltic, ready for operations against Poland—and, in accordance with existing plans, against Russia, too.

★   ★   ★

"Got you!" As the other boys hurtled out of her orchard, Betty Haigh collared the youngest and smallest. Kicking and punching in his efforts to escape, he screamed up at her, "You let me go! My dad'll come, an' 'e's a boxer!"

"Listen to me," she answered, breathless but calm. "You don't frighten me with that kind of talk, so don't try. I'm going to let you go, don't worry. But if you want apples, come and ask for them, all right? There are plenty of them, and I'll give you some. But what you're doing is stealing — d'you understand?"

Still holding the urchin tight with one hand, she reached up and picked an apple. "There you are. That's much better than the ones on the ground." He snatched it from her, baffled and suspicious. "It's all right," she said. "That's for you. And when you want more, just come and ask." With a sudden twist the boy broke free and ran off. As he ran, he turned, throwing the apple hard at her, and yelled again, "My dad'll come! 'E's a boxer!"

Over lunch in the lighthouse — their nickname for the three-story detached house that was both home and workplace — Betty told her husband of the episode. "It's so depressing, Michael," she finished. "I don't think he understood anything I said."

He nodded. "The same sort of thing happened to me in a different way the other day," he replied. "I haven't mentioned it before — it's not really important — but a little lad came into the office. He knocked on the door before he came in, very respectfully, shut the door behind him; and then he knocked again, on the closed door. Then, when I asked him what his name was, you'd never guess what he answered: 'Dunno — Jimmy or summat.' He wasn't just being shy. The kid honestly didn't know his own name."

One day, Michael Haigh would achieve the distinguished title of Emeritus Professor of Social Medicine. In the summer of 1939, that was many years away, but he was put on the road to his caring academic distinction by much of what he saw with Betty in the suburbs of Birmingham. At that time, Britain's second city seemed to contain all that was worst and unhappiest in the nation: severe economic depression, high unemployment, dirt, poverty, and all the illnesses that went with them. The red brick "lighthouse" was an intensely ugly building, uncomfortable and inconvenient in many ways. The fireplace in the living room smoked badly; the wooden floor tiles were loose, clattering under foot, always threatening to trip you up; apart from the smoky hearth, there was no other main heating; fungi grew on the cellar walls, and, for lack of other space, the dispensary had had to be set up in the garage. However, the house had two acres of land, including the very prolific apple orchard, and the Haighs knew how fortunate they were, compared to most of their patients. Close by, living on the banks of the canal, were the vagrants and the gypsy types, the pub owner who beat his wife — and who once, when she had called the doctor for help, had turned on him, too. Behind the house, on Balsall Heights, were long straight rows of low-income housing; inside them you could smell the vermin. Delivering babies there — something that happened about once a week — Dr. Haigh could feel the fleas as they jumped onto his wrists and ankles and, even as the mother gave birth, could see the flat, bloodsucking bedbugs writhing around her and the newborn infant.

After such sessions he always needed to scrub down from head to foot, standing naked on a large white bathtowel; it was the only way to be certain all the parasites were gone. But he did not resent it. The respect shown by almost everyone to him as a doctor, an educated man who could cure their ills, embarrassed him — they trusted him to do his best and did not blame him when he failed. Yet he knew how little he could really do and, with babies and children dying from measles, whooping cough, and diphtheria, how narrow were his resources. Chalk and opium for diarrhea; bismuth and chloradine for stomach complaints; bromide with strychnine as a tonic; quinine, insulin, and arsenic — until 1936, when antibacterial sulfonamides had been introduced, these had constituted the complete range of his effective drugs. Often, seeing in his office the large glass Winchester jars filled with different colored solutions, patients would know exactly which they needed — pink, white, or yellow — because it had worked before. What they did not know was that all the different solutions were simply solutions of aspirin. Convinced that the pink would fix them up and the yellow would do no good, they were given the pink, and, more often than not, it worked. Haigh was not really tricking his patients; it was simply the best that could be done within the system he and they had inherited. That was what he resented, and he wondered sometimes about the housing projects. Certainly they were better than the inner-city slums they had replaced, but people had been moved to them willy-nilly, in some strange new area they did not know, without shops or pubs or any of the neighborly things of the past.

"You know I'm not being romantic about slum life," he remarked to his wife. "God knows they were dreadful, but people don't seem to be healthier outside them, and every day I see how unhappy they are in these houses. I think it's possible a lot of their illnesses come from plain old-fashioned unhappiness."

★   ★   ★

"A conversation with the Duce in the morning," Ciano wrote dully in his diary. "His usual shifting feelings." Mussolini still thought the democracies would not go to war, and his latest worry was that "Germany might do good business cheaply, from which business he does not wish to be excluded." With the candor of privacy, Ciano noted that the Duce was also chicken. "He fears Hitler's rage . . ." Gnawing at the Italian leader's mind was the fear that, if he denounced the Pact of Steel or even came close to doing so, Hitler might abandon the Polish question altogether and turn his full wrath on Italy. ". . . All this makes him nervous and disturbed." As well it might, but dictators should not dither. The only thing on which Mussolini's mind appeared made up was a refusal to accept any further advice on foreign affairs from his Foreign Minister, and so Count Ciano turned his mind to a more congenial subject and made ready for an official visit to Albania.

About the same time, Sir Percy Loraine, Britain's ambassador in Rome, was sending another report home to London. The first part of it might have reassured Mussolini — or at least helped him to make up his mind — had he cared to listen: One of Ciano's senior officials, who had accompanied the Count to the Berghof in Berchtesgaden, was convinced that, unless Danzig was surrendered, Hitler had definitely decided to take it and then march on Warsaw. But the second part of Loraine's report would, no doubt, have thrown Mussolini off beam again, for the same official judged that "Herr Hitler's language and behavior showed clear signs of mental abnormality."

Count Ciano should have taken some little consolation from the fact that, even if Mussolini ignored what he said, he would at least listen to him. Herbert von Dirksen was itching to present von Ribbentrop with his assessment of the likelihood of British involvement in a war. On that subject — which had, after all, an undeniable bearing on Germany's best move — von Dirksen was probably the best informed person in the Reich; yet, try as he might, he could not get an interview with von Ribbentrop. In exasperation, he decided to go on holiday to Silesia, as he had intended all along. From there he would write to von Ribbentrop — but not directly. He would send his letter through Ernst von Weizsäcker, Secretary of State at the Foreign Office. That way, the Foreign Minister might be forced to take a look at it.

Meanwhile, in Warsaw, Ambassador Kennard was having no success at all either with Colonel Beck or with the Polish Commander-in-Chief, Marshal Edward Smigly-Rydz. Both were as immovable as Marshal Voroshilov — "absolutely obdurate," Kennard reported to London. Under no circumstances would the Poles consider allowing Soviet troops to pass over their country. They had two central reasons. First, Beck judged that, if he were to agree, Hitler would go over the edge: "Given his anti-Bolshevik complex, he would see red and not hesitate to precipitate a war." There was something in that; undoubtedly the Führer would regard such an agreement as provocative. Smigly-Rydz gave the other reason, one that encapsulated centuries of battered Polish pride: "With the Germans we risk losing our lives," he explained, "but with the Soviets, our souls." Apparently he did not consider the possibility that persistent refusal might result in Poland losing not only its life but its soul as well.

This was the essence of *Spannung,* the war of nerves. For the politicians and diplomats most closely involved — and for the ordinary people, too — these weeks constituted the toughest many had ever known or ever would know. A decision, any decision, could offer release from increasingly awful uncertainty. But, in the meantime, life carried on as best it could, with all its enormously differing degrees of innocence and experience. Returned safely to the isle of Foula and back with the few friends the island offered, Nanette Smith cavorted again, riding the backs of cows, while her uncles in Bressay gloomily told each other that disaster was coming. In eastern Australia, following the politics of Europe and communism as closely as possible, Charles King prepared the next edition of *World Peace.* In rural Devon, Kit Dennis and her farming family followed the season, with harvesting and hunt balls and meetings of the Young Conservatives. In the state of Maine, Vacationland, USA — perhaps the farthest removed of all from Europe's desperate situation — Barkley Goodrich prepared for a visit to the New York World's Fair to get a look at the "World of Tomorrow." In the English towns of Bradford and Newcastle, firmly planted in their world of today, Elspeth Harmes and Molly McAndrew sold ribbons and lingerie — Elspeth happy with her fleeting visit to the sea and her silver bracelet, an unexpected birthday present from a friend in the shop, and Molly happy with the thoughts of Ernie, her fiancé. In Northern Ireland, David Howarth pondered the BBC's radio talks for the coming week, while in London, on his last day of holiday, Francis Vanek could not resist going straight out to his cycling club; and in East Sussex, Bob Leaney, a parish priest, was walking through the tranquil village of Mountfield.

In time, like Dr. Haigh in Birmingham, the priest would also become a professor — the Reverend Professor Robert Leaney — but, in August 1939, just thirty years old, he was still a humble

Anglican vicar, ministering to the 600 or so souls in his parish. It was a job that he enjoyed enormously. He and his wife Liz had been there only a short time, and they found nothing humdrum about the quiet little village nor anything unpleasant about their lives in it. Indeed, before coming to Mountfield, they would hardly have believed that such a place still existed. Both had been born and bred in Birmingham, and, after studying and being ordained in Oxford, Bob had returned to the Birmingham suburb of Oldbury to take up his first post as a curate. It had been ghastly in almost every way. Facing the same social conditions as Dr. Haigh, he had felt even less able to deal with them effectively; anyone could see the need for a doctor and would go to him if they were physically unhealthy, but the need for a curate was not so obvious. For Bob Leaney, life in Birmingham and the depressed industrial midlands had been a deep well of unhappiness and frustration.

He would have agreed with Dr. Haigh's suggestion that unhappiness caused illness; in Birmingham he, too, had spent much time with the poor and unemployed. Mountfield was like another world — as if, in a flash, one had been taken back forty or fifty years to a more stable England before the Great War. Because of a prosperous gypsum mine outside the village, there was hardly any unemployment. Being a small place, it was easy for him to get to know all his parishioners — each afternoon, after studying, preparing sermons, and gardening in the morning, he would visit several households — and best of all, he was welcomed by all. Even those who did not go to church at all (and he knew they were the majority) felt the village needed a vicar.

There was no deception in Mountfield's traditional atmosphere and appearance. In its center, the level crossing of the railway line from Hastings to London was one of the few signs of any intrusion by the nineteenth century, let alone the twentieth. In the graveyard surrounding the small, sturdy church, generations of Mountfield villagers were buried. Its registers went back to 1517; in one of the earliest, Bob Leaney had been delighted to discover a record of the burial of one Mercie Leny — no relation, he was sure, but it made him feel at home. The vicarage, orig-

inally an Elizabethan farmhouse, was an enormous rambling
building, all tile-hung walls and tall heavy chimney stacks.
Opposite was the entrance to the drive of Mountfield Court,
residence of Commander Sydney Egerton—and he, the vicar
reflected, was one main cause of the village's character, for he
virtually ran it, filling to a T the role of squire.

In this idyllic, archaic setting, the Reverend Leaney sensed
himself blossoming into his task and position. Yet no one and
nowhere were immune that August. *Spannung* touched everyone,
creating a sense of imminent evil even in Mountfield's rural
obscurity. It felt as if a poisonous mist were creeping through the
hedgerows and across the sunlit fields, a mist that you could not
see or smell but that you knew was there and that might at any
instant rise and choke you.

But the priest did have one defense. For him the more serious
crisis was not one of politics but of conscience, and, with the help
of his bishop, George Bell of Chichester, he had faced and
overcome it. It was the classic dilemma of a Christian: If war
came, what would he do? One by one, Bishop George had asked
all his ministers the same question. In his modulated voice, he
had spoken of General Montgomery; the memory still amused
Bob. "Favorable to our work—helps chaplains," the bishop had
said. "But he's queer, you know; he's Irish, you know . . ."
However, it was something else that had helped Bob to his
solution. Bishop George knew Dietrich Bonhoeffer well;
indeed, he was probably the closest English friend Bonhoeffer
had. For six years the German theologian, a Lutheran pastor, had
opposed the Nazi regime in every way he could; in 1943, he
would be arrested, and in 1945, only thirty-nine years old, he
would be executed. Talks with Bonhoeffer gave a special insight
into the nature of the potential enemy. Under other circumstances, Bob would probably have been a pacifist, but not against
the Nazis. A war against such a creed would be, he decided, the
nearest possible thing to a morally justified war. He had discussed it with Liz, and she had agreed; so it was arranged that, if
necessary, he would become chaplain to a battalion of the Royal
Sussex Regiment, a part of the Territorial Army.

There was nothing further he could do; whatever happened next was out of his hands. Once the decision had been made, the weight lifted; his crisis was over. With confidence in God, he gave himself back to his family and his ministry. *Spannung,* the time of tension, ceased to affect him. But for others that Friday, August 18 — others less fortunate in faith — tension was reaching its highest pitch.

"I don't usually take tickets in the 'dates' lottery," wrote Sir Nevile Henderson from the British embassy in Berlin. "But I did venture to write to the Secretary of State [Lord Halifax] early in July to the effect that I foresaw the big crisis around about 27 August. I am afraid that I may not be far out."

Cadogan was dining at home that evening with his wife Theo. They were just finishing the meal when the Government's chief diplomatic adviser, Sir Robert Vansittart, telephoned "in a high state of excitement." Vansittart had just been talking on the phone to Halifax and now was so worked up that Cadogan could barely grasp what he was saying: Halifax *must* come back at once, and the Prime Minister, too. Realizing there was little point in trying to make sense of this over the phone, Cadogan insisted that Vansittart should come round at once and talk; when he arrived, Cadogan noted later, "I have never seen a man nearer nervous collapse." Providing his distraught guest with a cold supper, he heard the reason: "His source has told him Hitler has chosen war, to begin between the 25th and 28th." Cadogan did not entirely credit the report. *Still,* he thought, *one can't ignore it,* and telephoned Halifax himself. Before long it was agreed that the Foreign Secretary would come to London the next day but that the Prime Minister need not be summoned yet.

"Eventually calmed Van down a bit," the phlegmatic Under Secretary wrote, "and packed him off about 11:00. This is the beginning of the 'War of Nerves.' And I have seen the first casualty!"

It was just about then that a telegram was sent from Joachim von Ribbentrop to Ambassador von der Schulenburg. Its priority coding was "Most Urgent." Von Ribbentrop understood Commissar Molotov's caution at the German Foreign Minister's proposal to bypass the usual system of diplomacy by coming in person to Moscow. "We too, under normal circumstances, would naturally be ready to pursue a realignment of German-Russian relations through diplomatic channels, and to carry it out in the customary way." But that would take time, and "the present unusual situation makes it necessary, in the opinion of the Führer, to employ a different method which would lead to quick results." To be more precise, that meant von Ribbentrop's "imminent departure for Moscow." Von der Schulenburg should make this possible. "Please," von Ribbentrop concluded, "emphasize that German foreign policy has today reached an historic turning-point."

★   ★   ★

On that Friday, *The Times* published a letter signed by no less than 375 notable academics. It was an appeal to the Prime Minister to drop his prejudice against Winston Churchill and include him in the Cabinet again. On Saturday, August 19, "at this grave hour" and "on behalf of some of my friends here informally assembled," Captain Alfred Henderson-Livesey of the Army Educational Corps sent Churchill a private letter. "We pray," wrote the captain, "that God will give you health and strength to discharge the great task which awaits you. We feel that the continued exclusion of yourself from the ranks of the Government is a monstrous scandal which cannot long continue. We note that you have been spending your vacation inspecting the defenses of France, while the First Minister of the Crown has been absorbed in the mysteries of rod and line in remote Highland streams. At this juncture your name alone can do for the people of this country what that of Kitchener did in 1914."

The letter was ponderously worded but honestly meant; throughout the country, there was a powerful feeling that putting Churchill back in government would be the clearest possible sign to Germany — specifically, to Hitler — that, if it came down to it, Britain meant business. At that moment, Churchill was in Dreux, fifty miles west of Paris, resting after his tour of the

Maginot Line in a château belonging to his cousin Consuelo Balsan — "some sunshine days," he wrote later, "with a pleasant but deeply anxious company." One of his fellow guests was the wife of the British Minister of Transport. "She was expecting him to join her. Presently he telegraphed he could not come and would explain why later . . . . I found painting hard work in this uncertainty."

On the same morning — a brilliantly sunny morning in every part of Great Britain — a young man named Andrew Hole, a schoolmaster in Plymouth, received a letter from his Uncle James, who had lived in Germany since 1910. "Can't quite believe Hitler will go to war," said Uncle James. He should know, shouldn't he? He'd been there for twenty-nine years, since before the Great War. He'd seen that through, and, after Germany's defeat and humiliation, he'd seen the Weimar republic, the depression, the rule of President von Hindenburg, and, since 1933, the renaissance of national spirit and confidence. It wouldn't be thrown away on a whim, on a throw of the dice — would it? He should know. But Andrew Hole was, he wrote in his diary, "very depressed." He was twenty-nine years old and had grown used to his pupils' jokes about his name — A. Hole — and that was not the cause of his mood. Uncle James might well be right, "but there's little sign of tension slackening or of weakening in the German policy over Danzig."

In Warsaw that day, Colonel Beck had a session with Léon Noël, the French Ambassador to Poland. Like his British counterpart Sir Howard Kennard, Noël did his utmost to gain permission from the Polish Foreign Minister for the passage of Russians across Poland; and, like Kennard, Noël failed — Beck's response was *"un 'non' catégorique."*

At noon, as arranged, Lord Halifax, Sir Robert Vansittart, and Sir Alexander Cadogan met in "the Office." Cadogan had already written down his proposals for an approach to Mussolini. By 1:00 P.M. they had agreed to send a telegram to Rome, to draft a letter for the Prime Minister to send to Hitler, and to let the Prime Minister stay a little longer in Scotland. Since he was due to return early on Monday morning, there seemed no point in bringing him back two days early; they could handle all that needed to be done in the meantime.

Chamberlain's holiday had two main purposes: to relax and strengthen him in preparation for whatever might come next, and to maintain, so far as possible, an air of normality in the country and in Britain's dealings abroad. Nations might be panicked into war, but no one had ever been panicked into peace. Merely being on holiday did not mean, however, that he was unreachable or even out of regular touch with developments; daily telephone calls to and from London kept him up to date, while key telegrams and digests of the situation were continuously forwarded to him. One such, sent this day, was a 1,000-word letter drafted by Cadogan and signed by Halifax, summarizing recent events, action taken, and action proposed. Government and diplomacy did not go to sleep, but, as usual in any parliamentary recess, their continuing work was more or less invisible to ordinary folk. The system functioned as well in this recess as in any other, and Chamberlain would have been going against his nature to have altered it. But whether this recess was publicly or politically appropriate in the August of 1939 was another matter. The intended signal of confident stability could easily be misread at home, as Henderson-Livesey's letter to Churchill made plain: "We note that you have been spending your vacation inspecting the defenses of France, while the First Minister of the Crown has been absorbed in the mysteries of rod and line." This was less than fair to the Prime Minister; for better or worse, Churchill was not a member of the government, and he had toured the Maginot Line as a private citizen. Since 1933 he had advocated increased defensive and offensive preparations for Britain; his tour was as natural a reaction for his pugnacious character as was fishing for the Prime Minister. In their different ways, both were striving for peace. What if they had changed places? What if Churchill had traveled in an official governmental capacity? The questions are unanswerable today, except theoretically, and they were just as unanswerable then, when it was all real and urgent.

1. With an elegance to rival that of any royal court, senior Nazis and their guests gather for a concert in the Berlin house of Reich Foreign Minister, Joachim von Ribbentrop. In his Field Marshal's dress uniform, Hermann Goering sits at the left of the picture, next to Frau von Ribbentrop; the Führer is in the place of honour; to his left, the actress Olga Tschechowa, and beyond her, on the far right, Frau Emmy Goering. Also visible in the second row are the Japanese Ambassador, General Hiroshi Oshima; Frau Gertrud Scholtz-Klink, leader of the Reich Women's Movement, and Major-General Wilhelm Keitel, Chief of the High Command of the Armed Forces.

2. Behind the facade of cultural appreciation, however, is the reality of a nation where even children and teenagers are already semi-militarised. In the middle of August 1939, the subjection of Czechoslovakia is symbolised by a contingent of Hitler Youths marching with banners flying through the Invalidenplatz in Prague...

3. ... while in Germany, where the growth of the armed forces leads to a civilian labour shortage, the harvest is gathered in by numerous members of the *Bund Deutsche Mädel*, the League of German Maidens.

4. Across the border, by the third week of August, the Polish Army is also ready – not merely the famous, archaic cavalry, which rode vainly against German tanks, but also fully equipped soldiers sufficient to make Poland the world's fifth military power, with an army larger than that of France.

5. Wednesday 9 August: breaking his holiday at Balmoral Castle in Scotland, His Majesty King George VI has travelled overnight in the Royal Train to Weymouth Bay on England's south coast. There, 133 warships — the British Reserve Fleet — await his inspection, the ceremony marking their mobilisation. Wearing the uniform of an Admiral of the Fleet, he boards HMS *Effingham*, the Fleet's flagship.

6. Tuesday 15 August: at Salzburg airport in Austria, Count Galeazzo Ciano, the Italian Foreign Minister, shakes hands with Joachim von Ribbentrop, Reich Foreign Minister, after two days of discussion with him and the Führer. A German spokesman states that complete unity had been achieved on all questions concerning the Axis; yet over the next two weeks, Ciano will successfully do his utmost to save Italy from fulfilling the obligations of its Pact with Germany.

THE ILLUSTRATED LONDON NEWS

The World Copyright of all the Editorial Matter, both Illustrations and Letterpress, is Strictly Reserved in Great Britain, the British Dominions and Colonies, Europe, and the United States of America.

SATURDAY, AUGUST 12, 1939.

"UNDER THE SPREADING CHESTNUT-TREE," SUNG BY THE ROYAL FAMILY DURING THEIR VISIT TO THE KING'S ANNUAL CAMP FOR BOYS AT ABERGELDIE, ON THE BALMORAL ESTATE.

By invitation of its royal founder, the King's Camp for boys from Public Schools and Industrial Areas took place this year at Abergeldie Castle, on the Balmoral estate. Some 200 boys from 17 to 19, were the guests of the Royal Family for tea at Balmoral on August 6. On August 7 the King and Queen, with Princess Elizabeth and Princess Margaret motored the two miles from Balmoral in perfect weather to visit the Camp, and above they are seen with Captain J. G. Paterson, the camp commandant (seated next to the King), and boys joining in the action-song. "Under the Spreading Chestnut-Tree," conducted by the song-master, Mr. Robert Hyde, director of the Industrial Welfare Society, from among whose member firms the boys are selected. The little Princesses joined in with appropriate gestures. *[G.P.U.]*

7. [*Opposite*] 'Back at Balmoral'.

8. [*Right*] Sir Reginald Plunkett-Ernle-Erle-Drax (left) and Joseph Doumenc (right): on Saturday 5 August, on board *City of Exeter*, the British Admiral and French General, heads of their respective military missions, look cheerful enough at the start of their long journey to Moscow in search of an alliance with Russia. Knowing their task will be difficult, they do not realise that centuries of anti-pathy between Russia and Poland will make it virtually impossible.

9. Biggin Hill RAF Station, Kent: on Tuesday 8 August, pilots sprint to their machines. Not only fifteen groups of the Civilian Observer Corps, but also 500 barrage balloons, 1,300 aircraft and 1,400 anti-aircraft guns are engaged in a test of British air defences and counter-offensive strikes. This is the beginning of the most comprehensive air exercises ever planned in Britain.

10. [*Opposite above*] Tests of barrage balloons have already begun: the first five hundred are ready by 28 July, moored in a circle 14 miles across and centred on Tower Bridge. From 2,000 feet up – their maximum daytime flying height – the Albert Hall's dome is dwarfed, and the Albert Memorial becomes a tiny spike. In war conditions the balloons will fly at altitudes between 20,000 and 30,000 feet, forcing attackers above the zone where accurate bombing is possible.

11. [*Opposite below*] Gradually the strange and abnormal becomes a familiar, comforting sight. On 3 September, the day war is declared, hundreds more balloons are in position, and at ground level their huge size is apparent: even when partially inflated, they dominate the busy thoroughfares of London.

12. Conscription in Britain: compulsory military training began at the end of April 1939. By the beginning of June, 234,000 20-year-old men were registered; in July, 34,000 of them were called up. By mid-August, when this photograph was taken, enrolment centres were inundated...

13. ... and even statesmen put on uniform. Anthony Eden, Member of Parliament and ex-Foreign Secretary, was also a major in the Territorial Army. On Sunday 13 August, at the head of his TA unit – the 2nd Battalion The Rangers (King's Royal Rifle Corps) – he marches from his Bloomsbury headquarters to Waterloo Station, *en route* for their training camp in Beaulieu, Hampshire.

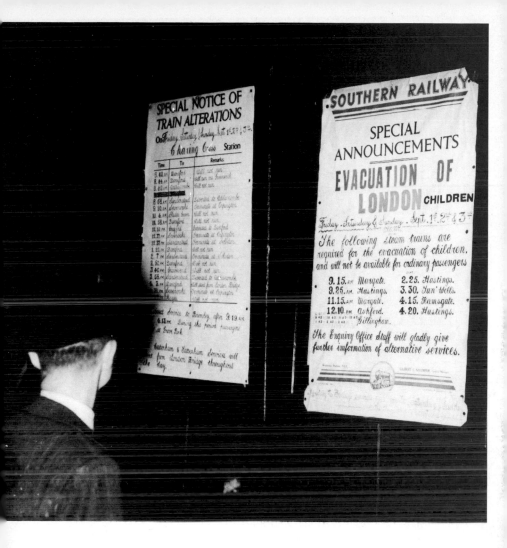

14. Beaming with optimism at the apparent strength of French defences, Winston Churchill arrives at the Gare de l'Est in Paris on Thursday 17 August. Although, like Eden, he is out of office and acting as an ordinary backbench MP, he has just returned from an inspection of the Maginot Line – while, as many people note despondently, the only line the Prime Minister is inspecting is his fishing line: Chamberlain is on holiday in Scotland.

15. The eve of evacuation: on 31 August posters in every railway station in Britain herald the greatest migration of British people ever known. In four days, more than 1.4 million children and crippled, blind or elderly men and women will be moved from the urban centres to places of comparative safety. Already well rehearsed, the whole vast operation is outstandingly successful, without a single accident or casualty taking place ...

LCC

0341

ENGLISH MARTYRS

16. ...except, of course, the traumatic, inevitable separation of children from parents. After a last brushing of the hair and straightening of the socks, and wearing the knapsacks made by their father, 11-year-old John Brown of Clerkenwell Green, London, leads his brother and two sisters, aged 10, 9 and 4, away from home. There is no promise they will see their parents again...

17. ...and yet for some it is all a great adventure. Leaving for the West Country, pupils from a Roman Catholic school in the south-east London suburb of Walworth are exhilarated by the prospect of a long train journey, and with unintended irony, wave the banner showing their school's name.

18. For those left in the cities, other posters indicate what they may have to endure. In Covent Garden, London's great fruit and vegetable market, porters read of air-raid warnings and the possibility of poison gas attacks...

19. [*Opposite left*] ...and even away from the city centres, it is sensible to take precautions against air-raids. Wielding unfamiliar tools, a mother and daughter make wooden shutters, after covering their windows with sticky tape to minimise the danger of flying glass...

20. [*Opposite right*] ...while some fathers come to terms with the outrageous new realities by reducing them all to a more manageable scale.

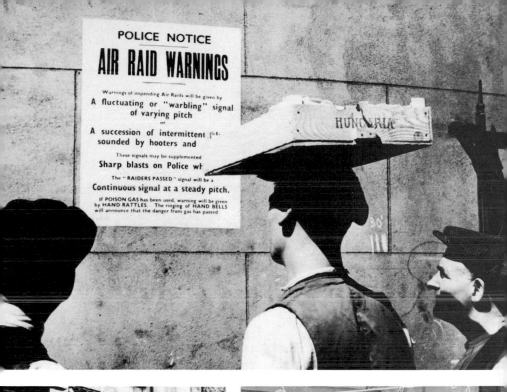

POLICE NOTICE

AIR RAID WARNINGS

Warnings of impending Air Raids will be given by

A fluctuating or "warbling" signal of varying pitch

or

A succession of intermittent _____
sounded by hooters and

These signals may be supplemented

Sharp blasts on Police wh _____

The "RAIDERS PASSED" signal will be a

Continuous signal at a steady pitch.

If POISON GAS has been used, warning will be given
by HAND RATTLES. The ringing of HAND BELLS
will announce that the danger from gas has passed

21. [*Opposite above*] But as the nervous strain increases, practical activity is the best means of coping. Everywhere, busy groups of soldiers and civilians are filling sandbags: outside the Royal Eye Hospital at St Geroge's Circus in London, women volunteers help nurses fill the bags.

22. [*Opposite*] For months, the Government's repeated advice has been 'Take your gas mask with you'. By the end of August, slung in a box over the shoulder, they have become a part of nurses' uniform, and by Christmas even toy dolls will have them too.

23. Friday 1 September: war may be only hours away. The Bank Rate has been doubled; the price of gold has leapt, and Britain's reserves have been massively depleted, with up to thirty million pounds' worth leaving the country in a single day. Now even the Stock Exchange is closed…

24. …and although heavy-handed, whether posed or not, a bit of humour helps to keep things in perspective. *'What – again?'*: these men from the Royal Artillery are too young to have fought in the Great War, but the memory of victory bolsters morale.

25. Wednesday 23 August is Soviet Air Day, and, accompanied by Foreign Commissar Vyacheslav Molotov, Defence Commissar Marshal Kliment Voroshilov and other high-ranking Soviet officials, Stalin watches an air-war exercise over Moscow's Tuchino Aerodrome. This marks the humiliation of Drax and Doumenc: their mission has failed entirely, and Communist Russia's impending pact with Nazi Germany has just been announced.

26. Both the King and the Prime Minister returned from their Scottish holidays well before the end of August, and on Friday 1 September were together at Downing Street. In bowing to his Sovereign, Chamberlain observes the ritual formalities, yet looks exactly as he feels – old, sad and terribly worn.

27. On Wednesday 30 August, steel-helmeted men of the SS crouch beside a grenade thrower near the Polish border...

28. ...while in Danzig harbour, crowds assemble under a welcoming banner to stare at the German cruiser *Schleswig-Holstein*. Within 24 hours, the grenades will be launched and the cruiser will bombard the city.

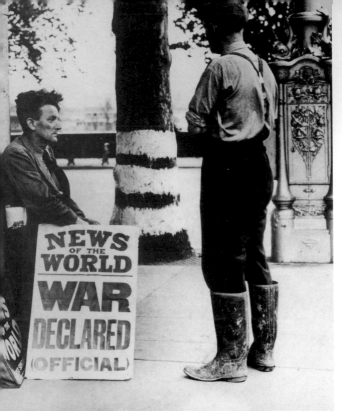

29. Sunday 3 September: Great Britain declares war on Germany. For once the paper's name is entirely appropriate. On a London street-corner, by a tree striped white for the blackout, a news-vendor's face shows the unutterable bleakness of the future...

30. ...while the artist Henry Moore sees people swimming below the cliffs of Dover. With pencil, wax crayon and water colour, he gives them hideous, mechanical, mask-like faces; the world has changed for ever, and no one will ever be the same again.

Chamberlain was as fully informed and aware as any individual could possibly have been. He knew that the military talks in Moscow were temporarily halted until a reply came from Poland. He knew the Poles had not yet given in to diplomatic pressure. He knew that Hitler might respond to a visit from a German-speaking Englishman of high military rank or to a personal letter from himself. He knew of the predicted possibility that war might begin in as little as a week's time. "All this," Lord Halifax had written to him, "may have its place in the general nerve storm which we have been told was designed to rage during these weeks. . . . If the appreciation is in fact a true one, it is also a black one, and there is no time to lose." Chamberlain knew, too, that the Italians were frightened and were being encouraged in every way to restrain Hitler; in short, he knew that the diplomatic system was at full stretch in every country, but was still functioning and might yet succeed.

But, in Moscow that afternoon, Saturday, August 19, Ambassador von der Schulenburg was trying hard to persuade Commissar Molotov to shortcut the system. Naturally, Chamberlain did not and could not know this, and at first it seemed to von der Schulenburg that his efforts had failed. The Commissar could not be persuaded to act with speed but kept on putting up problems, arguing details, and apparently doing all he could to avoid making any commitment. Von der Schulenburg left disheartened; then, only half an hour later, he was asked to return.

He had no idea what had happened in the interim, but, as soon as he got back to the Kremlin, it was obvious that somehow a transformation had occurred. Welcoming him in, Molotov apologized for the inconvenience of a second meeting in one day and, without more ado, presented him with a draft pact of nonaggression and an invitation for Reichsminister von Ribbentrop to come to Moscow the next week.

10

I have them!

For a moment the ambassador's heart leaped. At once, and correctly, he assumed that Stalin must have intervened personally. Never mind why—the important thing was that Molotov had done an about-face. But then, as the Commissar continued to speak, the ambassador realized that there were, as there were bound to be, conditions attached. First, the trade agreement being negotiated by Julius Schnurre and Georgi Astakhov must be concluded and signed as a preliminary; second, because the reception for a guest as important as Reichsminister von Ribbentrop would take time to prepare, a week must be allowed before his visit.

As conditions went, they scarcely seemed onerous. With a handshake, a bow, and a murmur of thanks, von der Schulenburg took his leave and went directly back to his embassy's communications room. At 7:10 that evening, Saturday, August 19, his message was received in the Foreign Ministry in Berlin, where it caused mixed delight and consternation—delight because it was an enormous advance, something firm to build on, and consternation because of the two seemingly light conditions. Those conditions were actually critical to the timing of Germany's—and Europe's—immediate future. Negotiations on the trade treaty had been concluded the night before with complete agreement: Germany would extend to Russia a merchandise credit of 200 million Reichsmarks at 5 percent annual interest to finance industrial plants, machine tools, armor plating, and optical instruments; Russia would repay the loan with raw materials. Signature of the treaty had been expected today, but Julius Schnurre had just reported a delay: His Russian counterparts were awaiting instructions from Moscow.

This could hardly be coincidence. The Russians had maneuvered themselves into a position of complete control. Worse yet, from von Ribbentrop's and Hitler's points of view, they had put a timetable on the possibility of continued peace in the East. A minimum of seven days must elapse, they said, between the signing of the trade agreement and the signing of the nonaggression pact. Therefore, if the treaty was signed tomorrow, the twentieth, the pact could be signed on the twenty-seventh. But all German plans in motion were targeted on an assault on Poland taking place at dawn on the twenty-sixth. Captain Dönitz's U-boats were in position. The pocket battleship *Graf Spee* was on alert in the Atlantic. General Heydrich's Operation Himmler, the pseudo-Polish attack on the German radio station at Gleiwitz, was ready. German troops in sealed trucks were being moved to points on the Polish border. Yet, if the attack should be launched with Russia unallied, what then? Before August 26, Russia must become a German ally — or else remain an imponderable, perhaps an unacceptable, risk.

Some people might have seen a certain irony in this. Hitler had inaugurated *Spannung,* and now he was falling prey to it himself.

*   *   *

Locked in the Rosau barracks in Vienna, Hilda Richter was all alone. There were other female prisoners there, but none of her family. She was not certain how much her jailers knew. Nor was she certain where her husband was, only that he had left Vienna for Britain. So had the Reverend Grimes. Her twenty-three-year-old son Richard was there already and had been for the past three years, since he had left the Hitler Youth. Now he was living just outside Kenilworth, close to her brother Edward. Indeed, Richard was well settled, with a clerical job at A. C. Wickman's machine tool company in Coventry. Thinking of her family made her feel less alone — they would get her out of this place. But, until they or someone else did so, all she could do was wait, hope, keep quiet, and try to avoid giving anything incriminating away.

She had not been badly treated — yet — but it was a strange thing, to say the least, for a girl from Tipperary to be a prisoner of the Gestapo. *It's been a long way from Tipperary, indeed,* she thought unhappily. Her husband was Austrian born but had become a naturalized Briton nearly forty years ago. After the Great War he had joined British Intelligence, and, when their son Richard was six, the family had moved back to Vienna, ostensibly so that Mr. Richter could take up a job with the British Council in the Wöhlnerstrasse. Actually, he was continuing his work for British Intelligences, the Vienna operation used a cardigan factory as its cover. It had been a pleasant life, spending Saturday nights at the English Club in the center of Vienna; working for Christ Church, opposite the British legation in Lustigprienstrasse; watching Richard grow up — he had had all his schooling in Vienna and had learned to speak German like a native. Smiling sadly, she remembered how, even when he spoke English, he had a pronounced German accent. *I wonder if he's lost it yet? Probably not — probably never will.* He had joined the Hitler Youth simply because everyone else at school did; his parents, treating the organization like a suspicious form of the Boy Scouts, knew that he was sufficiently levelheaded not to fall for the propaganda side of it, and, when he had decided he would like to try and join the British Army, his father had instigated his return "home" to a country he had not seen for fourteen years.

That had been in 1936; then, after the *Anschluss* last year — the forcible union of Hitler's homeland, Austria, with Germany — life in Vienna had begun to change radically. In the first two or three weeks, it had not been as bad as they had all feared, but then the Gestapo had arrived. Their threat to all Jewish people was self-evident; she had seen for herself old Jewish men being forced, on hands and knees, to clean streets with sacred scrolls, degraded, humiliated. If they refused, the sneering Gestapo laughter stopped, and they were kicked and beaten mercilessly; she had no doubt that some died.

It was then that the Reverend Grimes, a tall, lean, reserved man already in his sixties, had begun secretly baptizing as many Jews as possible into the Christian faith. Hilda Richter had helped him. Both had understood that they were placing themselves at some risk; but neither realized that they were doing so to no effect. Under Nazi race laws, simple baptism did not purge a person of the crime of being Jewish.

Eventually the Richters had sold their house and moved into a hotel, the Malek. It had seemed a sensible precaution; in an emergency they would be able to leave the country swiftly. Then, unexpectedly, the Gestapo had come — it had been pure coincidence that Mr. Richter was away. They had taken Hilda from the hotel garden one afternoon; wearing her housecoat, she had not even been allowed to change but had been peremptorily invited to step into a waiting car. Such invitations were not open to refusal.

At the barracks, her passport had been confiscated, and she had been interviewed by an English-speaking officer. Where was her husband? Where was the Reverend Grimes? Since she was not an accomplished liar, she had been relieved to be able to answer truthfully that she did not know; but then, with a surge of apprehension, she had remembered that in the pocket of her housecoat was a completed baptismal certificate, waiting for a ceremony that had not yet taken place. In sudden fear, she had asked if she might go to the lavatory. To her astonishment, she had been allowed to go unescorted, and she had been able to flush the incriminating paper away.

They had released her then. At once she had gone to Captain Thomas Kendrick, passport control officer at the British legation. Without hesitation he had given her a new passport and had advised her to get out as soon as possible. Perhaps, if she had gone directly to the airport, she might have got away, but she had returned to the hotel. She should not have done that; she was promptly rearrested. An Austrian clerk in the legation — himself under threat from the Gestapo — had overheard her worried discussion with Kendrick and had reported it all.

Since then, only four or five days had passed, but it seemed an eternity. What day was today? Counting up, she realized it must be a Sunday — Sunday, August 20. What could she do? Nothing but go over in her mind again and again the things she had said, the answers she had given; wait, and pray that she would be released before a war began. *Hold on — hold on.*

★   ★   ★

"Hold on, Zofja — here, take my hand." At the quayside in Gdynia, Tadeusz Olszolwski helped his wife down the ship's gangway to the shore. Their trip to Copenhagen, anticipated so happily, had been an ordeal that Zofja never wanted to repeat. The outward voyage, 300 miles across the sheltered southern waters of the Baltic, should have been pleasant, and was — until suddenly she had understood who the majority of their fellow passengers were and why they were there. At first she had thought only that the ship was unusually crowded, but gradually she had overheard snatches of conversation. Some of it had been in Polish, some in a German-sounding language she had not recognized at once. All had sounded tense and nervous, and, in a sickening instant of comprehension, the whole scene had made sense: the complete families huddling together as if for protection, the mothers with confused large-eyed children, the old women, the long-bearded men dressed entirely in black, pebble glasses under wide-brimmed hats. "Tadeusz," she had whispered urgently, "are all these people Jewish?"

He had looked at her in mild surprise and nodded.

"But where are they going? I mean, so many of them — what are they doing?"

He had answered in one word: "Escaping."

"But what from? Surely they're Polish? I heard some speaking Polish."

"And Yiddish. I expect they're all Polish, or most of them. I suppose some might come from the Corridor. But that's what they're doing, anyway — getting out while they can. I don't suppose they really need to, but I don't blame them; I expect we'd do the same in their position."

Dizzy with the intensity of her realization, she had leaned against him, clinging to his arm. With concern in his voice, he asked, "Zofja, are you all right?" For a moment she had been unable to answer. Taking the carpets and the silver from the villa to safety in Warsaw seemed suddenly like some kind of game. Taking the children to Moniaki had felt, more than anything, like part of a family holiday. She was not stupid; she read the papers, listened to the wireless — but it was not until she saw for herself all these poor people in this horrible ship that she had truly grasped, deep inside, what kind of a reality might be coming. *I expect they're all Polish* — and yet they were fleeing from Poland . . . She had known then what she must do. From its coldness, she had been aware that her face was still white with shock, but she had straightened up, opened her eyes, and spoken as firmly as she could.

"Tadeusz — I want to go back as quickly as we can. I must go to the children."

He had looked at her steadily, silently, sadly, before replying, "Yes . . . you must go to the children."

That had been two days and nights ago. Until they had reached Copenhagen, Zofja had only felt the distance between them and the children increasing. In the beautiful Danish capital, she and Tadeusz had walked hand in hand together, both trying to be cheerful. They took coffee in Tivoli park, admired the intricate spire of the Börsen, the stock exchange — it was formed by the spiraling tails of four dragons — and strolled out along the Langelinie promenade to see the Little Mermaid. Perhaps this had been a mistake; the statue's delicate, chaste innocence spoke to Zofja only of their own small children. "Of course, they're not all like that," Tadeusz had remarked. "Mermaids, I mean. Lorelei, and the Greek ones, the Sirens, looked beautiful and sang delightfully, just in order to lure sailors onto the rocks, to their doom." He had grunted and smiled. "But then Lorelei was a German mermaid, so what could you expect?"

"Dear God, Tadeusz — I don't know what to expect at all." His attempt at a joke had not worked, and that night in bed, he could only hold her until, tired of crying, she fell asleep at last.

Now, on Sunday, hastening from the ship, they found their car, went quickly to the villa, and set off on the drive southeast to Lublin. There, they had agreed, Tadeusz would leave Zofja with one of her aunts to stay overnight, before she proceeded in the morning to Moniaki; he would have to return at once to Gdynia to be ready for work the next day.

As they traveled, Zofja could feel her spirits rising again. It was a long drive, 300 miles or so; while they were on the road, two crucial developments took place in Germany. The first, at 2:00 P.M., was the signature of Germany's commercial treaty with Russia, delayed since the day before by lack of instructions from Moscow. With that signature achieved, Commissar Molotov's timetable came into effect; Reichsminister von Ribbentrop could visit him in seven days. But for Adolf Hitler that would be too late — by then, he intended to have commenced his attack on Poland. The possibility, remote as it might be, of Russian aid then coming into Poland was an unacceptable risk; he could devastate Poland, no doubt, but at what cost and for what result? At the cost of an eventual German defeat and without gaining either the minerals or the land, the *Lebensraum* he so avidly sought — without even gaining the humiliation of Poland, a nation he had learned to loathe. No, it could not be done in this way. Yet, to retreat from his plan was equally unbearable. For hours he struggled with it, conscious that he was for once in the hands of another, that Josef Stalin the Communist had out-maneuvered him, the Nazi, just as surely as he himself had in the past outmaneuvered the democracies and bloodlessly gained for the Reich the Saarland, the Rhineland, Austria, the Sudetenland. At length he decided.

If the message that followed at 4:35 P.M. had not been of such importance, its address would have appeared ridiculous: "Herr J. V. Stalin, Moscow." A personal appeal from the leader of the Nazi world to the leader of the Communist world — diametrically opposed ideologies, the opposite extremes of politics. But extremes can meet and touch. The Führer welcomed sincerely the new commercial agreement; it was the first step in a proper adjustment of relations. With a few small reservations that no doubt could be swiftly clarified, he accepted the Russian draft of a nonaggression pact. But speed was vital. Herr von Ribbentrop would have plenipotentiary authority: Let him come at the earliest opportunity, the twenty-second or twenty-third.

It was impossible to tell what the unconventional move cost in pride for Hitler; though couched in the language of a dictator, it was a begging letter. Nerves stretched taut, he could only wait in the Berghof, pacing in agitated silence to and fro. No one dared to speak to him. *Geduld — halt' aus*. Patience — hold on.

Galeazzo Ciano's patience was also close to breaking point. The previous day he had left Italy to visit Albania, going first to Tiranë — or, as he called it, Tirana. He had been much encouraged by the country's spiritual and material progress, and he felt confident that, in a few years, Albania could be the richest region of Italy, "if we can work in peace." He was especially gratified to receive news that the Collar of the Annunziata had been conferred on him, making him an honorary cousin of the King of Italy. But still he was distracted by thoughts of what was going on in Europe, events "serious and sad." He proceeded by steamer, the *Duke of Abruzzi,* sixty miles down the coast to an enthusiastic welcome in Vlorë (which he called Valona). His first thought on seeing it was *What misery!* Tirana, a humble enough place, was a metropolis in comparison. Nevertheless, there was an excellent bay, the sea was rich, and the locality was beautiful; all that was needed was a few years' work.

But then a telegram reached him: He should be in Rome that evening. Canceling the rest of his tour, he returned at once to the Italian capital. "This is what had happened," he wrote later. Though the British had sent Mussolini an appeal to try to settle the dispute peacefully, the Duce had finally made up his mind "to support Germany at any cost." Ambassador Attolico, who was in Rome, was to return to Berlin with a communication stating that intention. Pressing Mussolini for his reasons, Ciano was exasperated to find they were feeble in the extreme: If the Pact of Steel was broken, "the whole world would say that Italy is cowardly, that she is not ready, and that she has drawn back in the face of the specter of war." The fact that Italy's genuine military unreadiness made withdrawing from the Pact common sense, not cowardice, cut no ice with the Duce; he was not going to have

people saying he was a coward. *Holds very stubbornly to his idea,*
Ciano noted. By pushing hard and using the British appeal as an
excuse, he managed to get the final decision deferred until the
morning, and he left the conference with some hope remaining;
but he saw that Attolico departed in tears.

It was about then that Ambassador Kennard in Warsaw was
making up his own mind about a telegram from Lord Halifax.
The Anglo-French-Russian military talks must not be allowed to
fail because of Polish noncooperation. "I am convinced," wrote
Halifax, "that such failure must encourage Herr Hitler to resort
to war, in which Poland would bear the brunt of the first attack.
On the other hand, I fully believe that the conclusion of a
politico-military agreement with the Soviet Union would be
calculated to deter him from war."

From his conversations with Colonel Beck two days before,
Kennard knew at first hand that Beck's assessment was exactly
contrary. He had told Halifax so, of course, but he realized that
the firsthand emphasis had not come across; things looked
different in London, as somehow they always did. For his own
part, he sympathized with the colonel's point of view and, feeling
there would be no point in trying any new arguments on him,
told London so. By then, however, as the Prime Minister was
settling into his sleeping cabin in the overnight train from
Scotland, Lord Halifax was pondering a cryptic message from
Berlin. It proposed that Hermann Göring, Commander-in-
Chief of the Luftwaffe, should secretly fly to London, meet the
Prime Minister, and explore any remaining avenues of peace.

Adolf Hitler could not sleep that night. Prowling through the
rooms of the Berghof, he seemed near to nervous collapse. Close
by, his doctors kept a discreet but watchful eye on him.

★ ★ ★

"The very confident attitude of the crews deserves special mention," Captain Dönitz recorded on Monday, August 21. "In my
opinion it is a sign that the broad masses of people have great
faith in the government." He certainly seemed to have such faith:

That day he moved his command ship 170 miles eastward to Swinemünde. Since he had previously decided to move 120 miles *west* to Wilhelmshaven "if *Fall Weiss* should develop into a major war," it appears that he was still not expecting any serious conflict in the West. Ironically, Swinemünde today is called Swinoujście and is part of Poland.

Meanwhile, deep in Poland, Zofja Olszolwska was traveling with an almost light heart from Lublin toward Moniaki. This last three-hour stage of the journey was always her favorite. In winter it would be made by horse-drawn sleigh, with people's ears protected from the brisk cold by foxtail muffs; in summer, as now, the conveyance was a horse and trap. As they bowled along, the clop of the hooves, the rumble of the wheels, and the merry musical jingling of the harness combined into a lively harmony. Quietly she hummed and sometimes sang softly little songs of love and Poland. Her emotions were mixed: She was nearly with the children, but Tadeusz was already back in Gdynia. When they had parted last night, it had been with a prayer that very soon they would all be reunited; yet now, as the journey passed, her fear began to slip slowly away, to be replaced by a growing confidence that all would be well. In fact, Tadeusz and Zofja did not see each other again for more than five years.

While Chamberlain's train drew into London that Monday morning, Sir Alexander Cadogan picked up Lord Halifax early and, at 11:30, took him to Number Ten Downing Street. "Discussed letter to Hitler, and all phases of the crisis," Cadogan noted two days later. "Frightful day, but don't remember all details."

Among other things, they agreed to accept the suggestion that Göring should come to London, and accordingly they made secret arrangements for August 23. From William Strang, head of the Foreign Office's Central Department, they also learned of a drastic French initiative in the Moscow talks, communicated by Charles Corbin, French ambassador to London. Acting on the advice of the French ambassador in Moscow and of General Doumenc, the French government had decided to override Colonel Beck's refusal to allow Russian troops across Poland.

The talks, Corbin pointed out, were due to resume — indeed, should be under way even now — and, as soon as he was authorized, Doumenc was going to give consent in principle to the Soviet demand. Corbin requested that Great Britain should cooperate with this and, when asked on what basis such consent could be given, explained that Colonel Beck had insisted his refusal should not be made known to the Russians. It might be a pretty loose interpretation of Beck's request, but giving consent in principle would certainly keep knowledge of his refusal secret. "In short," said Strang to Cadogan, "the French government has gone ahead without consulting and now asks for our support." And he gave his own view: "It may well be that their judgment of the Polish attitude is the right one."

But it was already too late. That very morning, to his great excitement, Admiral Drax had at long last received the written credentials authorizing him to negotiate. Marshal Voroshilov, however, had decided that, pending a definite answer on the Polish question, the talks should be postponed indefinitely. The foreign delegations agreed reluctantly, but, before they parted company, both sides spoke their minds frankly. Voroshilov had it put on record that he and his colleagues could not grasp how the negotiators had been sent without exact instructions on the passage of Soviet troops across Poland — "such an elementary matter." Drax and Doumenc responded in kind: The Soviet insistence on "difficult political questions" was beyond their understanding. Complete mutual incomprehension was all the two sides shared.

★   ★   ★

Shortly after 12:00 noon, a message was sent from the German embassy in Moscow to the Berghof. Seizing and scanning the paper, Hitler cursed in frustration: Count von der Schulenburg would not be permitted to see Commissar Molotov until 3:00 P.M. In Germany, that would be the early evening.

Mussolini and Ciano argued all day. As soon as Ciano arrived at the Palazzo Venezia, the Duce confirmed his decision to go along with the Germans. Vehemently opposing this, Ciano came up with a new line: "I went to Salzburg in order to adopt a common line of action. I found myself face to face with a diktat. The Germans, not ourselves, have betrayed the alliance . . . We were to have been partners, not servants." Sensing that Mussolini had not thought of that angle before, he followed it up dramatically: "Tear up the pact. Throw it in Hitler's face, and Europe will recognize in you the natural leader of the anti-German crusade."

He knew that to be thought a coward was the one thing that would make Mussolini act. Hitherto it had seemed to the Duce that reneging on the pact would be seen as cowardice. On the contrary, declared Ciano, it would be cowardly to follow in Hitler's footsteps. Proud defiance, not humble servitude, was the proper reaction for Italy. "Do you want me to go to Salzburg? Very well, I shall go and speak to the Germans as they should be spoken to."

Finally, by needling, cajoling, and thundering, Ciano got the reaction he was after: Mussolini approved his proposal to invite von Ribbentrop to a meeting at the Brenner Pass "to reaffirm our rights as Axis partners." The Duce made it clear he did not want the Axis to collapse. *If it should,* Ciano thought, *I would not be the one to weep over it.* They tried to telephone von Ribbentrop but could not get through to him until 5:30. The German Foreign Minister stalled, explaining that he could not answer at once; he was waiting for "an important message from Moscow" and would telephone Ciano later that evening. *Strange* . . . For the time being, however, Ciano put that to the back of his mind and conferred again with the Duce. Between them, they drew up a list of four points covering what seemed all possible eventualities. Privately Ciano felt that three of the four were irrelevant, *but one is fundamental: We shall not intervene if the conflict is provoked by an attack on Poland.*

★   ★   ★

Harold Nicolson, author and member of Parliament, dined on shore that evening. During the adjournment debate of August 2, in spite of his own deep doubts about its wisdom, he would have accepted the government line. In the end, though, he had given his support again to Churchill — "I cannot let the old lion enter the lobby alone" — and had commiserated when the majority of members had decided they should all go on holiday. Since he personally could do nothing further, Nicolson did go on holiday and had been enjoying himself enormously. The previous year he had borrowed £2,000 ($9,360) from his wife, the writer Vita Sackville-West, and had bought a yawl, a small two-masted yacht. "Really, this is just the boat I wanted," he had told her in the spring of 1939. "I didn't really want a swank boat, even as I never wanted a Pekinese." But it was not until the summer that, accompanied by his son Nigel and close friend, John Sparrow, he was able to get some decent sailing in; due to the course of later events, he would never sail his yawl again.

Unlike David Howarth in Northern Ireland, learning by trial and error how to sail single-handed, Nicolson employed a professional crew of two, sometimes three, under a skipper named Captain De'Ath. Confronted with his employer's light-heartedness, De'Ath turned out as humorless as his name. "We tried all yesterday to cheer him up," Nicolson had written to Vita in the middle of August. "We threw a mattress into the sea (not a smile); we shot at jellyfish with the air-gun (not a flicker of interest); we fished for jellyfish with the canvas bucket (not the slightest attention paid to us, until we dropped the bucket overboard and it sank: He then said, 'There's the bucket gone, and one can't get buckets in France.'" It was not until they had run into heavy seas and fog off the dangerous rocky coast of Ushant that De'Ath had been able to show his skills. "The captain, when tiresome things occur, is perfectly charming," Nicolson wrote. "I am getting to like him."

They had hoped to sail to Brest, but, judging it too risky, they headed back across the Channel "feeling cheated, frustrated, but wise," and ended up in the Cornish port of Fowey. After seventeen days on board, the idea of dinner in the Fowey Hotel was irresistible; but, when the meal was over and they were walking back down the hotel corridor, reality set in. From the wireless in the hotel office they could hear the news. "It looks as if the Germans have arranged with the Italians . . . to stage their coup at once. The Germans are half-mobilizing and the French are doing the same." With a sense of "terrific imminence," the small party rowed out across a satin-smooth harbor to the boat; on board Nicolson jotted in his diary, "How strange it is that this war which I have dreaded for six years and which I have so repeatedly forecast now seems close upon us." Three months ago, he had thought there was some chance of a negotiated settlement over Danzig, but "we have missed that chance as usual. It looks like war. I am glad that fate has given me these weeks of happiness before the great ordeal begins."

In the Berghof, Hitler dined late. The meal was tense and silent, his own mood dominating that of the others. Among the guests were Alfred Speer, his favorite architect, and the photographer Heinrich Hoffmann; all were trying to diminish the clink of their knives and forks when a messenger came in and handed a telegram to Hitler. Everyone paused. Appetites already dwindling because of the strained atmosphere vanished altogether. Covertly they watched him read the telegram. His face turned scarlet with passion. He put the paper down and gazed unseeingly out of the window, then abruptly turned back toward his guests, clenched both hands into fists, and crashed them onto the table so hard that the plates jumped. *"I have them!"* Speer recalled that Hitler's emotion was so powerful he could scarcely speak, and he said it again in pure ecstasy: "I have them!"

That was all; he did not explain but, evidently worn out, lolled back in his chair and signaled to the others to continue eating. They did so in unbroken silence. It was not until after they had finished that, calling for champagne, he revealed that the telegram had come from Stalin. Von Ribbentrop could go to Moscow on the twenty-third; the nonaggression pact would be signed in time for *Fall Weiss*. Instantly, the mood in the dining room changed to huge excitement. Amid the hubbub of toasts and congratulations, everyone present knew that they had just heard the first news of one of the century's most important strokes of diplomacy.

By an odd coincidence, the day before, Hitler's cry of delight had been foreshadowed 600 miles away by Winston Churchill, but in a grim, somber tone. At his cousin's château in Dreux, accompanied by the French artist Paul Maze, he was painting the Moulin. He and Maze had been friends for over twenty years by then; the Frenchman was one of the first to encourage him in art. As they had sat side by side at their easels, Churchill had suddenly turned to Maze and said, "This is the last picture we shall paint in peace for a very long time." It had hardly been a sentence calculated to help Maze's concentration, and Churchill's ability to think hard and simultaneously about painting and war had astonished him. From time to time as they had worked, the Englishman had thrown out further remarks about the French and German armies. Maze later recorded some of them in his diary. "'They are strong, I tell you, they are strong,' he would say. Then his jaw would clench his large cigar, and I felt the determination of his will." *I have them!* It is almost as if Churchill anticipated the Führer's distant shout of joy, for Maze, in his diary, noted Churchill's own resolute remark: "'Ah,' he would say, 'with it all, we shall have him.'"

11

The day is charged . . . and full of threats

By midnight on August 21, it was known in every press agency and government office in Europe. In Britain, on the morning of Tuesday the twenty-second, *The Times* summarized it in four headlines:

Full Cabinet Today
Growing Tension
German Troops Massing
Nazi Pact with Russia

"The sinister news burst out upon the world like an explosion," Churchill wrote later. "A complete bombshell," said Leslie Hore-Belisha, British secretary of state for war. "A sensation," wrote Paul Schmidt, "to Germany and the world." In Westphalia, a young German soldier called Bernt Engelmann heard his "Uncle Franz"—no relation, but an old friend of the family—say pensively, "This can't possibly turn out well." In Australia, Daphne King saw her father turn pale as he listened to the announcement. He opened his mouth, stood up straight, closed his mouth again, and left the room without a word. Charles King, the Communist editor, was experiencing his first terrible doubt about the Party. "A tactical masterstroke," said Ulrich von Hassell, "and at the same time . . . proof of absolute unscrupulousness and lack of principle." Harold Nicolson, sailing from Fowey to Plymouth Sound, did not hear the news until the evening. "This smashes our peace front . . . . How Ribbentrop must chuckle," he wrote. "I feel rather stunned by this news and sit on deck in bewilderment with the fishing smacks around me." Holidaying at his parents' home in Sheffield, the teacher Andrew Hole was no less bewildered: "What on earth can it mean?" In unheard answer, Harold Nicolson added, "I fear it means we are humbled to the dust."

Galeazzo Ciano's reaction was unusually muted: "A new act opened . . . There is no doubt that the Germans have struck a master blow." But it did not take a politician to see the implications, which Andrew Hole expressed as well as anyone: "It has given Germany a big fillip towards confidence and action."

Just how big a fillip would be known in London by the end of the week. Not a minute was being wasted in Germany. Early in the morning, armed with the Führer's final instructions — "to make every offer and accept every demand" — Reichsminister von Ribbentrop left the Berghof for Berlin. Shortly afterward, a line of staff cars with fluttering swastika pennants raced up the winding road to the Mountain Court. Senior military commanders followed by their Chiefs of Staff strode over the crunching gravel, up the famous flight of stairs, and into the spacious reception hall. There, facing an enormous desk, a semicircle of chairs was ready. Greeting each other, the officers settled themselves, and then Hitler came in. As one, his audience stood up, their right arms rigidly outstretched in salute — "Heil Hitler!" The hall echoed.

The Führer's excitement was obvious. As he spoke, some of the officers took notes, and one, a general, passed his to a member of his staff. Later this man, in turn, gave them to a journalist in Berlin, who passed them on again to the British embassy. They were immediately forwarded to London. From newsreels and wireless broadcasts, Hitler's rasping, metallic voice was almost as familiar there as it was in Germany, and reading the notes was a peculiar experience, almost as if one were standing outside a window at the Berghof eavesdropping.

". . . There are only three great statesmen in the world — Stalin, myself, and Mussolini. Mussolini is the weakest, for he has been able to break the power neither of the Crown nor of the Church. Stalin and I are the only ones who visualize the future. So in a few weeks I shall stretch out my hand to Stalin at the common German-Russian frontier and with him undertake to redistribute the world. Our strength lies in our quickness and our brutality . . . . I have given the command and I shall shoot everyone who utters one word of criticism, for the goal to be obtained in the war is not that of reaching certain lines but of physically destroying the opponent."

He spoke like a man possessed, in an atmosphere filled with the vibrant dominating intensity of his will and confidence. "I have put my Death-Head formation in place with the command relentlessly and without compassion to send into death many women and children of Polish origin and language. Only thus can we gain the living space we need. . . . Poland will be depopulated and settled with Germans." Prime Minister Chamberlain and Premier Daladier of France — "Those poor worms" — might institute a blockade but would be too cowardly to attack. "As for the rest, gentlemen, the fate of Russia will be exactly the same . . . . After Stalin's death — he is a very sick man — we will break the Soviet Union. Then there will begin the dawn of the German rule of the earth."

As he continued, his language became coarse and crude. He admitted that he had one worry — "namely that Chamberlain or some other such *Saukerl* will come at the last minute with proposals. . . . He will fly down the stairs, even if I personally have to trample on his belly in front of the photographers. No, it is too late for this. The attack on and the destruction of Poland begins on Saturday, early." Explaining that German soldiers disguised as Poles would open the attack, thus giving a reason for Germany's assault, he added, "Whether the world believes it is *Scheissegal* [shit-equal]. The world believes only in success."

He had begun by speaking of the greatness of Genghis Khan; he ended in the same way, telling his commanders that, for them, an era of fame and honor was opening such as had not been seen for centuries. "Be hard," he exhorted them, "be without mercy, act more quickly and brutally than the others. The citizens of western Europe must tremble with horror. This is the most humane way of conducting a war — it scares the others off."

At that point, according to the notes, "Göring jumped on a table, thanked bloodthirstily, and made bloodthirsty promises. He danced like a wild man." Perhaps he did, but different perceptions can give quite different accounts of one event. Years later, on trial for his life at Nuremberg, Göring indignantly denied this particular episode. "I want you to know," he told his judges, "that the speech was made in the great hall of Hitler's private house. I do not have the habit of jumping on tables in private houses. That would have been an attitude completely inconsistent with that of a German officer." Nevertheless, as Hitler's speech in the Berghof ended on the morning of August 22, 1939, his audience responded with enthusiastic applause — some because they believed it all; others because, if nothing else, they believed the threat that any opponents would be shot.

★ ★ ★

As the Nazi officers applauded their Führer, Winston Churchill was being driven from Dreux to Paris. There had been enough in the news bulletins to be profoundly unsettling, but there were too few details. He felt he must go home and explained apologetically to his hostess, "At least there I can find out what is going on." During the drive his secretary, Mary Shearburn, took notes from his dictation. When he finished, they sat in silence as the car proceeded, and watched the passing countryside — a beautiful pastoral scene of wide cornfields, the crop ripe, heavy, and waving gently like an undulating sea. Churchill gazed at it for some time, deep in thought, looking more and more grave, until at last, slowly and sorrowfully, he voiced his thoughts: "Before the harvest is gathered in — we shall be at war."

His return through Paris gave him the opportunity of inviting to lunch his military host, General Joseph Georges. Over the meal, they discussed the relative strengths of the French and German armies. General Georges had all the figures to hand and was able to classify the divisions by quality as well as quantity. Churchill was deeply impressed by the results. Digesting the balance sheet of potential war, he said something he had never said before to the French: "But you are the masters."

General Georges hesitated — war, they both knew, was not a simple matter of accountancy. After a moment he replied, "The Germans have a very strong army, and we shall never be allowed to strike first. If they attack, both our countries will rally to their duty."

For the British people, Churchill believed it; he had faith in them. Looking closely across the table at Joseph Georges, he sensed that the French general had the same faith in the French people. "Yes," he answered. "They will both rally, as you say. And now, if I may say it, *bon appétit.*"

* * *

The formula for the sudden recall of Parliament was fairly well known in Westminster; as Chamberlain had pointed out, it had been used at least six times in the past four years. Whatever feelings it hid or provoked, its style was calm and authoritative:

> I, Edward Algernon Fitzroy, Speaker of the House of Commons, do hereby give notice that I am satisfied, after consulting with His Majesty's Government, that the public interest requires that the House should meet at an earlier time than the 3rd day of October.
>
> By virtue, therefore, of the Resolution of the House of Commons of the 2nd day of this instant August, I now give notice that the House shall meet on Thursday the 24th day of August.
>
> Given under my hand this the 22nd day of August, 1939.
>
> E. A. Fitzroy,
> Speaker.

The recall was only one result of a three-hour meeting of the Cabinet that afternoon, its first session since the adjournment eighteen days earlier. The mood in the Cabinet room was of concentrated high anxiety, the imminence of peril emphasized by a ghastly announcement made that morning by the Town Clerk of Westminster: Parents and guardians residing in the area were asked to "bring their infants up to two years of age to one of the below-mentioned centers during the week commencing Thursday 24 August . . . to be fitted with gas helmets."

That was the reality of late August 1939. If anyone beforehand had failed to grasp the full seriousness of the threat the country faced, the dreadful idea of having to fit infants with gas helmets brought it savagely home.

The Cabinet meeting was hectic but productive. Lord Halifax briefed his colleagues on developments in Moscow, both of the Anglo-French mission and the astounding new initiative from Germany, and pointed out that the critical problem was still Danzig. Solving that problem was still the only way to preserve peace, whatever might transpire between Ribbentrop and Stalin. By 6:00 P.M., the ministers had agreed to make preparations for evacuation; to activate Civil Defense, including blackout; and to call up a further 5,000 naval reservists, as well as all squadrons of the Auxiliary Air Force, including balloon squadrons, and key groups of all coastal defense and antiaircraft units. The remainder could be called up without reference to the Cabinet at the discretion of Leslie Hore-Belisha, the War Secretary. They also agreed to prepare measures to stem an alarmingly large outflow of gold from the Bank of England — in one single day, 30 million pounds' worth ($140.4 million) — for, as the Chancellor of the Exchequer, Sir John Simon, pointed out, what was left was "the minimum required for our War Chest." After prolonged discussion, they agreed that Chamberlain's letter to Hitler should be sent, but perhaps their most important agreement was to declare publicly that, whatever arrangement Germany and Russia came to, it would make no difference to Britain's obligations toward Poland.

The question of the letter had been difficult. Some ministers felt that a public announcement would be just as effective; others did not want to drop the idea of a personal emissary, even someone — a soldier, perhaps — from outside the diplomatic community. Chamberlain's own view was that a firmly worded letter with practical proposals for a solution would be the best: Hitler would have to pay attention, while he could ignore a public announcement; a trained diplomat would handle the delicate situation best; and, since Parliament's duty on the twenty-fourth would be to pass the Emergency Powers (Defense) Bill, that would be the best time for the letter to be sent. As the ministers were debating the matter, they were interrupted by the arrival of a telegram from the British Consul-General in Danzig. Ernst von Weizsäcker of the German Foreign Ministry had sent a colonel there, pleading for an emissary to come while Ribbentrop was away. Whether an emissary or a letter was sent, it would have to be by the next day. Faced with such urgency, the Cabinet chose the letter. Just after 6:00 P.M., Sir Alexander Cadogan was called over from the Foreign Office "to give effect to their decisions." At 9:50 ("awful rush,") he noted, the letter was sent. Sir Nevile Henderson, British ambassador in Berlin, would take it personally to Hitler the following afternoon.

By the time the letter was dispatched, Ribbentrop and his team of thirty were past Danzig and in the East Prussian port of Königsberg. Two large Focke-Wulf Condor aircraft, their tails emblazoned with giant swastikas, had been provided for their transport and the Park Hotel taken over for their accommodation. Among the delegation, to his own astonishment, was Paul Schmidt, Hitler's interpreter. Hauled unwillingly out of leave yet again, he had known no more than anyone else about the impending pact until he had arrived in Berlin. Even then he had not seen what use he could be because he did not speak Russian; nevertheless, he had been assigned to report on and record negotiations and agreements. Once over the initial surprise, he had rather liked the idea, and friends had envied him his journey to "the distant planet." But it was not exactly a holiday. At Königsberg, Ribbentrop kept the team frantically busy, preparing material for the forthcoming discussions, constantly telephoning Berlin and Berchtesgaden ("asking for the most un-get-at-able papers," Schmidt remarked), and filling sheet after sheet of paper "with notes in handwriting which grew larger and larger as the night wore on." At one point Schmidt and some of the other younger delegates were able to get away "from this statesmanlike activity" to the Park Hotel bar. Back in Berlin, people had generally been pleased at the possibility of a pact with Russia, feeling it would obviate war. Schmidt disagreed. In his judgment, Hitler would become still rasher and more irresponsible if a pact were concluded; so, in the bar with his colleagues, he drank "a farewell toast to peace."

In Moscow, the Anglo-French missions had spent the day in a fever of frustration. At last, with their governments' authority to override the Polish refusal, they had been ready to present Marshal Voroshilov with the answer he wanted; but, mysteriously, he had been unavailable all day. They did not track him down until the evening, and, when they found him, he made it absolutely plain that they were too late. "The question of military collaboration with France," he told Doumenc, "has been in the air for several years, but has never been settled. Last year, when Czechoslovakia was perishing, we waited for a signal from France, but none was given. . . . The French and English Governments have now dragged out the political and military discussions too long. For that reason," he concluded, "the possibility is not to be excluded that certain political events may take place . . ."

That same evening the British Ambassador, Sir William Seeds, gained an interview with Molotov. It was little less than a confrontation. Infuriated at the Russian's secretive system, Seeds accused him face to face of having acted throughout the military discussions in bad faith. It was hardly diplomatic language, Seeds knew, but he was sure now that it could do no harm; and, "after months of patience and self-control," he was glad to have the chance to say what he really felt.

In 1939, the port of Königsberg was nearly 700 years old. It had been founded by the Teutonic Knights in 1255 and, in the Middle Ages, had been the capital of East Prussia; it was German through and through. As Joachim von Ribbentrop worked there in nervous excitement through the night of August 22, the last thing he could have imagined was that, by the end of 1945, as a more or less direct consequence of his efforts, little would remain of the original town, and Königsberg rebuilt would become Kaliningrad, a major naval base and the third largest port in the Soviet Union.

★ ★ ★

"Of course, with the naval base more or less just down the road," Frank Harding said thoughtfully, "I suppose that, if the worst comes to the worst, we might be rather a good target."

"Really, dear," his wife protested, "I do wish you wouldn't say such things. Or if you must, then not in front of the baby." Richard — thirteen months old that morning — gave no sign of being interested in anything apart from breakfast.

"Sorry . . . Just thinking aloud. I see Parliament's going back tomorrow. About time, too, lazy so-and-sos. Not much they can do about this extraordinary Russian business, I imagine. Perhaps I ought to stand as a member — must be easier than selling furniture."

His wife, engaged with the baby, had not been paying full attention, but now she looked at him in surprise. "And leave Harding's? Surely not!"

Smiling, he shook his head. "Of course not. Harding's without a Harding — Grandfather would turn in his grave. Anyway, I'd better be off now. Don't forget, I'll be late back; ARP tonight."

"Yes, of course, darling. I'll keep something hot for you." Following him to the front door, she added, "I wonder how many people they'd have for ARP if the instruction took place somewhere else — a church hall, say, instead of a pub."

"Oh, just as many, I'm sure; they all take it pretty seriously. The Tamar's very suitable in many ways — good-sized room. It's not as if we actually practice in the bar, after all. Lucky little fellow," he said, fondly stroking his small son. "Lying in a pram on silken pillows while Daddy's hard at work. Well . . . off we go."

At the roadside, turning back for a moment, he saw his wife holding Richard's tiny hand up in a farewell wave. It was only a short bus ride from Hartley to the family store in the center of Plymouth. Happy but apprehensive, Frank looked out at the city. It certainly would be a target. Curious to think that his brother Denis, for all that he was a soldier, would probably be in less immediate danger in the barracks in Rangoon than they would at home. If . . . if "Air Raid Precautions" — there was a sinister ring to the phrase. "ARP" sounded so much less ominous. Yet "precautions" had a sensible sound as well. Be prepared.

As the bus trundled along, on the other side of the city Harold Nicolson was walking grimly toward North Road railway station. Waking to a warm, cloudy, almost windless morning, he had hoped at first for a pleasant little potter around in the yawl, but then he, too, had read in the papers the announcement that the House of Commons was to be summoned next day. Leaving his son Nigel and his friend John Sparrow on board, he had said good-bye with a sad heart.

While it was 8:30 A.M. in Britain, it was 10:30 in Moscow. By then the two Condors had been in the air for two and a half hours, droning over the apparently endless Russian plains. Peering through the windows, Paul Schmidt saw vast forests below, separating widely scattered villages and isolated farms with dark thatched roofs. He was particularly struck by that: German farms had red tile roofs, which looked bright and cheerful from the air. These, in contrast, looked very dour, very somber—very Russian.

In Paris, citizens were being advised to leave the capital if possible. Trains and aircraft were already filling steadily with Britons and neutral nationals making hasty returns to their own countries. In London, the American ambassador Joseph Kennedy came to express his concern to Lord Halifax. Referring to the latest development between Russia and Germany, he said, "I believe there's a real danger that the Poles just don't appreciate their true position," and added that, in his view, pressure must be brought to bear on them. Halifax's reply—that it was impossible—jolted him badly. He sought and gained an interview with the Prime Minister. What, he wondered, could now be done? There must be something.

Chamberlain, seeming deeply depressed, did not think so. "I have done everything I can think of," he said unhappily, "and it seems as if all my work has come to naught." Then, in a sudden access of angry energy, he told Kennedy what was upsetting him most. "The futility of it all," he burst out. "That is the thing that's frightful. After all, we cannot save the Poles—all we can do is carry on a war of revenge. And that will mean the destruction of the whole of Europe."

Yet that had always been a possible outcome of the prime minister's method of coping with Nazi Germany.

The Condors landed punctually at noon. During their final approach, the entire German delegation, including Ribbentrop, had been staring, fascinated, from the aircraft windows. Schmidt's first thought on sighting Moscow had been that, from the air, it looked exactly like London or Berlin, a sea of houses; but, once the airplane was on the ground and taxiing to a halt, he was overwhelmed by a sense of unreality. It was all so completely improbable, yet it was happening: there was a shield with "Moscou" written on it in French, and there was the red and gold hammer-and-sickle flag leaning across the black, white, and red swastika flag in a most friendly manner. There was the Italian ambassador, Rosso, in the welcoming committee — Schmidt had known him in Geneva — and their own ambassador, Count von der Schulenburg, and, along with a bunch of high Soviet officials, Molotov's deputy, Potemkin. *Couldn't have had a more appropriate name, thought Schmidt.*

With his colleagues, he allowed himself to be ushered into one of a fleet of Russian cars, large and comfortable, looking like American Buicks. The motorcade sped off toward the capital, down a straight, very broad road. It reminded him of the autobahns at home. *Dictators seem to delight in the magnificence of broad roads,* he reflected, deciding at the same time that the immediate surroundings were unutterably bleak and dreary. First stop was the German embassy, where the delegation had a hurried meal; and at that point, to his consternation, Schmidt discovered that his suitcase had been mislaid somewhere between there and the airport. It contained his only dark suit, which "even in Moscow" was regarded as essential for formal occasions. Without it, he could not go any further, and von Ribbentrop, who was in a great hurry, was definitely not going to wait around. The Reichsminister was taken to see Commissar Molotov, and Schmidt, to his chagrin, had to remain at the embassy.

To make up for this, his host's wife (who spoke perfect Russian) suggested that they go for a tour of Moscow. Schmidt accepted, and they walked for several hours; but, apart from the incongruous luxury of the underground railway system with its chandeliers and marble walls, he found the Soviet capital unexpectedly dull. At first he thought it was merely that it looked like any other great European city, but then he realized "the essential difference": No one looked at all cheerful. The people were clean and neat but colorless in faces and clothing, and "a melancholy gray pall seemed to hang over everyone and everything." He wished again he was with the delegation; it was frustrating not to know how they were getting on.

In other towns and capitals, other people were equally on tenterhooks. "The day is charged with electricity," wrote Ciano, "and full of threats." Mussolini had authorized him to give the British ambassador, Sir Percy Loraine, a plan for a solution. First, Danzig should be returned to the Reich; then negotiations and "a great peace conference" would follow. Rome was intensely hot, and, either through emotion or the heat, Loraine fainted—or nearly fainted—in Ciano's arms. In Warsaw, in one final joint effort, Ambassadors Kennard and Noël were again trying to make Colonel Beck change his mind. In Washington, President Roosevelt was writing an appeal for peace to Hitler; and, in the Berghof, Hitler, highly agitated, was reading, in Chamberlain's letter to him, that Britain's guarantee to Poland still stood.

Late in the Moscow afternoon, von Ribbentrop hurtled back from the Kremlin to the German embassy, "positively bubbling over with enthusiasm," and over another quick meal told Schmidt again and again that things were going splendidly with the Russians. Molotov and he had discussed how to carve up Poland; he had checked with Hitler to see if Russia could have the Baltic ports of Libau and Windau. Within half an hour, the reply had been there: *"Ja, stimmt."* Yes, agreed. Now, confident there would be a pact that evening, Ribbentrop raced back to the Kremlin with von der Schulenburg and the head of the embassy's legal department in tow, and, once again, because the

Reichsminister did not want a new face cropping up in the discussions, Schmidt was left behind to wait.

"Papa says that war is inevitable," Niusia Zamecka wrote in her diary. "I asked Papa why Hitler wants to attack us, and Papa said it's because he's a greedy bully." It was as accurate and concise a description of the Führer as anyone could hope to make, and, thinking it over, the ten-year-old Polish girl concluded primly, "I only hope he knows that peaceful people don't think him very nice."

It was about then that Colonel Beck relented at last. The Anglo-French mission could tell Voroshilov "for certain that in the event of common action against German aggression, collaboration, and the technical conditions to be settled subsequently between Poland and the USSR are not excluded." For the colonel this was an enormous step to take, but it was still far from what Voroshilov had wanted; and anyway, it was much too late. While Gauleiter Förster, by decree of the senate, was being made Head of State in Danzig, Hitler had just set *Y-Tag*. Much calmer in speech and action than he had been in the morning, he summoned Ambassador Sir Nevile Henderson to receive his written reply to Chamberlain. It was suitably long — over 1,000 words in translation — and it was uncompromising: Responsibility for the existing political tension in Europe lay with Poland and Great Britain. "Only after a change of spirit on the part of the responsible Powers can there be any real change in the relationship between England and Germany," he declared. "I have all my life fought for Anglo-German friendship; the attitude adopted by British diplomacy — at any rate, up to the present — has, however, convinced me of the futility of the attempt. Should there be any change in this respect in the future," he concluded, "nobody could be happier than I." Naturally, though, he did not mention his latest decision — that, at 4:30 A.M. on Saturday, August 26, in less than sixty hours' time, Poland would be invaded.

★ ★ ★

"How we did blackguard each other in the past!" Midnight in Moscow. With a jovial chuckle, Stalin bade farewell to his visitors, and von Ribbentrop found it easy to beam in response. For the past three years, he had based his political work on the Anti-Comintern Pact, jointly signed by Germany, Italy, and Japan. Now all that, of course, was out the window, in the most radical about-face anyone could have conceived. Perhaps it should have felt like a betrayal, but it did not; on the contrary, to discover he was capable of making such a rapid, successful, and fundamental switch was gloriously exhilarating.

At the same moment, Sir Alexander Cadogan was at home, tired and confused. In the course of the day — "the kind of lull that comes in the middle of a typhoon" — Halifax had asked him, "Do you think this means war?"

"Yes," Cadogan had replied. "I think it does, but I believe it doesn't." All his staff had been recalled from leave; diplomats had been sent back to their posts. Now, sitting down to dinner, he thought wearily, _These crises really are too tiresome. We can't go on living like this in Europe. There's no point in it._

Harold Nicolson dined with Sir Archibald Sinclair, leader of the Liberal Party, and Sir Maurice and Lady Violet Bonham-Carter. Throughout the evening, they discussed the meaning of the Russo-German agreement. Might Ribbentrop be kept hanging about, humiliated, like the Anglo-French military missions? Nicolson did not think so. "I doubt whether Ribbentrop would have been such a fool as to go to Moscow," he said, "unless he was pretty certain that he would be exposed to no humiliating delays."

Even then, Paul Schmidt was hearing from von Ribbentrop himself just how swift and stimulating the negotiations had been. There had been a nasty moment early on, when, reading Ribbentrop's preamble to the German draft, Stalin had shaken his bearlike head and growled in obvious disagreement. Turning nervously to his interpreter, Ribbentrop had learned that the Communist leader felt it was going too far to talk about friendly German-Soviet relations. "He says his government could not suddenly present their people with a German-Soviet declaration of friendship after they had been covered with, er—" The interpreter hesitated. "With, ah, pails of manure by the Nazi Government for six years." With the flowery passage instantly struck out, everything had proceeded without a hitch, and at 11:00 P.M. the pact had been signed. For the next ten years, "both High Contracting Parties obligate themselves to desist from any act of violence, any aggressive action, and any attack on each other, either individually or jointly with other Powers . . ." This part would be made public, but the final protocol would remain secret. Poland's territories would be divided between Russia and Germany, and later they would determine whether or not any independent Polish state would be permitted to exist.

After the signing of the pact, many toasts had been drunk, led by Stalin, and, in the German embassy, the celebration continued into the early hours. In London, Harold Nicolson left his dinner companions at 10:15 P.M. and drove home. On the way, he saw something he had never seen before: a motorcyclist wearing a steel helmet. It was, he noted, "a sinister sight" and, though the night was "very hot and still," he shivered.

12

Action will begin

On the morning of the twenty-fourth, Ciano visited his king in Sant' Anna di Valdieri, ostensibly to thank him for the Collar of the Annunziata. They hardly spoke of it; instead, the king wanted news of the situation. Ciano told him all he knew, including the four points agreed with Mussolini as an approach to the Germans. The king approved them, especially the third — the one about neutrality. Not only was he openly hostile to Germany but also he assessed Italy as being "absolutely in no condition to wage war." Ciano got it straight from the shoulder: The army was in a pitiful state, a military review and maneuvers had revealed the unpreparedness of all their major formations, their frontier defenses were insufficient; the king had inspected them thirty-two times and was convinced the French could go through them easily:

"The officers of the Italian Army are not qualified for the job. Our equipment is old and obsolete. To this must be added the state of mind of the Italians, which is distinctly anti-German: The peasants go into the Army cursing those 'damned Germans.' We must therefore await events and do nothing. Six months of neutrality will give us greater strength."

The king ended emphatically: If "supreme decisions" had to be taken, he would be in Rome. He particularly wanted "not to be left out."

At the same time, King George VI was traveling back from Balmoral to London, guided by a similar instinct: His place was in the capital, at the head of his people. By an equally natural instinct he wanted his wife the queen to stay in Scotland with their children, as safe as could be from any possible harm. Her mother-in-law, Queen Mary, wrote to her from the West Country: "I feel deeply for you, I having gone through all this in 1914,

162

when I was the wife of the Sovereign." For the time being, Elizabeth obeyed.

Now that she was with her own children, Zofja Olszolwska felt more secure than for several days past. In the family estate of Moniaki, with a comforting sense of perpetual safety, everything was as it had always been. It was a beautiful, prosperous place. Eight thousand acres surrounded the house and its garden, studded with tall, old trees. The fields were full of hops, corn, and beetroot. In the meadows, cows munched steadily; astrakhan sheep and lambs bleated, and the family's herd of 140 horses ran and rolled under hot sun and clear skies. Ann, her sister, ran the household, and Zofja was able to do much as she pleased. She read, wrote letters, played tennis, and played with her children, delighting to see them with their cousins in the sunshine. With Josephine, the fat, bad-tempered, but excellent cook, she made preserves of strawberry, black currant, and red currant; and even Josephine's bad temper was welcome because it was so normal. She put the shattering memory of the refugee ship firmly to the back of her mind. Over the days the tensions from Gdansk and Gdynia faded; and, if only Tadeusz had been able to be with her, all would have been perfect.

In another part of Poland, in a scene of equal innocence, Niusia had fallen in love with, she wrote in her diary, "the most adorable little baby girl I have ever seen." Irka, the maid, had returned after a successful confinement, "absolutely glowing with pride, although she was shy at first." Her daughter was illegitimate, but almost everyone was entranced. Niusia was fascinated by the infant:

"She has a few hairs on top of her head, navy blue eyes, and she hardly ever cries. And when she does, the noise doesn't come out immediately. First, she waves her arms about, then she crumples her face, and only after that the sound comes out. Her hands are very tiny, and her toes are no bigger than peppercorns."

The infant's precise origin, however, remained a mystery. Niusia's brother Jurek had told her that babies grow inside their mother's stomach, which she found incredible. *Could Irka have eaten her own baby? No, that's too ridiculous altogether.* But now the observant girl noticed that Irka's tummy was much smaller than before. Still skeptical, she noted, "It does seem that Jurek could have been right." Only her grandfather was unimpressed. According to her mother, little babies bothered him. Leaving the others to coo, he made himself some sandwiches and went for a ride on Samson, the horse.

So, in their different ways, the two families were able to ignore — or, at least, to be distracted from — the news that filled every newspaper in Poland and Britain: the text of the Nazi-Soviet Pact. The official Polish reaction was that it merely demonstrated Germany's basic weakness, and the government expressed complete confidence that, if there was a war, Poland would win with the help of France and Britain. But from Berlin, Sir Nevile Henderson reported to Lord Halifax, "I anticipate an ultimatum to Poland. Whether an eleventh-hour attempt of the Polish Government to re-establish contact will avail, I much doubt. But I regard it as the *last* hope, if any, of peace — if there is a last hope."

Harold Nicolson thought not. "I see mighty little chance of peace," he wrote to his wife Vita. "It may be that Colonel Beck will lose his nerve and fly to Berchtesgaden. But even that would be a bad catastrophe."

And, in the British Foreign Office, with the terms of the pact public knowledge, Sir Alexander Cadogan's advice to Lord Halifax was simple. In his judgment the only thing to do was to encourage Mussolini's peace moves. "We can't urge the Poles to agree to Danzig's incorporation into the Reich," he explained. "But if Hitler will agree firstly that Polish rights must be safeguarded and secondly that a settlement must be internationally guaranteed, then it would give us a basis on which we could approach the Poles." Halifax agreed; so did Chamberlain; and before lunchtime a telegram was sent to Rome. Such speedy action was almost unheard of — "almost Totalitarian!" Cadogan said with a quick smile. *But otherwise, he thought, everything is as black as black.*

As this was going on, a curious meeting was taking place in a country house called Karinhall. Field Marshal Hermann Göring, head of the German air force, was talking earnestly to a Swedish businessman named Birger Dahlerus. Göring's stepson was on Dahlerus's staff, which was how the two men knew each other; it was not the first time they had talked, nor was the subject new. But, on Thursday, August 24, against a background of crisis, their discussions had a real intensity; theory was replaced by urgent reality. The idea was that Dahlerus, as a neutral with business interests and good connections both in Germany and Britain, could act as a go-between, an unofficial intermediary between Berlin and London, and perhaps pull off an agreement where professional diplomats had failed. It was a possibility, at least, and Dahlerus accepted Göring's invitation to Berlin. The portly Field Marshal squeezed himself in behind the wheel of his neat little two-seater car, and the conversation continued as they drove.

From Threadneedle Street, home of the Bank of England, came a startling announcement at midday: Until further notice, the bank rate was increased from 2 percent to 4 percent — the first rise in seven-and-a-half years. For many British people this seemed, both then and in later years, to be the moment when the crisis of 1939 became real; you could joke about gas masks and sandbags but not about a doubled bank rate — things must be serious indeed.

Lord Halifax lunched alone with King George. The king seemed "very calm and steady"; and at 2:45 in the afternoon ("a Quarter before Three of the Clock"), the House of Commons reassembled — "a very full meeting," noted Victor Cazalet, the Member for Chippenham. Immediately after the traditional opening prayers, the motion was put that an Emergency Powers (Defense) Bill should be brought forward — "a Bill to confer upon His Majesty certain powers which it is deemed expedient that His Majesty should be enabled to exercise in the present emergency" — and that it should be passed through all its stages on the same day. Chamberlain spoke at length, summarizing events since the House's last session. Sitting directly behind him, Henry ("Chips") Channon, the American-born Conservative Member for Southend on Sea, was able to see Lloyd George and Churchill — "those twin apostles of Russian friendship" — look-

ing "old, and dejected. Winston held his face in his hands."
Thinking of the Munich crisis of the previous September, Channon remembered "all the excitement then" and wondered at the
difference today. "The House was calm, bored, even irritated, at
having its holiday cut short by Hitler."

The Prime Minister's speech set the mood of the House.
Dignified and calm, thought Nicolson, *but without one word which
could inspire anybody . . . Exactly like a coroner summing up a case of
murder.* Privately, Channon agreed: *Clear and admirable, but with
little passion or emotion.* So did Cazalet: *A good but not very impressive
speech* was his conclusion. Nevertheless the vote on the motion
was almost unanimous. Recording the result, the ancient phrases
and biblical cadences of the House's *Journal* seemed particularly
suitable to the occasion:

And the Question being put;
The House divided.
The Yeas to the Right;
The Noes to the Left.
Tellers for the Yeas, (Captain Waterhouse)
                (Captain McEwen:)   427.
Tellers for the Noes, (Mr. Stephen)
                (Mr. McGovern:)   4.
So it was resolved in the Affirmative.

Members worked at full speed, while, in the Upper House, Lord
Halifax gave the peers an almost exact repeat of the Prime
Minister's speech, and from the Admiralty came orders placing
the Royal Navy at war stations. The French government, at this
stage no less certain of its obligations than the British, confirmed
its determination that, in the last extremity, France would stand
by Poland. For ordinary people like Derek Silver, all of this
combined to make "a most jittery day." Silver, twenty-two years
old, was a journalist working in the Essex town of Chelmsford.
He had come originally from Tunbridge Wells in Kent, and, as
he scribbled in his diary that night, "feeling war to be pretty near,
I wrote a more than usually passionate letter to my girl, who is

away on holiday." On hearing the news of the Nazi-Soviet Pact, Andrew Hole, the Plymouth schoolmaster on holiday in Sheffield, spent the morning stocking the house with food; it was, he thought, "the most resigned-to-war news there could be." And, as Hole bustled around the shops of Sheffield, a scene both farcical and frightening took place at Königsberg airport. The German delegation, led by Joachim von Ribbentrop, had wished to return home from Moscow at the first opportunity to present the signed pact to their Führer, and both Condors had been prepared for the flight. The first was to take von Ribbentrop to Berchtesgaden; the second, which left an hour later, was to take other members of the delegation, including Paul Schmidt, back to Berlin. From Moscow they had arrived without a hitch in Königsberg, where Schmidt assumed the same interval of an hour would apply. Deciding to take a stroll around the airport, he calmly watched von Ribbentrop's plane take off, and then, to his astonishment, the Condor in which he had traveled immediately followed suit. Later he rather wished someone had been there to take a picture of him — so often he had been photographed in formal situations with VIPs — but there was no photographer at Königsberg. As the aircraft left without him, he just stood and gaped

He had to get back. East Prussia was no good, he should be in Germany. Quick — the train. No good: "Rail connections with the Reich are suspended today." Over to the Air Office — better luck: An empty aircraft, a Junkers 52, was leaving for Berlin at any moment from the far end of the airfield. As fast as he could, he trotted toward it, gesticulating wildly; its engines were already running. He was glad to see them slow as he approached. He clambered aboard, and they took off at once, whereupon the pilot asked him for his pass. "As things are, one can't be too careful," he explained apologetically, adding over the roar of the motors that many Lufthansa airplanes had come under Polish anti-aircraft fire recently. "We're not so grand as those others," he went on, nodding ahead toward the invisibly distant Condors. "We get no fighter cover; but we fly far out over the Baltic, where the Poles can't get us unless they chase us with fighters and then force us to land." Just in case, Schmidt prepared his papers for destruction; but nothing happened, and they arrived in Berlin only half an hour after von Ribbentrop, whose plane had been diverted there because Hitler himself was already in the capital. "This whole episode," Schmidt wrote later, "brought home to me how near war between Poland and Germany really was."

Meanwhile, work in the House of Commons continued at an abnormal pace. To process a bill through all its parliamentary stages took time, even with the best will in the world, yet by 10:19 that night, the honorable members had completed their work, and the Emergency Powers bill had become an Act. They adjourned again, agreeing to reassemble a week later, on the thirty-first — or earlier, if Mr. Speaker was satisfied that the public interest required it. It had been a long, wearing day, and Cazalet and Nicolson joined Lloyd George and Churchill in the smoking room to talk over events. *Both very anti-Chamberlain,* Cazalet noted.

"He has let us into this mess," said one of the older men angrily. "We never ought to have given guarantees to Poland unless they had consented to allow the Russian army across their frontiers."

They had heard that Chamberlain had offered to resign if war came. Lloyd George was vehement: "We *must* be able to tell the Prime Minister that he must go." But perhaps the most remarkable event in Parliament that day was that Chamberlain had not gone; the king had refused to accept his offer of resignation. And this refusal by His Majesty had an unexpected effect far away, of which the grumbling M.P.s knew nothing and could not guess: Hitler had expected that, when his pact with Russia was made known, Chamberlain's government would fall. When it did not — the Führer learned that news the following day — he began to doubt the wisdom of attacking Poland, and hesitated for the first time in many years.

On the evening of August 24, however, Hitler was being entertained, indeed enthralled, by von Ribbentrop's vivid descriptions of business in Moscow. The pact was signed, sealed, and delivered, and at that moment it seemed that nothing could go seriously wrong.

About the same time, Sir Alexander Cadogan was recording in his diary that he personally had not had much work during the day. "There's really nothing to do. We've got to wait and hope. In one way, it's not so bad as last year. Then there was the awful question *ought* we to fight or ought we not? Now there's no question that in certain circumstances we *must*. It just depends on whether these circumstances — out of our control — arise."

For others, those circumstances arose within hours. Claud Kennerley, the Yorkshire doctor, had had a normal day's work. Throughout it, he and his wife Eleanor had tried not to think too much about what the future might hold. By late evening, weariness and the continuing insistent demands of normality had helped to blot out speculation. They were just going to bed when a phone call summoned the doctor to Listerdale Maternity Home; a woman was going into labor. "All right," he said, "I'll be there in fifteen minutes or so. Good-bye." Starting to dress again, he said to Eleanor, "Funny how many of them choose the middle of the night to come into the world. You go to sleep, love — I'll be back as soon as I can." A midnight birth was indeed nothing out of the ordinary, and Eleanor went calmly to sleep.

In Sheffield, Andrew Hole and his wife could not sleep at all for worry. Around 1:00 in the morning, deciding to get up and make a pot of tea, he found that everyone else in the house was still awake. They all assembled for tea in his mother-in-law's bedroom, but it did no good; no one could think of anything to say that made anyone feel any better. Andrew returned despondently to bed and lay awake; it was, he thought, "a most suicidal night."

At 2:00 in the morning, the shrill ring of the doorbell awakened Eleanor Kennerley. Tottering downstairs, she opened the front door to a messenger — she was never sure later whether he was a courier or a postman — who asked her name, handed her an orange envelope addressed to her husband, and sped off on a large motorbike into the darkness. Alone in the hall, she tore the envelope open and read the telegram: "Report immediately in uniform to Drill Hall in Rotherham."

Mobilization. And Claud was not there. Closing her eyes with a sudden feeling of faintness, she had a brief, vivid mental image of him at work at that moment, encouraging the new mother, coaxing the infant into life — dear God, what kind of a life? Reading the message again, as if the words might have changed, she found she was trembling all over. This was the reality of his Territorial Army training: He must go and might never come back. And all she could do was all she had ever done: give him her help and support and love. Clutching the telegram to her, still shaking, she walked up the stairs and began to lay out his uniform.

★   ★   ★

Daylight that morning, Friday, August 25, revealed a cool but very humid day in Sheffield. Dark-eyed through lack of sleep, Andrew Hole read over some of the public announcements issued by the office of the Lord Privy Seal: Find out the name and address of your local Air Raid Warden, if you have not done so already. If an air raid comes, there might be warnings from police whistles as well as warbling sirens, and, when the raid is over, a single continuous note will sound. If there is a gas attack — *My god, they really mean it* — the alarm will be sounded on handrattles. For a moment he could not think what was meant by that, then realized they meant the kind of clacking wooden rattle that soccer supporters would spin. It hardly seemed appropriate. The gas attack "all clear" would be given by ringing bells. *And heavenly bells if you've copped it, I suppose.* There was that old favorite again: "Take your gas mask with you. Those who ignore this advice may be running grave risks." And blackout: "Remember that, if your house is not blacked out when a 'no lights' warning is in force, you will not be allowed to have any lights on, because in that situation no lights at all are to be shown after dark. Black blinds and other curtaining materials are in short supply, but a heavy-weight beige material will do and will help to keep a room looking cheerful." No doubt; and no doubt it was all sensible advice. But Andrew remained depressed.

The same morning in Rome was cloudy and hot, and, when Count Ciano visited Mussolini, he found him in a "furiously warlike" mood — the last thing that Ciano wanted. More argument began, with Ciano using the king's opinions to back his own. Once again he managed to bend the Duce away from complete commitment to Germany; instead, there would be "nonintervention for the time being, pending a re-examination of our position and until such time as we have completed our preparations for war." Authorized to send a message on those lines to Hitler, Ciano left the Palazzo Venezia happily; he knew that those conditions meant abstaining from any conflict for at least three years.

For Berliners, the morning was warm and hazy with dust, the kind of muddy atmosphere that comes with prolonged dry weather, and Paul Schmidt was summoned to the Chancellery to provide Hitler with a translation of Chamberlain's speech given in Parliament the previous day. The Führer smirked when he heard that the pact with Russia had come as "a surprise of a very unpleasant character," but, though he said nothing, his expression changed as Schmidt continued: "In Berlin the announcement has been hailed with extraordinary cynicism as a great diplomatic victory that removed any danger of war, since France and ourselves would no longer be likely to fulfil our obligations to Poland. We felt it our first duty to remove any such dangerous illusion." The translation finished, Schmidt was dismissed and, as he left, he saw Hitler looking pensive and withdrawn.

In Washington, D.C., this busy morning, Franklin Roosevelt still hoped for peace in Europe; he said so in a press conference, during which he announced also that he had written both to Hitler and the king of Italy. The Danzig dispute must, he believed, still be open to negotiation and arbitration; he had suggested that the arbitrator should not be the United States but some other American nation, and he awaited Herr Hitler's response.

On the German-Polish border, the final moment of crisis was visibly approaching; "incidents" multiplied throughout the day, all the way from harassment and insults to shootings on both sides. In Makeszowa, near Katowice, German soldiers took over the courthouse and railway station; Poles broke into and wrecked the Katowice offices of a German newspaper. More Polish reservists were being called up, and cars and horses requisitioned. Nevertheless, foreign observers in the country assessed the national mood as still robust and optimistic; and, in Rome, Mussolini called Ciano back to the Palazzo Venezia to tell him that once more he had changed his mind. "He fears the bitter judgment of the Germans," the Count wrote, "and wants to intervene at once. It is useless to struggle. I submit and go . . ."

But, in the middle of the day, when all seemed set to topple over the edge, two simultaneous events brought some sudden hope. At 2:00 P.M. Hitler was to have issued the executive order launching the invasion of Poland. Just before noon, however, he gave instructions that the order would be postponed until 3:00, and at 12:45 he requested the British ambassador, Sir Nevile Henderson, to come to the Chancellery at 1:30. *Don't know what this means,* thought Cadogan when he heard of it. At the same time, in South London, the Swedish businessman Birger Dahlerus had just landed at Croydon airport and was on his way to the Foreign Office; with Hitler's concurrence, he had accepted Göring's proffered role of unofficial go-between, and, in all secrecy, Halifax had agreed to see him.

At the time that Henderson's interview with the Führer began, people in Broadgate—one of the main shopping streets of the English Midlands city of Coventry—were interested to notice a bomber flying overhead. Such things were not yet either a commonplace or an object of terror. Craning their necks in the crowded street, they stared, pointed, and discussed—and then there was an enormous explosion, or what seemed like an enormous explosion, and a flash of light followed by smoke and the crash of falling rubble. More than a dozen people were injured badly; five were killed. Of course there was panic and the instant assumption that somehow, unknown to them, war had actually begun. In one sense it had, but not with Germany: With quite a small (but effective) bomb, the IRA had struck, hoping to profit from the national sense of tension. They bombed Blackpool and Liverpool as well that day, and, as the bells of ambulances and fire engines clanged through these cities — bells that would soon become a daily, even hourly sound throughout England — Henderson was on the telephone from Berlin to Cadogan in London. His interview had ended at 3:00 P.M. with Hitler giving him a letter for the British government — a letter containing proposals to ease the international situation. Naturally, it was of great urgency, and Herr Hitler, saying it was his last attempt to secure peace, had offered a German plane to take him to Britain the next morning. Should he accept? Cadogan said he should, and went to tell Chamberlain and Halifax about it. But one thing none of them knew was that — as happened almost routinely with calls from the British embassy in Berlin — the conversation had been monitored by German intelligence. A second thing none of them knew was that at 3:02 — that is, as soon as Henderson had left the Chancellery — Hitler issued an order to his High Command confirming the schedule for *Y-Tag*. Poland would be invaded at dawn the following day.

★ ★ ★

At 2:00 P.M., while Henderson and Hitler were talking, an "ambiguous message" from the Führer was received in Rome. Accompanied by Hans Georg von Mackensen, the German ambassador, Count Ciano hurried once more to the Palazzo Venezia to read it. "Couched," he said, "in abstract language," it was not at all clear, but, as far as he or anyone else could make out, it said that "action will begin in a short time" and asked for "Italian understanding." It was actually the kind of cue Ciano needed, and he used it to persuade Mussolini to write to Hitler. The core of the message was simple: "We are not ready to go to war. We will go to war only if you furnish us with all the war supplies and raw materials we need." *Not the kind of communication that I should have wanted to make,* Ciano thought, *but it is something, anyway,* and, as soon as it was agreed, he telephoned it personally to Ambassador Attolico for immediate relay to Hitler.

Throughout the day, German naval and military reservists were being called up; throughout the afternoon, units of the regular army were on the move, truckloads of soldiers rumbling through Berlin, where the city's rooftops were weirdly decorated with antiaircraft guns, toward the Polish border. SS units already in place were put on standby alert, some changing rapidly from German to Polish uniforms in readiness for Operation Himmler. Everything was moving ahead smoothly; by 4:00 A.M. next morning, all that would be needed was the Führer's command, and blitzkrieg would begin — a smashing, lightning war so swift and devastating that, in all likelihood, Poland would be crushed before France or Britain could make any move to its assistance. And, after that, Hitler believed, they would not wish to move; for the sake of peace, his domination of central Europe would be accepted.

He had planned every move hitherto on the assumption that, in France and Britain, the desire for peace was stronger than the fear of dishonor. Since he had won his way thus far on every point — the occupation of the Rhineland, the remilitarization of the Saarland, the *Anschluss* with Austria, the dismemberment of Czechoslovakia — the assumption seemed correct. Yet it was basically mistaken: It had not been love of peace that had guided the Western powers in their dealings with him so far, but fear of communism. And now he was an ally of Stalin. Politicians in other countries could admit to an astonished professional admiration for the sheer dexterity of the coup, but, for almost all of them, it had removed any lingering thought that Hitler could be trusted. He had not grasped this.

Now, as he waited impatiently for a reply from London to the proposals he had given Henderson, it is likely that his final offer of peace was sincere — that is, to the extent that there would be no war if Britain was prepared to accept the sacrifice of Poland. "The German-Polish problem," he had said, "must and will be solved." In return, he had proposed to discuss limitations of armaments, to guarantee west European frontiers, and even to guarantee the existence of the British Empire, with German help "in any part of the world where such help might be needed." There is some evidence, too, that he was mentally preparing at least to delay *Fall Weiss,* the invasion of Poland, if a preliminary reply from London looked favorable — if London seemed ready to consider taking his bribe. A fully considered reply would be impossible in the short time available, but he assumed, again mistakenly, that Henderson would telephone the contents of the proposal to London at once, before taking the written version next morning, and that an initial reaction would come very rapidly. But, when telephoning to ask whether or not he should fly to England, Henderson had not divulged the details of the proposal; instead, he had sent them by cable. They did not reach the Foreign Office until late in the afternoon; and they were preceded by another message, one that Hitler would dearly have loved to have kept secret — the notes, taken surreptitiously by a horrified general, of his ruthless speech in Berchtesgaden three days ago:

> Decision to attack Poland was arrived at in the spring . . . .
> Our strength lies in our quickness and our brutality . . . .
> Poland will be depopulated and settled with Germans . . . .
> The fate of Russia will be exactly the same . . . . Then there
> will begin the dawn of the German rule of the earth.

And there was the date: "The attack on and the destruction of Poland begins Saturday, early." There could only be one British reaction to this. At 4:30 on Friday afternoon, the informal guarantee to Poland was formalized into the Anglo-Polish Treaty of Mutual Assistance, binding the two countries together. Within minutes — not through diplomats but through press agencies — the information reached Hitler. Paul Schmidt was with him, awaiting a visit from the French ambassador, Robert Coulondre. Hovering discreetly behind the Führer, he was able to read the report over his shoulder, "and then I watched him sit brooding at his desk until the French Ambassador was announced."

German radio carried the news of the treaty that evening. The young soldier Bernt Engelmann was having supper with his

Uncle Franz and Aunt Käthe in their hotel in Bielefeld when
they heard it. Uncle Franz was highly indignant. "That's all we
need!" he exclaimed. Loathing communism, he had for years
accepted Hitler's oft-repeated assertion that Germany and Britain were cousins and should be natural allies. "Now our
English friends have gone over to the enemy," he added
scathingly, "and *we're* allied with the Bolshevists."

Hitler's natural interpretation of the treaty was that it repre-
sented Great Britain's reply to his proposals. It did not; Chamberlain, Halifax, and Cadogan did not discuss those until much
later that evening, after dinner in Number Ten Downing Street.
Cadogan's reaction then, which the others shared, was impatience — "They aren't proposals at all." For all Hitler was really
offering was the same thing he had offered many times before —
namely a free hand for Germany in the East in exchange for
British freedom of action elsewhere. Nevertheless, the decision
in Number Ten that night was that they must be treated with
some seriousness, if only to keep Hitler talking. Each day that
peace continued could mean further chances of averting war
altogether. Agreeing that they must prepare a preliminary draft
before Henderson returned in the morning, they went back to
the Foreign Office at 11:30 P.M. and continued work, not knowing that, by then, Adolf Hitler had been through one of the most
humiliating evenings of all his years in power.

At 5:30 Coulondre had arrived. He was with Hitler for barely
half an hour. During the interview, Schmidt noted, "the Führer
made very much the same statement as he had made four hours
earlier . . . . I had the impression that he was mechanically
repeating what he had said to Henderson and that his thoughts
were elsewhere." He clearly wanted to end the meeting quickly,
and, when he had finished his own statement, he started to rise
from his seat to indicate it was ended. But Coulondre (whom
Schmidt, from ten years' acquaintance, rated highly as a diplomat) insisted on giving a reply. Lest there should be any misun-
derstanding, he said, "I give you my word of honor as a French
officer that the French army will fight by the side of Poland if
that country should be attacked." Raising his voice for emphasis,

he added that, also on his word of honor, France would do everything possible for the maintenance of peace.

Angrily, Hitler interrupted, "Why, then, did you give Poland a blank check to act as she pleased? It is painful for me to have to go to war against France, but the decision does not depend on me." He dismissed the ambassador. Already another was waiting outside: Bernardo Attolico, with the reply from Rome. The Italian squirmed with embarrassment as he produced Mussolini's letter to Hitler.

"In one of the most painful moments of my life," it read, "I have to inform you that Italy is not ready for war. According to what the responsible heads of the services tell me, the petrol supplies of the Italian Air Force are so low that they would last only for three weeks of fighting. The position is the same with regard to supplies for the army, and supplies of raw materials. Only the head of the navy has been able to acquit himself of culpable negligence; the Fleet is ready for action and supplied with sufficient fuel. Please understand my situation."

Please, Hitler might well have replied furiously, *understand my situation: The British have just allied themselves with Poland; you, my own ally, have just defected from my side; and in ten hours I shall launch an attack that may trigger a major war.* Certainly that was what he felt ("the letter," said Schmidt, "was a bombshell"), but he managed to hold his temper and contented himself with a frigid dismissal of Attolico. As Schmidt ushered the ambassador out, Field Marshal Wilhelm Keitel, Chief of the High Command of the Armed Forces, was summoned in. Within minutes he came rushing out again, with momentous news: The advance on Poland was to be halted.

All communications from Berlin to the outside world were temporarily suspended. At the same time in London — the early evening — Birger Dahlerus had been with Lord Halifax. The British Foreign Minister had been in an optimistic mood. Knowing nothing yet of the moment-by-moment developments in Berlin, he explained to Dahlerus that his services as go-between would no longer be needed; according to Nevile Henderson, Hitler himself had offered to reopen discussions. Looking back, it now seems a bizarre set of coincidences; yet, for both the British and the Germans, lack of knowledge and misinterpretation had combined to produce exactly the effect that Halifax wanted — a further delay. And while, in France, Prime Minister Édouard Daladier exhorted his people to be firm in the face of adversity, in Berlin Hitler, von Ribbentrop, and Göring began a conference with General Walther von Brauchitsch, Commander-in-Chief of the German Army, and Admiral Erich Raeder, Commander-in-Chief of the Navy. The session continued until the early hours of the morning. One of the first decisions made at 7:40 P.M., was to send a message to Mussolini requesting precise details of Italy's military needs. A few hours earlier Hitler had hoped that, if he announced a delay in *Fall Weiss,* it would be with the added information that once again he was on the verge of a diplomatic coup: that Britain would talk and that Poland was likely to fall bloodlessly into his hands. Of course he did not know that, even then, the British Foreign Office *was* preparing to talk, and, though there was no longer any possibility at all that Poland would be sacrificed as he had hoped, still it was deeply ironic that in this conference he was obliged to admit to his Commanders-in-Chief that *Fall Weiss* was canceled because it was too risky an undertaking.

That evening in his barracks, Bernt Engelmann learned that their expected "mobilization drill" had been postponed. One of his friends made a sarcastic, accurate comment: "Adolf got cold feet."

THE FINAL WEEK

August 26–September 3, 1939

13

To measure the unknowable

Late in the evening of August 25, Admiral Sir Reginald Plunkett-Ernle-Erle-Drax, head of the defunct Anglo-French Military Mission to Moscow, left the Russian capital by train with his British colleagues. At their departure, courtesies on both sides, Russian and British, were minimal and perfunctory. Behind them, they left a crushed and grieving man — their country's ambassador, Sir William Seeds. Of all the British people involved, he had had perhaps the highest hopes of a successful outcome to the talks; and, although he had guessed the Russians might choose an alliance with Germany, he was shatteringly disappointed when they actually did so. Now, still in a state of mental shock, he found himself "left holding the beastly baby!" It was unbearable; within four months, he, too, quit Moscow and left the diplomatic service.

At the peak of summer in that latitude, the hours of darkness are short. As the Soviet train rattled and shook through the brief night toward the Finnish border, Admiral Drax, uncomfortable, disillusioned, and bitterly angry, reflected on past days. The long sea passage through the Baltic had been deemed too dangerous for his team's return route; instead, they were traveling 700 miles overland to Helsinki, the capital of Finland, and from there they would fly to Britain. They would be home the following day. The journey out had taken nearly a week. His mission had become a degrading, abject failure, and the sad thought came to him that his life would probably be remembered for that, if it was remembered for anything. True, his naval career had not been outstandingly distinguished, yet he had played his part in some of the key battles of the Great War; he had always been a steady naval man; and he remembered that Nelson had once said something like "Any fool can't be an admiral." Well, well — but it was not much comfort. The real question was: Could the mission ever have succeeded? If they had flown out, for example? If they had been more thoroughly prepared, particularly as far as the blasted Poles were concerned? Seeds thought so; Drax was more doubtful. The military aspects of it were logical, indeed obvious; even now he could only agree with Voroshilov's view. But he had not been ready for the extraordinary depth of mutual dislike between Russian and Pole, a dislike that completely overrode military logic. Today, at the formal termination of the talks, Voroshilov, with passionate intensity, had suddenly exclaimed, "Were we to have to conquer Poland in order to offer her our help — or were we to go on our knees and offer our help to Poland?" Unanswerable, yet that was the truth of it. What Drax and General Doumenc — now on his way back to France to take up his command — had really been asked to do was not to negotiate a simple military treaty but to overcome enormous national pride and centuries of reciprocal antagonism. *No wonder we failed,* Drax thought, staring glumly out at the fleeting, shrouded Russian landscape. *It was probably doomed from the start.*

★ ★ ★

"You remember all that stuff in the Great War about 'gallant little Belgium'?" A thousand feet up the slope of Kinder Scout, in the Pennine Hills between Sheffield and Manchester, Andrew Hole and Jack Withers had stopped for a breather.

"I wasn't alive then, but I know what you mean," Withers answered. "What about it?"

"It just occurred to me: There's no comparable feeling now about 'poor little Poland.' The papers aren't even trying to work it up."

"That's probably why there isn't any such feeling," said Withers sardonically. "I doubt if our parents knew anything about Belgium except what the papers told them. And I don't really want to think about any of it, anyway."

"Nor me."

There was something about climbing high on a mountain or a hill that seemed to take one away from the cares of the world.

Mussolini had felt that in the middle of the month, when Ciano had come back from Salzburg. "Perhaps we are closer to the Eternal Father up there, if He exists, but we are surely more distant from men," the Duce had said. "It is useless . . . . This time it means war." For other lesser mortals, however, climbing brought a temporary but very welcome sense of release. Withers and Hole had left Sheffield that morning, Saturday, August 26, simply to get away for a while from the stressful urgency bred by newspapers and wireless bulletins. It was a good morning for climbing; with a slight breeze from the southeast to keep them fresh, it was warm but not too hot, hazy but not enough to obscure the widening view. Slowly they continued upward to the peak.

Derek Silver, the young journalist in Essex, was giving himself a similar kind of therapy. The day before he had cycled sixty-two miles around the county, noting with interest that the searchlights were in the positions they had been in all summer; there was only one he saw that could be towed. He had also spotted, and noted in his diary, approximately thirty fighters lined up around an airfield; but mindful of security, he had been careful not to write its name down. Likewise today, "much calmer," he rode from Chelmsford to London through Epping Forest, a distance of thirty-five miles or so, observing en route " — squadrons lined up ready for action at — aerodrome," and in the capital he was glad to find everything "normal and cheerful." The mood of the people was generally cheerful, indeed — reports that Hitler had made an offer contributed to that — and the soccer season had opened that day; but many odd things were happening as well. Outside Buckingham Palace, the guards' wooden sentry boxes were being replaced by curious conical steel shelters, looking like giant bells with doorways, each with a protective shield of sandbags. With backbreaking toil, more sandbags were being piled outside shops, offices, and public buildings. The National Gallery in Trafalgar Square was closed — for "picture storage," said apologetic posters. In Canterbury and York, medieval stained glass was being removed from cathedral and minster to safer housing, while in London (and most cities) alternating curbstones were being painted white, and white lines were being painted on trees and lampposts, to assist nighttime drivers in the event of blackout. (Silver subsequently discovered that one Essex farmer had painted white stripes on his cows for the same reason — although the farmer did not explain why he thought cows and cars might be in the same place after dark.) The trenches in Hyde Park, dug with such furious haste during the Munich crisis, were being repaired, and, moored at various points, a growing number of barrage balloons floated 2,000 feet above the city. Some had been in position, for "experimental purposes," since the middle of July. People had become accustomed to them and were reassured by the sensible nature of the additional precautions; so for that day at least, they could feel "normal and cheerful" in a London increasingly filled with signs of abnormality.

At 10:00 in Rome, the Chiefs of Staff of the three Italian armies and Antonio S. Benni, an industrialist who was also Minister of both Communications and Public Works, met at the Palazzo Venezia to see Ciano and Mussolini. Ciano had already heard of Hitler's postponement of marching orders. Now, he explained to the visitors, "Berlin is showering us with requests for the list of our needs." He paused before entering the Duce's room. "May I remind you, gentlemen, we need the whole truth on the extent of your stocks — none of your usual criminal optimism, if you please." There was a chorus of indignant protest, and, feeling half depressed, half cynically amused, the Count realized they had all come prepared to put the best possible gloss on the situation. They filed in and he closed the door. Two hours later they filed out again, more than a little dazed. Ciano had put them all through the wringer and at last had extracted an accurate list. Alone with the Duce, he remarked, "It's enough to kill a bull — if a bull could read it." Seventeen million tons of basic materials and 17,000 vehicles — Mussolini could hardly bear to acknowledge the extent of Italy's weakness. Reluctantly he helped draft a letter to Hitler explaining why their needs were so vast, concluding: "Italy absolutely cannot enter the war without such supplies."

At 12:10 the letter was telephoned to Ambassador Attolico in
Berlin. Ulrich von Hassell saw him in the German Foreign
Office, "obviously deeply worried." There was a pervading sense
of uncertainty: "Everything is up in the air; orders terribly
confused. The Reichstag is to meet within a few hours, nay,
minutes; thrice called into session and dismissed." Simultaneously, the German plane bearing Sir Nevile Henderson was
approaching London, and Birger Dahlerus was fidgeting in the
British Foreign Office, waiting for Lord Halifax. After their first
meeting the day before, in which Halifax had shown such optimism that he felt Dahlerus was not really needed, the Swede had
called Field Marshal Göring and learned that, in his judgment,
war might break out at any moment. That was the message
Dahlerus had just passed on, adding his personal opinion that
Göring was the only man in Germany who could prevent war,
and offering his own services once more. A personal message
from Halifax to Göring saying that England's desire for peace was
genuine would, he believed, work wonders. Frank Roberts (later
Sir Frank Roberts, ambassador to Moscow and Bonn) was then
on the Foreign Office German Desk and assessed Dahlerus as
well-mannered, possessed of some charm, sincere and honest,
but naive. "We knew definitely that Göring did not want war," he
recalled in later years. "Göring had too many of the good things
of life, and he wanted to keep his life-style, not gamble it all on a
war." This time Halifax was sufficiently impressed to relay
Dahlerus's offer to Chamberlain. The Prime Minister swiftly
approved; and, before 1:00, Dahlerus was being driven to
Croydon airport, a letter from Halifax in his case. As Roberts
observed, Göring was a devil, but at least he was a less warlike
devil than Hitler.

Sir Nevile Henderson arrived at Number Ten about 1:00.
There he found Cadogan, Halifax, and Sir Horace Wilson, the
Permanent Head of the Civil Service, "jiggering about with
words," as Cadogan put it, while they tried to agree on a draft
reply to Hitler. Since Henderson had nothing essential to add to
Hitler's message, they all adjourned for lunch, meeting again at
2:30, when Wilson and R. A. ("Rab") Butler, a member of the

Foreign Office, were given the task of improving the draft. Settling himself in the garden of Number Ten with the Prime Minister, Cadogan remarked, *"What* a party!" and "tried to put ginger into him. He, I think, quite receptive."

General Sir Edmund Ironside lunched at Chartwell with Winston Churchill. On the whole, their conversation was optimistic: Ironside was just back from Poland and brought very favorable reports of the Polish army; he had watched a divisional attack exercise under live barrage, and, though there had been casualties, morale seemed high. Churchill, for his part, was "full of Georges," Ironside wrote in his diary. "I found that he had become very French in his outlook and had a wonderful opinion of the whole thing he saw." Optimistic as they were, neither became carried away; all they could do was, in Churchill's words, to try hard "to measure the unknowable."

At that time, Bernt Engelmann's little radio team — consisting of himself, his friend Erwin (who had spoken of Hitler having cold feet), and a loathsome creature named Barczustowski (who, despite his Polish name, was a fanatical Nazi) — were sitting in their communications car with nothing to do except listen to all the available news bulletins. Years later, Engelmann remembered how "the British, and even Mussolini and the pope, were trying to find a successful solution to the conflict over Poland . . . . 'I hope they succeed,' said Barczustowski in a subdued voice."

Perhaps wiser — certainly freer — than the young German soldiers, Andrew Hole and Jack Withers were by then lounging on the top of Kinder Scout, as far as possible from any news bulletin. The views of moors and Pennines were magnificent. "Capital, capital," Withers said with satisfaction. "And what marvelous air . . . This was a first-class idea, truly it was; you've no notion, it makes me feel — well, ordinary again. It's a wonderful feeling."

"I know," said Hole. "It's just the same for me. I'd never thought of it before, but feeling ordinary can be a real luxury. Goodness, it was worth the climb."

Withers laughed. "But then comes the climb down, eh?" He remembered that, just yesterday, after hearing that an offer had come from Hitler, Andrew had said, "Can this be the first recognition that Britain can't be shaken?" and had assessed the three possible alternatives for the future: "Either we climb down; or war; or they climb down."

Today, it was a measure of Andrew Hole's relaxation that he laughed, too. "No, no — it won't be us who climb down — not us, Britain, I mean. As for us, you and me" — jumping to his feet, he pulled Withers up as well — "we'll have to be the grand old Duke of York!"

With the youthful, even boyish mood on them as they walked down the hill, they could not resist singing the nursery rhyme:

Oh, the grand old Duke of York,
He had ten thousand men,
He marched them up to the top of the hill
And he marched them down again.
And when they were up, they were up . . .

★   ★   ★

The song would have found an echo very far away, for echoes of Europe's profound abnormality had penetrated even to Schoharie County in New York, midway between the Catskills and the Adirondacks. There, two other young men, Ernest Kroll and Heinz Lindt, were vacationing for exactly the same reason as Hole and Withers: the need to escape the constant influx of unsettling news, the need to climb back to normality. As their names suggest, both were of German origin; Lindt was a refugee from the Nazi regime. Both worked for another refugee, Otto L. Bettmann. One-time curator for prints at the Berlin State Museum, he now owned the Bettmann Archive, a New York picture agency. Both, the day before, had traveled in the *Governor Clinton,* a great oval wedding cake of a ship belonging to the Hudson River Day Line, 120 miles up the river from New York City to Catskill, had bussed a further forty miles to Livingstoneville, and had checked into the Schoharie Rest, a small hotel run by a Mrs. Seidel, herself also of German origin. Finally, this morning of the twenty-sixth, both had got out of the hotel as fast as possible: Mrs. Seidel, motherly and thoughtful, had one blind spot; while serving their supper, she *would* keep on relaying news of Europe from her radio in the kitchen. "And what do you think of that, then, Herr Lindt?" she would ask. But neither Herr Lindt nor Herr Kroll wanted to think about any of it, and hence now found themselves walking in the rolling Schoharie hills. They had been told the Hudson was nicknamed the Rhine of America; the Schoharie Rest was just like a Rhineland pension; and, what with Mrs. Seidel's questions, Heinz, a stocky, blond alpinist, was homesick. But the hills beguiled him. With eager professionalism he took picture after picture while Ernest — who would become a noted poet — wrote down those things the shutter could not capture. Years later, Ernest recalled how, "with his photographer's eye for detail," Heinz had "found cows on a hilltop consorting with clouds enough to make him forget the absence of mountains." It was balm to the spirit. In order to enjoy a full week's holiday free from worries about European politics, they had only to ramble during the day and to evade Mrs. Seidel's well-meant questions at night.

★　★　★

. . . *And when they were down, they were down* . . . At 2,088 feet, the peak of Kinder Scout was just eighty-eight feet above the clear-weather daytime flying level of London's barrage balloons; yet the return to ground level, the level of everyday fear, did not affect Andrew Hole at once. On the way back to Sheffield, he saw soldiers boarding trains at Dore Station and felt interested rather than worried; as it had been for Londoners, Saturday for him had been a "cheerful day, not bothering about war." Yet, after a short time, it angered him again to remember Poland. *It's infuriating,* he thought, *that we let a decent country like Czechoslovakia go, if we are to fight for a lousy dictatorship.*

While *The Times* hinted it might not come to that — there could yet be some compromise over Danzig — more reservists were being called up in France. Cars, horses, and various useful blocks of French property were requisitioned; and, in Scotland,

Queen Elizabeth gave in to instinct. "If things turn out badly," she told a lady-in-waiting, "I must be with the King." Many of their subjects, advised to evacuate London, would feel the same: If you were going to be bombed, it might as well be at home under your own rubble. She traveled south that afternoon.

Meanwhile, with growing disbelief, von Ribbentrop was reading Mussolini's list of Italian requirements—7 million tons of petroleum, 6 million of coal, 2 million of steel, another million of timber . . . Before finishing it, he stared frigidly at Attolico and asked him when the Duce wished delivery of the items. Attolico, who, as much as Ciano, wanted to keep Italy out of war, answered on his own initiative. With a look of surprise, as if it was the most obvious thing in the world, he said, "Why, at once, before hostilities begin."

Outside, the city was baking under a clear blue sky; with the temperature in the high seventies Fahrenheit, many Berliners had gone to cool off and relax a little by the lakes. Attolico's request was so clearly impossible that for a few moments he thought von Ribbentrop might explode in front of his eyes. Yet somehow the German controlled himself. The requirements could be met but, unfortunately, with such short notice not immediately in full. No doubt the Führer would wish for everyone to do their best. If His Excellency would care to wait, he could have the Führer's reply very soon.

Attolico did wait, and, considering the circumstances, the reply was a model of restraint. At 3:08 he telephoned it to Rome: "Duce, I understand your position," were Hitler's words, "and would only ask you try to achieve the pinning down of Anglo-French forces by active propaganda and suitable military demonstrations, such as you have already proposed to me."

But, after the ambassador had gone, the corridors echoed with loud abuse of the Italian nation; and, at 3:22 General Franz Halder, Chief of Staff of the German Army, noted in his diary: "Attack starts September 1." *Y-Tag* had been rescheduled.

Sir Alexander Cadogan was even then redrafting the British reply to Hitler on which Wilson and Butler had worked. *"Quite awful,"* he said to himself as he corrected the worst errors. But it was not as if this was simply a chatty letter to a friend. Any diplomatic communication had to be scrutinized line by line and word by word, because, even in the best of times, it was at the very least embarrassing if one's intention — the national intention — was misunderstood, and these were hardly the best of times. There was no room for ambiguity or anything that might be open to misinterpretation, yet, without retreating, one had to avoid confrontation. It was a very narrow path, with the edge perilously close. And time was marching on; the redraft would have to go to the Cabinet at 6:00. Cadogan was sure they would still not like it. *Let them fight their own battle,* he thought, and rushed home for a quick dinner.

For the second time in a year, Henderson joined the Cabinet session at 6:30. It was not common for an ambassador to be part of those discussions, and he enjoyed the privilege; he was also rather relieved to be away from the Berlin embassy. Many British nationals fleeing the German capital had put their belongings there for safekeeping, and Henderson's First Secretary, Sir George Ogilvie-Forbes, had been left in charge of what he complained was looking more and more like a furniture depository.

While the British Cabinet meeting was going on, Mussolini and Hitler exchanged messages once more. Over this and the next few days, said Paul Schmidt, "verbal or written contact with ambassadors in Berlin and statesmen in London, Paris, and Rome continued almost without intermission. It was a sort of long-distance conference by telephone and telegraph." The latest message from Rome was a groveling apology and self-justification. Mussolini explained that Attolico's stipulation of immediate delivery had been an absurd mistake; naturally he did not expect anything from Germany for a year at least. Until then, of course and most unfortunately, he could do nothing to help. "I leave you to imagine my state of mind," he wailed, "in finding myself compelled by forces beyond my control not to afford you real solidarity at the moment of action."

"Never mind," said Hitler: "I respect the reasons and motives that have led you to take this decision." His ally had ratted on him; very well, Germany would go it alone. Asking for psychological support through the Italian press or other means, he added that, during the winter or at the latest in the spring, he would attack in the West with forces at least equal to those of France and Britain, so — with a piece of refined sarcasm — it would be very helpful if the Duce could send over some Italian laborers to assist with industry and agriculture.

In London, the Cabinet learned much of interest. Halifax's assessment, with which his colleagues agreed, was that Sir Nevile Henderson should not be sent back at once, nor should their reply go that day, as "this might create the impression we. could be rushed." Tomorrow would be time enough. Hitler's present offer used the same old techniques: Trying to divide Britain from the French and the Poles, it pointed out that, with the Russo-German Pact, Poland's friends could not and therefore should not help her. Hitler clearly wanted to settle the Polish question; equally clearly, he wanted to avoid a quarrel with the British Empire. The question was, which did he want more? They had heard he meant to attack Poland any moment, but sending Henderson over by special plane did not seem to tally with that. Without identifying him, Halifax mentioned Dahlerus obliquely; Henderson expressed the views that the message sent through the "neutral person" was not open to misinterpretation, that there must be a secret protocol attached to the pact with Russia, and that this year was quite unlike last in that, compared with his feeling about the Czech leadership, Hitler was quite well disposed toward Colonel Beck in Poland. In short, there was still everything to play for. Inspecting the draft reply to Hitler (and rejecting it on the grounds that it should be stiffened up — Cadogan had been right) the single most interesting thing the Cabinet learned was the answer to the question of timing. If Britain had to declare war, when should it be done? Lord Chatfield, speaking with a report from the Chiefs of Staff, had the answer: "If an ultimatum is not to be issued until all essential preparations for war have been completed, the earliest date for the ultimatum will be Thursday, August 31."

Five days to go.

★ ★ ★

Derek Silver spent the evening in London at a concert, where he noticed among the audience an RAF corporal in uniform. In Berlin, Ulrich von Hassell, the ex-diplomat and secret anti-Nazi, passed his evening in the White Room of the Imperial Castle, attending the last night of the International Congress of Archaeologists. "In view of the situation," he wrote, "it was grotesque. Englishmen, Frenchmen, and Poles had already been recalled. Boring concert . . . my thoughts wandered elsewhere." There was a banquet afterward, during which he and Johannes Popitz, the Prussian Minister of Finance, shared a table with Bernhard Rust, the Prussian Minister of Education. "He played the host loudly and often tactlessly. A silent exchange of glances with Popitz at one moment almost cost us our self-control." Von Hassell did not say whether he and Popitz felt angered or amused by Rust, or both; but Popitz was another covert opponent of the Nazi regime and another who, in 1944, would be executed after the attempt on Hitler's life.

Hitler himself went to bed early that night, worn out. In Bielefeld, the young soldier Bernt Engelmann was also in bed by 11:00 P.M., but before midnight he was awakened and up again. His unit had been alerted and must move at once. At half past midnight Hitler, too, was roused: Birger Dahlerus was there to see him with Field Marshal Göring. Stumbling into wakefulness, the Führer presented a weird picture to the Swede, who, before this midnight meeting, had never encountered him in person. A glassy-eyed stare gave way to an amiable greeting, followed by a well-practiced monologue on the desirability of peace with England, which developed into a passionate indictment of the Poles. Dahlerus was brave enough (or naive enough) to interrupt with a remark about British and French armed preparations and their ability to blockade Germany. Walking to and fro, Hitler did not appear to register this at all; but then he stood stock-still and, as if hypnotized, began to repeat: "If there should be a war, then I will build U-boats, build U-boats, build U-boats, U-boats, U-boats — " It came out louder and louder: "I will build aircraft, build aircraft, aircraft, *and I will destroy my enemies!"*

Dahlerus turned in astonishment toward Göring, and what he saw astonished him even more: The Field Marshal beamed at him benignly as if nothing unusual was happening at all.

14

What's the use of worrying?

The Press had not noticed Birger Dahlerus's first visit to London, but at 1:00 P.M. on Sunday, August 27, a Lufthansa flight brought (as British newspapers put it) a "strange man" into Croydon airport. His arrival was notable because by then there were no civilian flights arriving from Germany; all normal air communication between the two nations had been stopped. Of medium build, clean shaven, dark suited, and carrying only a small briefcase, the same man, or one very like him, was seen arriving two hours later at the German embassy, from which he did not emerge until 6:15 P.M. Thereupon a reporter from the *News Chronicle* approached him with a simple question: "Can you tell me who you are, please?" The courteous journalist was thrown by the reply: "I do not know who I am."

For some reason the reporter got the stranger's times and locations in London wrong, but there is no doubt now as to his identity. *Ich weiss nicht, was ich bin; ich bin nicht, was ich weiss* — I know not what I am; I am not what I know. Perhaps, when giving that cryptic answer, Dahlerus had the old German poem at the back of his mind. The past twelve hours had been enough to tax anyone, and he, an amateur, was dabbling in things of worldwide importance, where a handshake might bring peace or a wrong word, a global war.

Newspapers could only speculate on his identity and purpose, implying in their articles that he must be part of some secret international negotiation. They were right, but, outside the Cabinet, scarcely a soul in Britain knew for certain — indeed, apart from Chamberlain and Halifax, not even the rest of the Cabinet had known Dahlerus's name until the middle of the afternoon. As far as the general public was concerned, the full weight of Anglo-German diplomacy was borne by Sir Nevile Henderson.

It was the same in Germany: "There is news everywhere," von Hassell wrote, "but it is not easy to verify. This day may go down in history as the day of a very great decision. Whether there will be a world war or not will ultimately depend on what Henderson brings back today from London."

Andrew Hole made one solitary entry in his diary that Sunday: "No climb down from Germany yet." On Hampstead Heath, Derek Silver watched troops filling sandbags. The sky over the whole city was dotted with barrage balloons. In their respective capitals, Halifax and Hitler were both at work, the former still struggling with the draft reply to the latter, who in turn was replying to a message from the French Prime Minister. Édouard Daladier, reminding Hitler of the Great War, lamented the possibility that France and Germany might fight again. If they did so, he predicted that a second war would be longer and more deadly than the first. Hitler agreed. "As an old frontline soldier, I know, as you do, the horrors of war," he said sympathetically and, in a blatant attempt to separate his possible opponents, added that there need be no quarrel between France and Germany: The entire present situation was the fault of Great Britain, because of the encouragement it was giving to Poland. Without that, he was sure the Poles would have been reasonable. But the same morning, as Dahlerus was flying to London, Hitler refused to accept an offer from two Polish diplomats of similarly secret, semiofficial negotiation. In addition, he forbade von Ribbentrop's staff to listen to any further such offers; he forbade military, naval, and air attachés to leave Berlin until further notice; and he ordered the beginning of rationing. "The higher-ups are in a 'state' and the people in the throes of great unrest and anxiety," von Hassell observed. "Mobilization goes on apace. War weddings for weeping couples. Ration cards, scarcity of foodstuffs — all that even before war begins."

★   ★   ★

Dahlerus met Chamberlain for the first time at 2:15 P.M. Halifax and Cadogan were present. The three Englishmen listened carefully but, Dahlerus sensed, with skepticism as he did his best to persuade them of his own view that "Mr. Hitler himself is not in favor of war." Much later—when the war was over—he wrote that, at that time, he already considered Hitler "patently unstable"; on August 27, however, he limited himself to saying that Hitler's "temper is at times uncontrollable." Chamberlain asked the Swede what he personally thought of the Führer. Dahlerus hesitated before answering: "I shouldn't like to have him as a partner in my business." Otherwise grim throughout the conversation, the Prime Minister did smile a little at that.

"He didn't add much to what we know," Cadogan commented afterward, adding that, although the Cabinet was due to meet at 3:00 P.M., "we didn't finish with D. till 3:40." Halifax put the same thing another way to his colleagues; telling them of the current efforts, he said regretfully that Dahlerus "was not a man who came very quickly to the point." Nevertheless, he had brought with him at least one new piece of information: Hitler had specifically demanded that Danzig and the existing Corridor should become part of the Reich, with a corridor for the Poles to Gdynia. Dahlerus had also made a suggestion that they had accepted: He should return to Germany that day ahead of Henderson. That had required a telephone call to Göring, who had spoken to Hitler, gaining his assent; if nothing else, it won an extra day.

A further item for the Cabinet's information was that, during the session with "Mr. D.," Halifax had been asked to receive a telephone call: Ciano had been on the line from Rome, recommending British acceptance of Hitler's present proposals (which Chamberlain indicated they might well do) and repeating Italy's wish to cooperate in the search for peace.

What none of them in London knew was that Ciano was positively seething with indignation, because the first he had known about Hitler's proposals to Britain was from the British. "We are entirely in the dark," he fumed to Mussolini. "Hitler proposes to the English an alliance or something like it. And this was naturally without our knowledge." The Duce's assessment was that it had happened because Hitler must feel a successful

Italian intervention would raise Italy's prestige at the expense of
Germany. With a snort of contempt, Ciano dismissed that idea
outright: "For me there is a simpler explanation, namely that the
Germans are treacherous and deceitful. Any alliance with them
becomes a bad alliance after a while." He liked talking to Halifax;
the English Foreign Secretary was always courteous and cordial.
What a contrast to his German counterpart! "Could there ever be
a more revolting scoundrel than von Ribbentrop?"

In Poland, Colonel Beck had reached a difficult decision: He
was willing to consider the possibility of an exchange of German
and Polish populations in the disputed areas. Nevertheless, being
suitably cautious, he also ordered Polish mobilization. Meanwhile, in London — as "C," the head of the Secret Intelligence
Service, passed to the Foreign Office a report that General
Halder and Admiral Raeder were both convinced that Britain
would fight and had warned Hitler of the danger of a double-
fronted war — "Mr. D." was hidden in Cadogan's office, while
Cadogan himself, talking to the French ambassador, Charles
Corbin, in the Foreign Office waiting room, denied all knowledge of a "mystery man." "C" had also produced a spy he wanted
to send back with Henderson. "Arranged that," Cadogan noted
laconically. As for the draft reply to Hitler, Leslie Hore-Belisha
found it "obsequious and deferential," a judgment with which
his Cabinet colleagues agreed, sending it back to the Foreign
Office for further work. In Cadogan's view, "Cabinet did
nothing."

The Cabinet adjourned at 4:30 P.M. An hour later in the
Chancellery in Berlin, Adolf Hitler was in conference. "A secret
meeting," Ciano wrote, with "the Deputies of the
Reichstag . . . . I don't know what he said, nor has Attolico been
able to tell me." What he said, as noted by one of his audience,
was simple and crucial: He stated his minimum and maximum
demands. Colonel Hans Oster scribbled them down: "Minimum demands — return of Danzig, settling of Corridor question. Maximum demands — 'depending on military situation.' "

Rather less than three hours later (according to the *News
Chronicle*), at 7:20, "the mystery stranger's plane left Croydon for

Heston." Cadogan had insisted that Dahlerus should not leave Britain by the same route as he had entered the country, and, in an effort to maintain secrecy, he had the Swede ferried first to the smaller airport. Dahlerus reached Berlin's Tempelhof airport well before midnight and went directly to Göring with news of his activities during the day. The Field Marshal passed on the information privately and, at 1:30 in the morning, telephoned him with Hitler's reaction. The Führer was delighted that Britain wished for a peaceful settlement. Should it take the form of a treaty or a pact? The suggestion that Danzig and surrounding issues should be settled by direct negotiation between Warsaw and Berlin was acceptable. In summary, said Göring, "if Henderson's note corresponds with your report, we should reach agreement."

Within half an hour Dahlerus was briefing Ogilvie-Forbes at the "furniture depository," the British embassy in Berlin. After a few hours' sleep, he breakfasted on the morning of Monday, August 28, with Göring. The Field Marshal's subordinate commanders were hopeful that war could be avoided, but Göring did not agree. As far as he could tell, the Führer and von Ribbentrop still wanted open conflict in Europe.

★ ★ ★

A letter from George Bernard Shaw, querulous but articulate as ever, was published in *The Times* that morning. Hitler was now under Stalin's thumb; Stalin's interest in peace was overwhelming. "And everyone except myself," the playwright complained, "is frightened out of his or her wits. Why? Am I mad? If not, why? Why? Why?"

He did have some measure of the British people. Back at work in Essex, the indefatigably observant journalist Derek Silver noted that some of the printing firm's staff were taken off their regular work and put to filling sandbags, while in Sheffield Andrew Hole decided the time had come to alter his holiday plans and, with a group of friends, took a trip to Leeds now, instead of later. Stopping on the way in "a very miserable café," they noticed "a very pathetic young woman obviously longing for company . . . . We were all frightfully hilarious, ate twice as much as we'd expected to, and made crude and contemptuous jokes about Goebbels and Göring." Looking grateful, the young woman cheered up considerably. At the same time in Edinburgh, Jim Latimer, a medical student aged twenty-four, noticed how petulant his golf-addicted grandfather had become. "Having business worries," young Latimer noted clinically, "and in addition is 'socketing' his mashie shots. Very dramatic manner of condemning Hitler, with a wonderful air of personal indignation." During the day, a family argument developed on the advisability of war, with Jim's parents and grandfather trying to balance the horror of dead children and babies against the loss of honor. On the whole, they thought the loss of honor was worse. With youthfully easy philosophy, Jim wondered what the bother was; war, in his view, was the greatest calamity in the world, but then the world had carried on regardless for millions of years. Even if he and they did not survive, he was sure the race would live to fight another day. "So" — to the exasperation of his elders, he ended his argument by borrowing a line of a song from the Great War, their war — "what's the use of worrying?"

It was, Harold Nicolson noted, "a lovely hot day." He bathed, wrote an article for the *Spectator,* and pondered. The one o'clock news said that the Mediterranean and Baltic were closed to all British merchant shipping; in Germany all private train traffic and even private post were prohibited. He could remember clearly the same month, twenty-five years ago, when the Great War had begun. Now he marveled at the contrast: "Then we were excited . . . . There was a sense of exhilaration. Today we are merely glum."

During the afternoon, Latimer sat sunning himself in his parents' Edinburgh garden, reading a book called *Privileged Spectator* — a curious title, under the circumstances. One day, when he was much older, he would be able to look back and understand that, like millions of other people, he, too, had been a privileged spectator, present on the eve of the greatest upheaval in the history of the world. Yet at the time, again like those millions of others, each in his or her individual way, he could only see what was immediately around him — in his case, the old stone wall of the property, its lawn, trees, and trim flowerbeds, and beyond, the roofs and chimneys of the Scottish capital. He did not know then that, while he read, Chamberlain was visiting the king again; that Arthur Greenwood, deputy leader of the Labour Party, visited Number Ten four times in the course of the day; that staff in the War Office practiced an air-raid alert, scurrying to the cellars; that the price of gold suddenly and sharply increased; or that Sir Nevile Henderson was on his way back to Berlin. Of course, none of these events was particularly secret; Latimer heard about some of them on wireless news that evening and saw more in the papers next day. One reporter, seeing Sir Nevile go, had wished him good luck. With a wave of his hat, the ambassador had replied, "Thank you; I shall need all the good luck I can get."

There were other events, small private ones, of which Latimer never knew at all, simply because, like his own life, they were not thought worthy of public record or announcement — for example, the activities of the Hawkers, Gerald and Betty; and of the Richters, Richard and his mother. Gerald Hawker was seventy-two years old, but he still worked as a consulting engineer. From his office in central London, he called his wife Betty at home in NW11 and suggested they might take a little trip out of town to Claygate, near Esher in Surrey. Together, they caught a train at 4:25 from Waterloo; and at the same time, Richard Richter was pacing up and down the Continental arrivals platform at Victoria, awaiting, with considerable agitation, the arrival of his mother from Vienna.

On the way to Claygate, Hawker explained to his wife what was on his mind: memories of the Great War. If things went wrong again with Germany, the capital might not be a very safe place to be, and he felt they ought to investigate the possibility of an out-of-town getaway. Claygate sounded very suitable: It was supposed to be attractive, and it was fourteen miles from the heart of the city. With a direct railway link, it was close enough to be convenient for work and quite far enough to be safe. Arriving at Claygate punctually at 5:00 P.M., they spent an interesting three-and-a-half hours inspecting five different houses, before returning to town on the 8:42. They stopped for supper at Lyons' Corner House in the Strand, compared notes, and agreed that the rooms offered by Mrs. Ashdown in Gatehouse Lane were far and away the nicest. The rent was reasonable, and they could move in whenever they chose; so, well satisfied with their evening, they returned to NW11.

Richard Richter, meanwhile, was doing his best to drive safely and listen to the chilling tale his mother had to tell of her summary arrest and imprisonment by the Gestapo. Slipping from English to German and back to English again, she did not notice that, even after three years in England and though he had a perfect command of the language, Richard's accent was still quite heavily German. But then, he had little chance to say anything, for she had scarcely stopped speaking since their emotional meeting in London. There seemed to have been even less reason for her release than there had been for her imprisonment; a few days ago, an Indian maharaja, or someone who appeared to be a maharaja, had visited the prison and seen that, among the female prisoners, there was one British national — perhaps he had had something to do with it. It sounded like a wild idea, but no more so than anything else; and, for both Richard and his mother, the only important thing that evening was that she was safe in England. But he could hardly square his own happy memories of the Austrian capital with his mother's description of it since the *Anschluss,* and, as he drove her to his little house in Kenilworth, he decided that one day he would go back to Vienna and, if possible, find out who in the embassy had reported her to the Germans.

On Monday, August 28, 1939, these were just two of the many episodes in other private lives that Jim Latimer, drowsily reading in Edinburgh, never knew of at all. And years passed before he learned from history books what else happened in secret between public people that same sunny afternoon. The Cabinet had met at 12:00 to finalize the reply to Hitler. To help them they had Dahlerus's report, forwarded by Ogilvie-Forbes, in front of them. It was extremely encouraging: Hitler would accept international guarantees for Poland and was willing to negotiate directly with the Poles. Knowing that, the Cabinet agreed on the final text of their reply; Chamberlain described it as dignified and firm, yet quite unprovocative. As soon as the session was over, Sir Alexander Cadogan was ushered in to draft a momentous telegram, which Lord Halifax telephoned direct to Warsaw at 2:00 P.M. It asked if the Poles would accept direct negotiations with Berlin. Remembering how obdurate they had been about the Russians, their answer could be crucial. (Coincidentally, this day was also Admiral Drax's fifty-ninth birthday; he spent it at home quietly, still coming to terms with the failure of his mission.) For two hours, while Ambassador Kennard hastened to see Colonel Beck, the diplomats, politicians, and civil servants in London waited in suspense, until at 4:00 P.M., just before Henderson's departure, the reply came back. It was a simple affirmative: Beck was willing to negotiate.

But just about then, General Franz Halder, Chief of Staff of the German Army, received via General Walter von Brauchitsch, Commander-in-Chief of the same force, a most important document from the Führer: his schedule for the invasion of Poland.

★ ★ ★

At 9:00 P.M. Henderson arrived in Berlin and was whisked directly to the British embassy where, among the stacks of unfamiliar furniture, his First Secretary had a message waiting for him. "Must be at least a dozen sets of dining room things alone," said Ogilvie-Forbes ruefully. "If it goes well with Herr H. tonight, we could have a party—no trouble in finding somewhere to sit, if one doesn't mind climbing a bit." Henderson did not appear to be in the mood for levity. Asking for a half-bottle of champagne, the message, and dinner, he began to prepare himself for what he suspected might be an ordeal. Ogilvie-Forbes put the mood down to the pressure of work and to the nervous and mental strain they had all been under for so long, but he did not know—for Henderson had kept it secret from everyone—that the ambassador was also in constant physical pain. After a recent medical operation, he had been diagnosed as suffering from terminal cancer. He ate and drank hurriedly, reading the message; it was the full text of the British reply:

> Everything turns upon the nature of the settlement and the method by which it is to be reached. On these points, the importance of which cannot be absent from the Chancellor's mind, his message is silent, and His Majesty's Government feels compelled to point out that an understanding on both is essential if further progress is to be achieved.

The British government would not be bribed at Poland's expense — "could not, for any advantage offered to Great Britain, acquiesce in a settlement which would put in jeopardy the independence of a State to whom they have given a guarantee." In a paragraph added at the last minute, the Note proposed direct negotiations between Poland and Germany, explaining that the Polish government had given its definite assurance of willingness to negotiate, and it concluded:

> A just settlement of these questions between Germany and Poland may open the way to world peace. Failure to reach it would ruin the hopes of better understanding between Germany and Great Britain, would bring the two countries into conflict, and might well plunge the whole world into war. Such an outcome would be a calamity without parallel in history.

That's telling him, thought Henderson. *Could any reply be more precise or straightforward? It makes it easy for Hitler to avoid war, if he really wishes to do so.* Such was the British point of view; from the Axis side, as Count Ciano noted, things looked somewhat different. When he saw an outline of the text later that night, one of his thoughts was that "the British action has induced Poland to become more conciliatory. This is probably the key to the whole situation." Even so, his basic reaction to the Note was one of relief: *Not bad; in fact it leaves the door open to many possibilities.*

During Henderson's meal, another message was brought in: The Führer wished to see him as soon as possible and suggested 10:00. Henderson put off the meeting until 10:30 — more haste, less speed. In fact, at 10:00, another call was made, this time from von Ribbentrop to von Mackensen, German ambassador in Rome. Von Ribbentrop wanted to quell at once the rumors in Italy that Germany was about to back down. On the contrary (von Mackensen was told), "the armies are on the march." And Henderson, making his final preparations to see Hitler, did not know that his colleagues in the British Foreign Office had just received more information from Dahlerus: All German forces would be positioned ready to attack Poland by the night of August 30–31, only two nights away.

At 10:30, fortified by his half-bottle of champagne, the ambassador arrived outside the Reich Chancellery after being driven the short distance through pitch-dark streets — blackout in Berlin. There had been a small crowd outside the embassy; a much larger one waited outside the Chancellery. Both were silent, and in the darkness the drumroll from a guard of honor sounded unnaturally loud.

★ ★ ★

When they heard of it a little later, even those in the diplomatic service who did not particularly care for Sir Nevile agreed that he had managed the interview skillfully. His hosts had gone out of their way to set him at ease; even von Ribbentrop was polite, and Hitler, looking well, "was absolutely calm and normal," Henderson reported. "No fireworks or tirades of any kind." Von Ribbentrop was present throughout the hour-long interview, and Paul Schmidt, translating, was surprised at how quiet the Führer was; he never even came close to losing his temper and actually appeared to be interested in the British proposal.

There was only one aspect of Henderson's report that did cause concern in London. To his British colleagues the day before, he had put forth the idea of a nonaggression pact between Britain and Germany. With the Prime Minister and Lord

Halifax, Cadogan noted, "I managed to kill this." But Henderson still thought it a feasible idea. In the interview with Hitler, he emphasized repeatedly that the whole British nation supported the Prime Minister's stand, that the time for a final decision had arrived, "and it rested with Herr Hitler . . . . Herr Hitler must choose between England and Poland." Accepting that, Hitler expressed ("in moderate terms") his view that the Poles were incapable of being reasonable. Von Ribbentrop then intervened: Could Henderson guarantee that the Prime Minister would still have unanimous British support if his policy was one of friendship toward Germany?

"There is no possible doubt whatever that he could and would," Henderson answered, "provided Germany cooperated."

In that case, Hitler inquired smoothly, would England be willing to accept an alliance with Germany? "I said," Henderson wrote in his official account, "speaking personally, I did not exclude such a possibility provided the developments justified it."

That was way beyond his brief; it was neither the time nor place for an accredited ambassador, acting as spokesman for his country, to express personal opinions. "A treaty, Yes," wrote Sir Robert Vansittart, the British Government's Chief Diplomatic Adviser, when he read the account. "An alliance, No. An alliance means a military alliance if it means anything. And against whom should we be allying ourselves with such a gang as the present regime in Germany? The merest suggestion of it would ruin us in the United States." Halifax agreed that the notion was preposterous: "An alliance raises all the difficulties in most acute form that we felt yesterday when discussing the 'nonaggression pact' idea." A stern warning came swiftly to Henderson, telling him not to allow the subject to crop up again. But it *had* come up, and, even if the answer was only a personal one, the idea had not been rejected out of hand; as far as Hitler was concerned, that was the important thing. When the interview ended at 11:30 P.M., in a mood of self-congratulation, he immediately summoned his own cabinet to tell them how well his plans seemed to be working. An alliance with Britain was not impossible; if it took place, it would be a coup on a par with the Russian pact, probably splitting the western allies and certainly greatly reducing the risks concerning Poland. Further, he had worked the British into persuading the Poles to negotiate, and one had only to recall Austria and Czechoslovakia to see where such negotiations would lead. Schmidt should not have been surprised at the Führer's even temper; everything appeared to be falling into place.

At the same time in Warsaw, Sir Howard Kennard was finding sleep difficult. While Henderson had been with Hitler, he had been with Colonel Beck. The Colonel would not accept his advice. Poland continued to mobilize.

15

And still we wait from day to day

In Saint James's Park in central London, on the morning of Tuesday, August 29, three people were to be seen walking and talking earnestly together. One of the gentlemen was immediately recognizable because of his tall, lean, rangy figure; the less familiar lady at his side was correctly assumed to be his wife. The second man was much shorter and slightly built, yet had an air of authority and seemed to be leading the discussion. Sitting down together on a bench, they were joined presently by another couple. Again, the newly arrived lady must be the wife of the gentleman with her, and again, there was no mistaking his handsome, famous face. The five strolled on together.

No one outside the quintet could hear their conversation, which was evidently private. No one had the temerity to follow them, and, if anyone walking in the opposite direction passed them, a respectful greeting was courteously returned, and the discussion paused until the passerby was out of earshot. It was another day of high humidity, but the sun ascending had burned off a morning fog and, though it was still early, was once again edging the temperature into the seventies. Grateful for the pleasant weather, Sir Alexander Cadogan, Prime Minister and Mrs. Chamberlain, and Lord and Lady Halifax continued to talk over Birger Dahlerus's latest report.

The Swedish go-between had telephoned at 7:00 A.M., after being briefed by Göring at 1:15 in the morning on Hitler's reaction to the British note. Apparently the Führer "was in fact only considering how reasonable he could be" and was about to extend an invitation to the Poles for discussions in Berlin. Dahlerus, enthusiastic and eager now that his efforts seemed to be paying off, gave a strong recommendation that they should accept. Yet the feeling that Dahlerus might not be entirely trustworthy was spreading in the Foreign Office; and ironically, that was one view with which von Ribbentrop would have agreed — he thought Dahlerus might be a British agent.

★ ★ ★

"The only bad news that I can see is the cricket — Surrey beating Middlesex. I ask you!"

"Well, I didn't ask you, and I think cricket's a stupid game anyway."

Tempers were fraying in the Woodward household in East London. At breakfast, Mr. and Mrs. Woodward had not disguised their worries about the future, and it had rubbed off on their sons Ed and Jack. Although they were grown men — Ed was twenty-one and Jack nearly nineteen — they had been bickering like boys. Ed's show of disdain for events outside cricket grounds maddened Jack. He hated to sound frightened, but he tried to ram home the reasons for his fear: "You know what I saw? Blue lights in the train, that's what. They're so dim you can't even read." He shrugged his shoulders. "OK, nothing much. It just gives me the willies, that's all."

"Scared by blue lights?" His brother sneered. "You read too many ghost stories, that's your trouble."

"Ed — " Torn between impatience and apprehension, Jack's voice was almost pleading. "You like to pretend you're as thick as a plank, but you must have grasped it. If there's war, who d'you think's going to be doing the fighting? Among others."

"Soldiers, of course. And sailors and pilots. Who d'you think, cloth-head?"

"I've got to go. But I'll tell you who I think — *you and me*. We're the right age. I'll bet you a quid we're both soldiers inside a year. G'bye." Angry with everything, he slammed the door.

Ed stared after him and smiled. "That's a quid you'll owe me then, little brother," he said to himself. "I'm going to join the navy."

Andrew Hole began digging an air-raid shelter in his mother's garden that morning. The soil was heavy clay, and it was backbreaking work. *A year ago,* he thought as the sun climbed and he toiled and sweated below, *she wouldn't have a stone moved.*

The Scottish medical student, Jim Latimer, was in a thoroughly bad temper. Somehow he had got a bad sore throat, which he regarded as a professional insult. His morning was entirely spent in Aberfeldy, trying to get his car fixed; during the afternoon he had to go visiting with his parents in Perth; and in the evening, to his utter disgust, he had time for only nine holes of golf. His father read in the paper that his lucky number that day would be six, "so he backed the sixth horse in every race at Birmingham, thus backing six losers." Jim found some sardonic pleasure in that. His dad had rendered him utterly speechless at one point with the suggestion that the best way out of the present pickle would be for Hitler to rent Danzig and the Corridor from the Poles. Though he did not say it out loud — he had learned it was not worth arguing — it was beyond young Latimer's grasp how dim some people could be. But, with his sore throat and "everyone twittering the same thing over and over again," Tuesday, August 29, was altogether "an aggravating day."

In Essex, Derek Silver found that his jitters had inexplicably and completely vanished. From Chelmsford he wrote to his girlfriend in Tunbridge Wells, saying with complete confidence that he would see her the following Sunday, September 2. Another young journalist, twenty-four-year-old Michael Dowering, returned home with his wife to Surrey after a holiday in Eire to find, as he wrote in his diary, "everyone very het up — apparently a crisis on." Three months ago, he had reckoned "on good authority" that Hitler would attack Poland on September 5. "Heaven knows what all the fuss is about . . . . If we knew then, why are people getting so worried now? We ought to be fully prepared!" He was one who vehemently did not support the Prime Minister. Blanking out his own oaths, he added: "Presumably it was that — — — —Chamberlain's fault for openly asserting that there was no reason to expect a crisis in the near future." That, he seemed to remember, had been a week or two before they had left on holiday. "And now there is a crisis. He knew there would be one all along."

The seventy-two-year-old consulting engineer, Gerald Hawker, went to his office at 10:30. There was no work to do, and "my very capable secretary, Gladys Flight, strongly advised our getting out of London at once, because evacuation of children was expected at any moment." He decided she was probably right—she usually was—"so phoned my wife to this effect. Had some trouble to get her to agree because of our elder daughter Brenda being left alone in our home." Fortunately, Brenda was quite happy to go and stay with a friend, so Hawker, with touching confidence in the Royal Mail, was able to telegraph and write to their prospective landlady in Claygate, Mrs. Ashdown, telling her they would arrive that evening. In Sheffield, Frank Peters, a thirty-five-year-old clerk, was "waiting to hear what our government will tell Hitler, and wondering if he will explode or climb down in view of the determined opposition. Will Mr. Chamberlain say much in the House? I don't think so—only the usual vague talk. Getting a bit tired of the big headlines in the papers and the crisis news . . . . Not seen much about 'No war this year' in the *Express* lately. No explanation yet," he finished with suitable skepticism, "but I am prepared to be reminded of their ability to foretell events if this blows over."

Another normal morning in abnormal times. "Nothing much," Cadogan concluded. "Further messages from Dahlerus, who seems to think that things are going well."

Harold Nicolson heard the same thing from another Member, General Sir Edward Spears, who in turn had it from Count Edward Raczynski, the Polish ambassador to London. Far from being desperate, Raczynski was reported as saying, "Things are going very nicely," and, when the House reassembled early in the afternoon, it was with a distinct air of optimism. There had been no attack over the past weekend, as most people had expected, and Henderson being shuttled back and forth seemed a hopeful sign. So, though anti-gas doors were being fitted and sandbags piled against the basement windows, Members only found them amusing. "The House is more cheerful than it has been for weeks," Nicolson wrote when the short session was over. "I think also they are proud of themselves for having behaved so well, so calmly, so unitedly today."

They had indeed—even Winston Churchill and Anthony Eden. They were photographed entering the building together. Their shared strong opposition to Chamberlain's previous policy of appeasement toward Germany was internationally known; because of it, in Germany—and sometimes in Britain, too—both had been repeatedly denounced as warmongers. Eden, the Member for Warwick and Leamington, had been Lord Halifax's immediate predecessor as Foreign Secretary but, after fiery arguments with the Prime Minister over foreign policy, had resigned in February 1938. This event had distressed Churchill deeply: "There seemed one strong young figure standing up against long, dismal, drawling tides of drift and surrender, of wrong measurements and feeble impulses," he had written. "Now he has gone." The photograph of the two men taken that afternoon was to be used in the *Tatler* magazine the following week, with the caption "Not a War Cabinet—unfortunately." In fact, by the time the magazine came out on September 6, Churchill *was* in the Cabinet, as First Lord of the Admiralty, and Eden—a major in the Territorial Army—was in uniform. But on August 29 they did not attack the Prime Minister, as they had done often before; Chamberlain's twenty-one-minute speech, explaining developments since the Members had last met, was so eloquent, balanced, and firm that scarcely anyone wished to criticize it.

The first words of the speech were designed to avoid any false optimism: "The catastrophe is not yet on us, but I cannot say that the danger of it has yet in any way receded." Chamberlain warned that the press should exercise the utmost restraint—"It is quite possible for a few thoughtless words in a paper, perhaps not of particular importance, to wreck the whole of the efforts which are being made by the Government"—and he apologized for being unable to give more than an outline of communications with Hitler. Honorable Members would understand that, "when issues so grave hang precariously in the balance, it is not in the public interest to publish these confidential communications." Describing the national mood as one of calm, united confidence, he went on to list some of the preparations in hand: air defense in a state of instant readiness, key points protected, the whole of the fighting fleet ready to take up war dispositions at a moment's notice, the merchant fleet under Admiralty control, and the Civil Defense regional organization on a war footing. Evacuation plans for schoolchildren, mothers with young children, expectant mothers, and the blind were prepared and had been practiced. He added, more ominously, that preliminary steps had been taken in hospitals to prepare for the reception of casualties. All this, he believed, contributed to and justified "the general absence of fear or, indeed, of any violent emotion" in the country; and he ended with a stolid but stirring declaration:

"The British people are said sometimes to be slow to make up their minds, but, having made them up, they do not readily let go. The issue of peace or war is still undecided, and we still will hope, and still will work, for peace; but we will abate no jot of our resolution to hold fast to the line which we have laid down for ourselves."

★   ★   ★

Moods were dictated as much by location as anything else. In spite of Ambassador Raczynski's optimism, Danzig itself was a place of high tension. There was good reason: No traffic was permitted through the Free City; on the other side of Poland's southern frontier, German troops were entering Slovakia, while to the east, Russian troops were moving into position. And, from what they had heard, the British and French were weakening in their determination to stand by them. Polish mobilization became general, over the protests of Ambassadors Kennard and Noël; yet Zofja Olszolwska and her large family in Moniaki were completely undisturbed in their rural tranquility, while Niusia Zamecka was happily preparing for the next term at school. She had a new satchel and pencil box, and a new black dress with a white collar, two pockets, and a belt. "Next weekend we are going back to Warsaw," she wrote. "The trees are tired after the long hot summer, and gossamer is floating in the air.

The autumn has crept in, and our holiday is almost over." The only disappointment was that her father would not allow her to take her bicycle. "I've tried to convince Papa that I could ride my bike in Warsaw's parks, but Papa said no. Papa can sometimes be as stubborn as Samson, the difference being that one can bribe Samson with sugar lumps." And so, being a philosophical child, she spent the afternoon with her mother, pickling pears and apples.

★   ★   ★

Gerald Hawker got home at 5:00 and settled down to sunbathe in the garden until 7:00, when he was called into the house for dinner. It did not take long; within an hour and a half, he and his wife Betty were at Waterloo in good time for the 8:42 to Claygate. Regarding the move as no more than a temporary precaution, they were very little disturbed by it, and they were not at all surprised to find Mrs. Ashdown ready to welcome them. She had, of course, received Gerald's letter of that morning, as well as the telegram, and everything was ready for them.

Jack Woodward's evening was spent with some friends digging up a wasps' nest in an East London wood — and putting up with the jibes of other ramblers, who helpfully pointed out that their air-raid shelter would have to be a lot deeper if it was to be any good. By then it was known in London's diplomatic circles that Mussolini had urged Hitler to accept the British note; and in Berlin, still quivering with indignation, Sir Nevile Henderson was writing the official report of his latest meeting with Adolf Hitler. He had waited the whole day for a summons to the Chancellery, with only a single worry: While every indication was that the Germans and Poles were feeling well disposed to each other, the only diplomatic representative in Berlin who had not asked to see him that day was Josef Lipski, the Polish ambassador.

Henderson had come to the Chancellery at 7:15 P.M., expecting the Reich Chancellor to be as calm and sensible as he had been the night before. Instead, with Henderson completely unprepared for the change, Hitler had reverted to the manic vituperative mode of diplomacy that he generally favored. Its immediate cause was the report in German newspapers of the deaths that day of five or six more Germans at Polish hands — reports that may or may not have been true, but that he at least feigned to accept. Gone was the semblance of sweet reason; in its place, a shouting fury. Henderson managed to extract a grudging acceptance of direct negotiation with Poland, but the Führer had said plainly that he was sure such talks would fail, expressing at the same time his deep resentment of British interference. It was when he had bawled at Henderson that the ambassador quite clearly "did not care how many Germans had been slaughtered in Poland" that Henderson had lost his temper, too. "I proceeded to outshout Herr Hitler," he wrote in cold rage, aware that this was a claim few could make; he had been honestly furious, for he was more pro-German than pro-Polish. "I told him I would not listen to such language from him or anybody. Such a statement was intolerable and an example of all his exaggerations. I added a good deal more, shouting at the top of my voice."

The message reached Cadogan about 10:00 P.M. *Looks pretty bad,* he thought, and promptly took it round to Lord Halifax. Together they went on to Number Ten and, with the Prime Minister, read Hitler's reply to the British note; it was an outpouring of abuse against Poland. "Barbarous atrocities which cry to heaven," "persecution of the German population of Poland," "the murder of Germans settled in the country, or their compulsory evacuation in the most cruel circumstances," "a state of affairs which is intolerable to a Great Power" — such was its general tone. "I glared at Herr Hitler the whole time," said Sir Nevile, with a touch of pride. But it was Hitler's final demand that, by its departure from normality, really irritated the British politicians. He was still willing to negotiate directly with the Poles — yet he insisted that a Polish plenipotentiary should come to Berlin for this purpose by the end of the following day. In London they agreed with Henderson's remark: The phrase sounded like an ultimatum.

There are two conflicting accounts of the immediate aftermath in Berlin of that stormy, undiplomatic interview. According to one, as soon as Henderson had left the Chancellery, Hitler had something like a nervous collapse and had to be given immediate medical attention. The other says that his mood changed instantly, that he declared gleefully that Poland would be finished within two months, and that a great peace conference would follow. Whichever is true — perhaps both, one state of mind following the other — it is worth remembering the testimony of Hitler's translator, Paul Schmidt: The reply to the British, with all its inflammatory accusations against Poland, had been written by Hitler and translated by Schmidt the night before.

That, of course, was not known in London then. Chamberlain, Halifax, and Cadogan sat up late working on a reply to the outburst. "Between us," Cadogan noted, "we knocked up a fairly hot draft by 12:30." They continued working on it for two more hours.

And still we wait . . . Far across the Atlantic ocean, Eleanor Roosevelt could not forget Europe. "And still we wait from day to day," she wrote, "hoping and praying for peace. I feel that every day that bombs do not actually burst and guns go off, we have gained an advantage." Nearer to the heart of events, however — and certainly no less concerned — Count Ciano closed his diary entry for August 29 with a portentous note: "The two armies are now within rifle range, and the slightest incident may cause a clash." And, at 2:00 A.M. the following morning, Wednesday, August 30, Sir Nevile Henderson was informed from Great Britain that Hitler's demand for the arrival of a Polish plenipotentiary that day was unreasonable. Britain would put no pressure on the Poles to comply.

★   ★   ★

Cycling to work on Wednesday morning, Derek Silver followed a route he had devised a few weeks ago — not the shortest but one that took him past a newsdealer. He liked to get any news as soon as possible. This morning the dealer's placards carried only two words: "Hitler Replies." He assumed rightly that this meant the reply was not to be made public — otherwise it would have said "Hitler's Reply" — and he did not stop. In the office, he got on with his usual first job of the day, plowing through all the national daily papers for material he could use in his weekly provincial one. It was a smooth morning's work with no sense of crisis. Outside, half a dozen men were still engaged in a leisurely way (they could hardly be called busy) in filling sandbags with earth and piling them against the machine room wall. Feeling the need for a smoke, he went out to join them — smoking was banned indoors, but not outside ("yet!") — and they all chatted and joked about ARP.

The conversation continued inside when, back at his desk, he found that another reporter, Chris Marley, had just got back from holiday in Cornwall. Silver asked him what signs he had seen there of military activity. "Oh, practically none to speak of," was the surprising answer. "Of course, every single village has its ARP on the go, and most of them an Auxiliary Fire Service, too; and naturally Plymouth's absolutely full of sailors. But that's about it, as far as visible signs go — no doubt it's all very hush-hush and underground, and we just don't get to see it. After all, if we could see it, so could everyone else."

"But even if we could see it, we wouldn't have to write about it," Silver remarked. "Look at these — the *Herald* and the *Mail*. They've both got a story about Hornchurch RAF station. And both say what type of aircraft is held there. I think it's shamefully irresponsible." Glancing at the articles, Marley nodded. "Frankly, I wouldn't have noticed it myself. Silver's unerring eye for security breaches strikes again. You'd be an utter beast if you were in charge of that kind of thing — but you're right. Talking of underground, though, I saw some wonderful caves on the Cornish coast. If they were furnished, they'd make the most perfect air-raid shelters imaginable. What d'you reckon to a little story about that?"

"It's a good idea, but you'd better not write about it."

Marley frowned. "Why ever not? Saboteurs might go and blow the caves up?"

"Not that. I don't suppose there's a single place in Essex that could claim to have a self-respecting cave. If Joe Bloggs reads that he can make himself into a caveman and keep his wife and aunty safe, he'll fill up the car with tinned peaches, rush off to Cornwall, and we won't have anyone left in the county to buy our papers."

ARP was also the first topic in Donald Richardson's office. Working in London, he was a solicitor in local government and, in common with more and more of his colleagues and friends, was undertaking air-raid warden's work in the evenings — he had been on duty until 8:30 the night before. However, there was little time to gossip; he had to go to Bow Street Police Court to prosecute a minor criminal. Over there, he found that, apart from sandbags round the door, the court looked quite normal inside and out; the only reminder of the outside world was when the magistrate referred briefly to the police having more than enough work at the moment. *The right attitude,* Richardson thought, nodding to show his agreement with the bench. He did not think this would be a difficult prosecution, but every little thing helped. In the Stock Market, reports that Hitler had studied Chamberlain's note with care led to a flurry of optimistic dealing; and, at 10:45, less than two miles away in Downing Street, Birger Dahlerus was ushered discreetly into Number Ten.

His latest secret concerned the conversation he had had with Göring in the early hours of the morning. It added two notable items of information to Henderson's report. The first was an explicit delineation of the geographical areas in which Hitler was most interested: Göring, in anger or panic, had dramatically pulled out an atlas, torn the appropriate page from it, and colored in the relevant parts. Danzig was specifically included; Gdynia, however, was left out, to remain a Polish port whatever happened. The second item was that Hitler was willing to accept a plebiscite on the matter; depending on the result, either the existing Corridor would become German, with a Polish right of passage across to Gdynia, or the existing Corridor would remain Polish and the existing German right of passage to Danzig would stay in force. But Danzig itself must become German.

Chamberlain, Halifax, and Cadogan were uncertain whether to believe Dahlerus. *"Says* Hitler *may* offer a plebiscite," Cadogan noted cautiously. But he added that, if it was true, "this throws a new light"; he and his colleagues decided that a few questions to the Field Marshal would be in order.

Andrew Hole's diary entry was simple: "Digging shelter in sweltering heat most of the day." By lunchtime in Bow Street, Donald Richardson had secured the conviction he was after. Without a second thought for the man now facing sentence, he had coffee at Lyons' and went on with a colleague to a nearby restaurant that catered especially to chess players. He found the game kept him in mental trim, but this time he was disappointed: He and his friend were checkmated into a long and tedious conversation with "a garrulous old gentleman who insisted on talking about the crisis" and who did not appear to notice how fidgety they were, until their lunch hour was over.

Harold Nicolson also lunched with a talkative gentleman, but he found it fascinating: Sir Ivone Kirkpatrick, now based in the London Foreign Office, had been First Secretary at the British embassy in Berlin from the time that Hitler first came to power until last year, and had met the German leader many times. Nicolson and their companions, Lady Colefax and Lady Cunard, asked him eagerly what the man was like.

"Socially, and when he is host in his own house, he has a certain simple dignity," Kirkpatrick answered. "Like a farmer entertaining neighbors. None of Mussolini's showy vulgarity. But, when one begins to work with him, or when one sees him dealing with great affairs, one has such a sense of . . . evil arrogance that it is almost nauseating. In fact," he confessed, "some of the interviews I have seen have made me physically sick. You've probably heard people speak of his eyes being hypnotic. Certainly they're a very bright, piercing blue, and when one actually meets him, they're virtually his only truly noticeable facial feature — photographs don't capture that quality.

Otherwise, I wouldn't say they're hypnotic at all." He thought carefully and continued, "They do look like the eyes of a mystic sometimes, but they dart with evil and treachery and malice. He is always laying down the law, and has a maddening way of talking—sharp, syncopated sentences—and gestures—he ends either with a sharp pat of his palm on the table, or a half-swing sideways in his chair, crossing his arms like Napoleon and staring at the ceiling in a suffering, detached way. He's terrifically impatient."

"Impatient, yes—but a sense of actual evil? What gave you that feeling?"

"I'll give you one example; I could give you fifty. You recall when Roehm was murdered?—the head of the *Sturmabteilung,* the stormtroopers? It's just over five years ago now. Hitler ordered that, of course, and flew from Godesberg to Munich to make sure it was done; and one of those who was with him on his return told me how he had been in the very highest spirits, describing the whole business to his secretary in minute detail— even mimicking the gestures of fear that Roehm had made." Kirkpatrick shook his head at the memory. "No, he is not just a simple sadist, but something far worse. I don't think I am overstating it when I say he is actually evil. I have never encountered that before, and I hope never to do so again. It is a very, very strange experience."

There was a silence around the table. Kirkpatrick smiled slightly: "I'm sorry. Hardly lunchtime conversation. Let me tell you something else a little more cheerful. Less sinister, at any rate. Even some of the highest Nazis can be amazingly disloyal to him at times. For instance, when Henderson was going in for some important conversation with him, the man—I don't remember the name offhand, but it's irrelevant—the man who took Henderson to Hitler's study whispered to him as he opened the door"—leaning forward, Kirkpatrick spoke in a hushed, conspiratorial tone, with a mock German accent—"'For God's sake, don't let him get away with it!'"

★   ★   ★

At 2:35, Betty Hawker took the train from Esher to London for an afternoon's shopping. From another direction, Jack Woodward, the not-quite-nineteen-year-old civil servant, was traveling up to work; during the crisis, his department was working in shifts, and he was on from 2:45 to 8:45. A small girl in the train was chattering enthusiastically to her mother: "Did you have blue lights last time, Mum? . . . I'm glad we've got black stuff for our windows . . . The shelters in the park are deeper than ours . . ." Chilly with apprehension, he tried not to listen, but there was no getting way from it; when he stepped out at the station, he saw with a deeper thrill of fear that armed guards were posted on every platform.

Gerald Hawker sat contentedly in his landlady's garden all afternoon, writing letters and reading *The Golden Bough* — an abridged edition, for he was not an ambitious reader. In Chelmsford, cycling out to cover the funeral of a local worthy for his paper, Derek Silver admired the white lines that were being painted down the center of the roads to help drivers in the blackout. *Going to mean pleasant night cycling without lights,* he thought. *Also strikes one that white lines everywhere are going to cut out a lot of guesswork in careless- and dangerous-driving police court cases.* It seemed odd no one had thought of it before, but then crisis made people think of a lot of new things. One such turned up at the office that afternoon: a thick green-covered book of about 100 pages, labeled in large letters "SECRET."

"The vindication of Silver, dear boy!" Chris Marley chuckled. "It's D-Notices — hundreds of 'em, listing all the things we can't write about. Plane types and locations, locations and numbers of troops, you name it — no doubt caves as well, somewhere. Makes you wonder what we can write about, without boring everyone to tears."

Flicking through the pages and nodding with satisfaction, Silver remarked, "It also makes you think why every newspaper, national or local, sounds so undisturbed. What was it Chamberlain said? 'The general absence of fear?' Of course that's how it seems. You can only judge the nation's mood by the papers, and what it amounts to is that we aren't allowed to say anything which could benefit the possible enemy—which includes reporting fear and frightening people more than they are already." Closing the heavy book and dropping it on the desk with a thump, he added, "Just as well, too, in my opinion."

Frank Peters, the Sheffield clerk, would have disagreed strongly. "Hitler's reply has come and ours has gone back," he wrote. "When do we get to know something? A year of crisis has left me feeling very calm. My wife made herself ill with worry last year and is determined not to do so this time." For him the most serious consideration was that, "if war comes, there is likely to be an immediate slump in our income. That is of more concern to us than bombs."

George Bernard Shaw's letter of Monday—"Everyone is frightened out of his or her wits. Why? . . . Why?"—received an epigrammatic reply in *The Times* that morning: "Who is frightened out of his wits? Who? Who? Who?" If there was one feeling that everyone shared, it was not fear so much as plain impatience with the seemingly endless waiting. "A waiting period of that kind is often very trying," Chamberlain had said in the House, and he was right. In Walton-on-the-Naze on the Essex coast—not far from Silver's office—a young tea merchant named Ross Mackay described it: "Everyone is feeling the strain, even in this out-of-the-way seaside town which never gets het up about anything." During the morning, while he helped to overhaul his van in the local garage, "people talked of nothing else, and every newcomer offered his own theory. The optimists and the pessimists seem to be about even, while there are few middlemen. All are at one in wishing something would happen to ease the tension . . ."

At 2:45, just as Jack Woodward was beginning his shift, Chamberlain sent a brief message to Hitler—not a reply, but merely to let the Reich Chancellor know that the continuing exchanges were welcome, that his most recent interview with Henderson was being considered "with all urgency," and that an official reply would follow shortly. By then, Birger Dahlerus had telephoned Göring from the Foreign Office. The Field Marshal could not be definite; however, repeating his hope of a plebiscite, he also hoped that Hitler's next proposal would not be in the form of a diktat, but a genuine offer. The only point on which he was certain was that a Polish plenipotentiary must come to Berlin that day. Both Cadogan and Halifax repeated emphatically that this was unreasonable. From Warsaw, Ambassador Kennard supported them in this judgment. In an early-morning telephone call, before Dahlerus had arrived in London, he had expressed his certainty that "it would be impossible to induce the Polish Government to send Colonel Beck, or any other representative, immediately to Berlin . . . . They would certainly sooner fight and perish than submit to such humiliation." Kennard had received a copy of the Hitler-Henderson interview demanding an immediate plenipotentiary, with instructions from London not to pass it on to the Polish authorities, and Joseph Kennedy, the American Ambassador to London, sent to Washington his own assessment that Chamberlain was more worried of getting Poland, than of getting Adolf Hitler, to reach agreement. He was right to an extent: There was concern in London that revealing the demand to Warsaw might result in a Polish reply so uncooperative that Hitler could feel at liberty to proceed as he chose. In that sense, the Poles were being protected from themselves. But there was still more to it; they were being protected from Hitler as well. Before passing on his demand, the British wanted to be absolutely certain that he was actually going to negotiate seriously and was not merely maneuvering for advantage so that he could give invasion a public justification.

By keeping the Führer's demand secret from the Poles, rightly or wrongly the British believed they were doing two things at once: first, deferring war — and a war deferred might yet be a war avoided altogether — and second, standing by the bottom line of their guarantee to Poland. If negotiations were to take place, they must be real, without the threat of force, and with Poland treated as a nation equal to Germany.

For weeks past, Hitler's most secret intelligence service, the *Forschungsamt* or Research Office, had monitored, recorded, and reported on every telephone conversation between London and the British embassy in Berlin. But, despite their skill, which was of a very high order, they — and consequently the Führer — did not know that his demand had not been forwarded to the Polish Government. In choosing this unilateral method of standing by its guarantee, the British Government was accepting a very great risk and a very grave responsibility, for, in Poland, mobilization carried on as if the demand had never been made, while in Germany, news of that continuing mobilization could only be viewed as a challenging refusal.

And yet it did cause Hitler to hesitate. General Halder's diary for the twenty-ninth read: "Basic principles: Raise a barrage of demographic demands . . . . 8/30 — Poles in Berlin. 8/31 — *Zerplatzen,*" [to burst, or blow up.] "9/1 — Use of force."

On the thirtieth, however, again on information from Commander-in-Chief General von Brauchitsch, Halder noted that the Führer had amended the strategy: "Make all preparations so that attack can begin at 4:30 A.M. on September 1. Should negotiations in London require postponement, then September 2. In that case we shall be notified before 3:00 P.M. tomorrow [the thirty-first] . . . . September 1 or September 2. All off after September 2."

By 4:30 on August 30, every Polish city was plastered with posters summoning all men up to the age of forty to report for enlistment. At 5:30, after reports had been received of German sabotage in Poland, another message came from London to Berlin: Germany must exercise complete restraint if Poland was to do so as well. At 6:50 the text of His Majesty's Government's reply was sent to Henderson. "We understand," it began, "that the German Government are insisting that a Polish representative with full powers must come to Berlin to receive German proposals." Nineteen of the twenty-four hours' notice given in the demand had by then elapsed, and this was to be the first official intimation to Berlin that a plenipotentiary might not arrive. When this reply was presented, it seemed scarcely credible — as if the British government had been sound asleep.

But it could not be presented yet. Lord Halifax was, in fact, asleep — he had gone to bed at 5:00 in the afternoon, exhausted — when the French ambassador, Charles Corbin, arrived at the

Foreign Office with, Cadogan noted, "an objection from his Government to a passage in our Note to Hitler. And Van [Sir Robert Vansittart] blew up. By desperate efforts managed to compose the differences and get P.M.'s approval. Home about 8:00 — mad with fatigue. Things must now take their course . . . . I can't help feeling Germans are in an awful fix."

★   ★   ★

There was a marked and sinister change in the tenor of German news broadcasts during the evening. In place of the previous night's main subject, Anglo-German peace efforts, almost every item spoke of alleged atrocities on German people in Poland — rapes, murders, burnings, beatings — while the police looked on indifferently and the government made belligerent preparations. The same propaganda process had been used before the destruction of Czechoslovakia, and many Germans accepted it as gospel — but, even so, by no means were all eager for a war of revenge. A couple of nights earlier, Ulrich von Hassell had been to the movies and seen a newsreel in which weeping women and children had been shown, describing their sufferings in Poland. *A disgusting example of how human misery is exploited for propaganda purposes,* he had thought, and noticed how the other spectators had remained "completely passive; there was only very weak applause at the showing of military pictures, not taken up by the bulk of the audience."

"Today," wrote Harold Nicolson on the evening of August 30, "when war seems a matter of hours, the absolute gloom of a week ago seems to have changed into determination, the gloom of anticipation melting into the gaiety of courage. It is as though we had taken our fill of apprehension and sadness and can absorb no more." Many other Britons, writing in their own diaries at the same time, backed this up. Jim Latimer, his mother, and his aunt all took part in their golf club's weekly competition and did rather well; his mother won the scratch prize, his aunt the first handicap, and he himself the second handicap. Andrew Hole went to the theater to see Shaw's *Geneva,* and, after listening to a

Bach promenade concert on the wireless, Derek Silver went to
the cinema, timing his arrival "just right—getting in just as the
frightful Kay Francis sobstuff second feature (*Comet over Broad-
way*) ends, and the news comes in."

Even those ordinary folk who, with their own eyes, could see
physical evidence of the times seemed less inclined than ever
before to be worried. Donald Richardson, the London solicitor,
went walking with his wife on Ealing Common after supper and,
noticing a searchlight, strolled over to have a look at it. They
"found it surrounded by a fair-sized crowd, seemingly in almost
holiday mood. A poor devil of a sentry marching up and down
the fence was being ragged by schoolboys, who had laughing
support from the crowd. When the sentry said, 'Keep back,' a
woman said, 'Listen to the voice of officialdom!'" Feeling sorry
for the sentry, Mr. and Mrs. Richardson turned for home, where
she went to bed early and he played checkers with his brother
until 11:00. Silver's film, *Stagecoach,* was over by then. "Well up to
expectations," he jotted. "Walked home with my head full of its
grand theme tune and got in just in time to hear 11:00 P.M. news
summary. This tells of much mobilization going on (reservists
called up in France; cars, cycles commandeered in Poland;
precautions in Switzerland), but, while this warlike activity goes
on, all seems much calmer on the diplomatic front. And so
calmly to bed to write this."

He could scarcely have been more mistaken.

16

I hear the wings of the angel of peace

At midnight on August 30, 1939, in a room where Bismarck used to work in the German Foreign Office, Joachim von Ribbentrop sat at a small table, almost shivering with excitement. His face was pale, his lips set, his eyes unnaturally bright. Opposite him, speaking mostly in German, sat Sir Nevile Henderson; between them, at the end of the table, was Paul Schmidt, the sole specta tor, translating whenever Sir Nevile's command of the language failed him. Beginning with the message that it was unreasonable to expect a plenipotentiary so swiftly, Henderson had just finished reciting the communications that he had sent in writing to the German Foreign Minister during the course of the day.

Von Ribbentrop's reply ignored it all. "The time is up," he said bluntly. "Where's the Pole your government was to provide?"

Henderson did not give a direct reply; instead, he handed over a letter from Chamberlain to Hitler, stating that Poland had been asked to prevent frontier incidents. Sir Nevile added that Germany should adopt a similar policy.

"The Poles are the aggressors, not we!" Von Ribbentrop retorted hotly. "You've come to the wrong address."

As calmly as he could, Henderson gave his government's suggestion that the Germans should follow normal diplomatic procedure and send their proposals through the Polish ambassador.

Folding his arms, von Ribbentrop shouted across the table, "Out of the question, after what has happened! We demand that a negotiator empowered by his government with full authority should come here to Berlin."

Schmidt saw Henderson's hands begin to tremble and thought he was frightened; he was not known in Berlin as a brave diplomat. But then, as the ambassador began to read the official

225

British reply, Schmidt noticed his face was flushed red; the tremble was not from nerves but anger. As Henderson read, von Ribbentrop's frown deepened. He interrupted repeatedly— "Ridiculous! Absurd!"—and, at the recommendation that troop movements should cease, burst out, "That's an unheard-of suggestion!" Unfolding and refolding his arms again, he stared at Henderson in direct challenge and shouted, "Have you anything more to add?"

"Yes," said Henderson in German, his own temper barely under control. "As a verbal addition to the written reply, my government possesses information to the effect that Germans are committing acts of sabotage in Poland."

Utterly enraged, von Ribbentrop roared at him; "That's a damned lie of the Polish government's! I can only tell you, Herr Henderson, that the position is damned serious!"

Henderson reeled in shock; then he, too, lost his temper completely and, wagging his finger like a schoolmaster, shouted back, "You have just said 'damned.' That's no word for a statesman to use in so grave a situation."

For a moment von Ribbentrop stared at him in disbelief; then, jumping to his feet, he bellowed, "What did you say?" Henderson jumped up, too. The two men leaned on the table breathing heavily and glaring furiously at each other.

Schmidt gulped. "According to diplomatic convention," he wrote later, "I, too, should have risen; but to be frank I did not quite know how an interpreter should behave when speakers passed from words to deeds." Thinking that at any moment it might well degenerate into a fistfight, "I therefore remained quietly seated and pretended to be writing in my notebook."

The least that can happen now, he thought, *is that the Foreign Minister of the Reich will throw His Britannic Majesty's Ambassador out of the door.* He did not find it the least bit amusing.

After a good deal more glaring and heavy breathing, however, there seemed to be an improvement. Looking up warily, Schmidt saw that "the two fighting cocks" were sitting down again, their composure evidently somewhat restored. Von Ribbentrop then began to read through Hitler's proposals to Poland, a list that became known as the Sixteen Points. He did so in German, naturally, and Sir Nevile, proud of his ability with the language, did not ask for an interpretation. But he was not as good a linguist as he thought. To him, it seemed that von Ribbentrop gabbled through the list; later, both von Ribbentrop and Schmidt denied this, Schmidt adding that the Reichsminister actually elaborated on the outline of some of the proposals. Henderson's lack of complete comprehension was unfortunate; but the real surprise, both for him and Schmidt, occurred when he asked for a copy to transmit to London. Schmidt wondered why he asked — to provide a copy was normal diplomatic practice — and could hardly believe von Ribbentrop's answer. "Sorry, no," the Reichsminister said, with an inappropriate smile. "I cannot hand you these proposals."

Henderson obviously thought he had misheard and asked the question again, only to receive the same reply. Throwing the document on the table, von Ribbentrop said, "Anyhow, as the Polish envoy has not appeared, it's out of date."

Schmidt "suddenly saw the game" and believed ever after that the proposals had only been put up for show, that there never had been any intention they should actually be used. They were generous; the Poles might have actually accepted them. He desperately wished he could intervene but was unable to; an interpreter putting forth his own view could only create confusion. Grinding his teeth, he saw a chance of peace "deliberately sabotaged" before his eyes. *So this is what Hitler and von Ribbentrop have been discussing,* he thought, and gazed at Henderson, mentally willing him to ask for an English translation, which von Ribbentrop could not have refused; Schmidt would then have translated slowly enough for Sir Nevile to take full notes. But the ambassador was not telepathic. The moment passed.

★   ★   ★

For many people it was a long and almost sleepless night. Henderson returned to the embassy convinced that the last hope of peace had vanished. He had put it to von Ribbentrop that, if the proposals were out of date, they had in fact been an ultimatum. Von Ribbentrop had heatedly dismissed this allegation as nonsense, whereupon Henderson had suggested that the Reichsminister should at least make direct contact with Josef Lipski, the Polish ambassador to Berlin. Von Ribbentrop's reply, "in the most violent terms," had been that "he would never ask the ambassador to visit him. He hinted that if the Polish ambassador asked him for an interview it might be different."

With that — the slenderest of hopes for Henderson — they had parted. By then, Birger Dahlerus was back in Berlin. As soon as Henderson reached his own embassy, he called Ambassador Lipski over to see him, while his First Secretary, Sir George Ogilvie-Forbes, informed Dahlerus of the ghastly interview with von Ribbentrop. By 1:30 in the morning of Thursday, August 31, Lipski was at the British embassy, and Dahlerus was in consultation with Hermann Göring. The Field Marshal had just been appointed head of a newly formed Ministerial Council for the Defense of the Reich, a War Cabinet. Now, listening to the Swede's reprimand — "This is no way to treat the ambassador of an empire like Great Britain" — he protested that the German proposals were extremely liberal, "formulated to show how extremely anxious the Führer is to reach an agreement with Great Britain." Very well, said Dahlerus, give them a copy.

By 3:00 A.M. Lipski was back in the Polish embassy, after Henderson had implored him to seek Colonel Beck's immediate permission to receive the Sixteen Points. Ambassador Kennard had already been in contact with Beck, at midnight, to give him the text of the British reply and, on Halifax's instructions, to ask for the earliest possible opening of discussions between Poland and Germany. Lipski, by telegraph to Warsaw, was able to add details of three of the Sixteen Points — the only three of which Henderson was fully certain. He also dispatched the Embassy Counsellor, Prince Lubomirski, personally to Warsaw to request permission for an interview with von Ribbentrop. At 4:00 in the morning, Henderson dropped into bed, confused and exhausted. At 5:35, Kennard reported to London that more delay was unavoidable; Beck insisted he must consult with his own government and could only promise that a formal reply would be sent to Berlin by noon. Less than one hour later, at 6:30 A.M., German troops were ordered to take up their positions.

★ ★ ★

On the last morning of August 1939, Count Ciano's first note was uncharacteristically brief: "An ugly awakening." Ambassador Attolico had telephoned him at 9:00, "saying that the situation is desperate and that unless something new comes up there will be war in a few hours." The Count went quickly to the Palazzo Venezia, thinking, *We must find a new solution.* By then Sir Nevile Henderson had already conducted three separate interviews, of which the third had been with Attolico. The first, at 8:00 A.M., was with Henryk Malhomme, First Secretary of the Polish embassy—Lipski himself had been too busy to come. In a voice filled with sadness, Henderson's opening words to his visitor were: "Malhomme, I do not like war." They had known each other from previous years when they both worked in Belgrade, and their meeting this morning was sad and friendly, Henderson still fuzzy from lack of sleep, Malhomme deeply concerned about the outcome of the next few hours. Above all, it emerged that the British ambassador wanted to tell a Pole exactly what he felt about Poland, especially since he had come to believe that many of them regarded him as a Nazi sympathizer. He was not. On the contrary, he said, he knew Poland well because of his passion for hunting; he liked the people and the country; he had done and would continue to do everything in his power to avoid a war that could only end in Poland's destruction. But, if he failed, Malhomme recorded, "he would like me, when the war was over, to repeat his motives to my compatriots." Despite the frightening augury for his own immediate future, Malhomme was touched by the un-British display of emotion and promised he would do as Henderson asked. As if neither wished to proceed with the day, their farewell handshake was noticeably long.

Over breakfast, Henderson's second visitor was another old friend, Ulrich von Hassell. Because of his curious position—an

ex-diplomat, opposed to the Nazi regime but still well connected — he could be used by those still within the administration who shared his dislike of Nazism. On this occasion, he
emphasized he was only there in a private capacity, without
orders: Ernst von Weizsäcker, von Ribbentrop's Under-Secretary,
had asked him if he could influence the British ambassador at
least as far as getting Lipski to announce before noon the intention of sending a plenipotentiary. Henderson had already done as
much as he could toward that, as he explained, adding that the
chief difficulty lay in Germany's methods — "particularly," von
Hassell noted, "the way in which we expected the English to
order the Poles around like stupid little boys." To this the
German answered that the Poles' persistent silence was also
objectionable. It did not occur to Henderson, but this was a
remarkable thing for von Hassell to say. He was a cultured,
educated, experienced man, yet even he accepted this one part of
the current Nazi propaganda. He put it down to Slavic
behavior — no doubt Henderson remembered that kind of thing
from his time in Saint Petersburg, before the Russian revolution.
That touched off the Englishman's fragile emotions again. "Ah,"
he said nostalgically, "I wish those times would only come back."

"Times in which you almost strangled your own ambassador?" In an effort to make a joke, von Hassell was remembering an occasion one night, when Henderson, thinking he had
disturbed a burglar, had tackled his boss. *Now,* von Hassell
thought, seeing Sir Nevile smile with a mixture of sadness and
anger, *he is in a mood to strangle others.*

As if reading his thoughts, the ambassador said with finality,
"It would be easy, you know, to reach an understanding between
England and Germany if it were not for the calamitous von
Ribbentrop. With him, it will never be possible."

The "ugly awakening" to the last day of August extended far
beyond Rome. Derek Silver's landlady declared herself "quite
shocked" at the sight of so many sandbags in Chelmsford. "All
round the 'ospital, they are, Mr. Silver," she said. "And the police
station, *and* the drill 'alls, and even the grocers are putting up
thick wooden shutters over their windows, so you can't see a

thing they've got inside. Not that they've got so much as usual," she added reflectively. "People do seem to be buying a lot. Makes you rather feel it's . . . a bit serious, doesn't it?"

In London, the solicitor Donald Richardson was having a good deal of trouble calming down his father-in-law — "rather jittery on the subject of mustard gas, some idiot having taken the trouble yesterday to explain in detail the way it works." As much as was possible, Richardson reassured him, using his skill at argument to invent an "authoritative (but highly inaccurate) account of how little danger there really is."

In Chartwell, his house near Westerham in Kent, Churchill was working that morning on his *History of the English-Speaking Peoples*. The four-volume work, commissioned in September 1932 for £20,000, [$93,600] was scheduled for publication in 1940. Other events intervened, and the first volume eventually appeared sixteen years late. While Churchill was out of office, writing and lecturing formed his sole source of income, and he knew intimately how hard such work could be. But these days, sleeping with a gun under his pillow and a guard at his door, "it is a relief," he admitted, "to be able to escape into other centuries."

But in Berlin there was no escape from the pressures of the morning, intensifying moment by moment. Henderson passed on von Hassell's assessment to Attolico, and at 9:15, soon after the Italian had left the British embassy, he sent it to London as well: "On the best possible authority . . . If nothing happens within the next two or three hours, i.e., possibly by midday, German Government will declare war." It was received in London at 9:30, just as von Hassell — through the agency of Olga Riegele, Göring's sister — was talking to the Field Marshal. His assertion, startlingly at odds with von Ribbentrop's, was that, if the Poles had not definitely refused to come, the proposals remained on the table. Von Hassell hurried back to Henderson — "He was greatly interested" — and then reported to von Weizsäcker, who promised to keep him up to date.

Those next two crucial hours were quite simply weird: a graphic demonstration of the rivalry and opposition that lay

between Göring and von Ribbentrop. At 10:00 A.M. Birger
Dahlerus appeared at the British embassy, bearing with him the
typed copy of the sixteen proposals he had received from Göring.
"Tired and depressed," Henderson listened to him and, deciding he could be used to pressure Lipski, sent him with Sir
George Ogilvie-Forbes over to the Polish embassy. Lipski was
not impressed. His staff were already packing up the embassy; he
himself was irritated at having Dahlerus, whom he had never
heard of before, introduced into the business. Finding it difficult
to credit Sir George's explanation that the Swede was a neutral
who had the confidence of the British cabinet, the British
embassy, and the German government—and just as difficult to
keep track of Dahlerus's excited ramblings—he asked him to go
and dictate what notes he had to a secretary in another room,
then told Sir George that the German plan breached Polish
sovereignty. It was, he declared, "a trap, and acceptance was quite
out of the question."

At 11:00, after consulting with Mussolini, Ciano telephoned
Halifax "to tell him that the Duce can intervene with Hitler only
if he brings a fat prize: Danzig. Empty-handed, he can do
nothing." Halifax refused the Duce's offer, saying the most
urgent problem was to get the Poles and Germans to agree to talk
to each other—could the Count help with that? Ciano said he
would try. But, while this conversation was going on between
Rome and London, Ernst von Weizsäcker (in the presence of
Ulrich von Hassell) was being told by von Ribbentrop in no
uncertain terms that Sir Nevile Henderson should *not* be given a
copy of the proposals. He himself would telephone Henderson
to say the Poles could have the proposals if they sent a plenipotentiary. Forbidding von Weizsäcker to have any further dealings
with Henderson, von Ribbentrop added that Hitler had ordered
any overtures to be rejected.

Thus, as midday on August 31 approached, the situation in
Berlin was more than a little confused. (As Ciano put it later that
evening, "There is something obscure about the whole German
attitude.") Von Ribbentrop and Göring, two of the most important men in the country, were operating without mutual liaison

in exactly contradictory ways. Officially — that is, as far as the Führer and his Foreign Minister were concerned — the Poles still did not know the detailed proposals, which might or might not be out of date and which therefore might or might not have been an ultimatum, and they would not know them officially unless they first agreed to send a plenipotentiary. Unofficially, the Poles did now have a good idea of the proposals, but they would not budge until they were told them officially.

"That was proof for Weizsäcker," von Hassell noted, "that Hitler and von Ribbentrop wanted war; they imagined their proposals had furnished them with an alibi. This seems nonsensical to me if the proposals are not given to the Poles. Von Ribbentrop further stated that, during the next half hour, it would be decided whether the proposals should be made public. If this is really under discussion, it is altogether incomprehensible why the proposals should not be given to Henderson, unless they want war." And from von Weizsäcker he heard the British point of view, as told to the Italians: "The only question now was one of honor: whether we asked Lipski to call, or whether he came of his own accord."

Twelve noon came and went without any reply from Warsaw to Berlin or any apparent change in the impasse. The von Ribbentrop-Göring clash was not the only difference of opinion on one side; when Henderson urged the British Foreign Office to put direct pressure on the Poles, Kennard's advice was a firm contradiction: "H.M. Ambassador at Berlin appears to consider German terms reasonable. I fear that I cannot agree with him from point of view of Warsaw." By 12:30 the Foreign Office had from Henderson a copy of the detailed proposals and, at the same time, received a telephone call from Dahlerus, speaking from Henderson's own office. Sir Horace Wilson took the call, and, as the Swede babbled excitedly on, was horrified to hear a German voice repeating his words.

"You'd better give this information to Henderson," he interrupted, but Dahlerus took no notice, saying that Lipski had described the proposals as out of the question.

"Don't get ahead of the clock," Wilson exclaimed in agitation — he could still hear the eavesdropping German voice. "If there's anything to say, Henderson should say it in the ordinary way." Still Dahlerus ignored him, announcing that the Poles were not going to give way and that it was obvious they were being deliberately obstructive.

"Shut up!" Wilson yelled — but even that did not stop Dahlerus. Wilson slammed the receiver down. It was the only way to end the grotesque indiscretions, and, fuming with rage, he promptly sent a stern telegram of warning to Henderson.

Within minutes the Foreign Office telephone shrilled again; Ciano was once more on the line from Rome to London, with a new suggestion: What about a peace conference, hosted by Mussolini, to take place on September 5? André François-Poncet, the French ambassador to Rome, was skeptical but thought it a good idea; Sir Percy Loraine, his British counterpart, welcomed it with enthusiasm; Lord Halifax was favorable but said he must ask the Prime Minister. Simultaneously — the time was 12:40 — Colonel Beck was talking to Lipski from Warsaw. More experienced than the amateur Dahlerus, he used a code for his message, which was that Lipski should request an interview with von Ribbentrop: Poland was "favorably considering" Britain's request to open direct negotiations. A formal reply would come soon. Meanwhile — and this was secret, for the ambassador's knowledge only — Lipski should not begin any concrete negotiations and, if asked to do so, should refer back to his government.

At 1:00 P.M. Lipski duly applied for the interview. To his mystification, von Ribbentrop did not seem particularly surprised to hear from him or particularly eager to see him. Some time in the afternoon would do; he would be told when. Uncertain and more suspicious than ever, the ambassador wondered what had prompted this unexpected lack of interest. It was a very long time before he knew the terrible double truth. The Research Office had not, this time, made the error of letting themselves be overheard. In spite of Beck's code, his entire message, including the secret section, had been intercepted, decoded, and delivered to von Ribbentrop even before Lipski's call at 1:00; and an hour earlier, at noon, Adolf Hitler had issued an order whose title would become infamous — Directive Number One for the Conduct of the War.

★ ★ ★

Donald Richardson, the London solicitor, did something he had never done before: He went to see a film, the latest one by Will Hay, at lunchtime and overstayed his lunch hour by 50 percent. The sense of guilt at such irresponsible behavior lessened his enjoyment of the film, but, when he returned to the office, he did not know whether to feel relieved or cross — no one had noticed his absence at all.

Jack Woodward, the young civil servant, was at work — his shift that day was from noon to 7:00 P.M. — unable to forget the latest things he had overheard on the way in, as two old ladies had gossiped morbidly: "They're clearing out all the 'ospitals . . . Doctors won't 'alf 'ave a time . . . They're digging an underground passage from the railway to the 'ospital . . . They've remembered everything, nothing left to chance . . . If a train's 'it they can take 'em into 'ospital quicker — poor fings might lie on the track for hours." He could not help thinking that soon he, too, might be one of those "poor fings."

In Edinburgh, Jim Latimer was recovering from "the shock of my life" — feeling something wriggling in his pocket, he had put his hand in without looking and pulled out a live and very angry wasp.

In Surrey, after a walk to Oxshott, Gerald and Betty Hawker were returning to Mrs. Ashdown's well satisfied with their choice of a getaway: "This place is a *beauty spot,*" wrote Gerald with pleasure.

In Essex, the journalist Derek Silver had just heard a shocking announcement on the 2:00 P.M. news: Evacuation of 3 million mothers and children from the "menaced areas" would begin tomorrow. The added information that this did not mean that war was regarded as inevitable reassured him somewhat. However, telephoning the local education department, he found both that they were preparing to receive evacuated children and that their own would not return to school as expected on September 4, but would remain on holiday until further notice. The railway station, too, advertised a "heavy curtailment" of normal services over the next four days; but, "far more unpleasant than the crisis," his main job that afternoon was to visit the father of a twenty-one-year-old RAF man whose bomber was believed to have crashed into the North Sea.

At Walton-on-the-Naze, the decision to start evacuating the cities caused great commotion. "Visitors have left in crowds while the going is good," Ross Mackay wrote, "and we may now expect thousands of children who will be everything from thrilled to bewildered." Business was brisk: "It takes little effort to sell tea just now. Nearly everyone is buying extra." He saw his first ARP rehearsal — "four inhuman objects in gasproof clothes" — and concluded in wonder, "Walton has never taken anything so seriously."

★   ★   ★

In a peaceful cemetery far away, Niusia Zamecka knelt down beside her mother and aunt at the foot of her grandmother's grave. Fresh crimson gladioli fanned out from its center, with two bunches of white and yellow dahlias. Close by were three new graves, one quite small. Niusia asked her mother who was buried in the little grave. There were pink ribbons on its bouquets and wreaths, and her mother said it must have been a little girl. Niusia was shocked; she had always thought that only old people died. "I should hate to be dead," she wrote, "when there is so much to live for. Every new day is as exciting as a birthday present. In fact, the more I live the more I like it."

"Grandmama dead" — the code words had stung Alfred Helmut Naujocks into action, ending his fourteen-day wait at Gleiwitz. As Niusia and her mother made arrangements with Father Jakob for the christening of Irka's infant daughter, SS Sturmbannführer Naujocks and Heinrich Mueller, head of the Gestapo, were carrying out the arrangements long planned by

General Heydrich. The canned goods were ready—a dozen "condemned criminals" dressed in Polish military uniform, administered with fatal injections, and subsequently shot. All was in order.

★ ★ ★

At 4:00 P.M. the OKW—*Oberkommando der Wehrmacht,* the High Command of the Armed Forces—issued instructions for the great assault, and the executive order was confirmed.

The Supreme Commander of the Armed Forces   Berlin,
OKW/WFA Nr. 170/39 g. K. Chefs. Ll   August 31, 1939.
MOST SECRET
Senior Commanders only   8 copies
By hand of Officer only   COPY NO. 2
          Directive No. 1 for the Conduct of the War

1. Since the situation on Germany's Eastern frontier has become intolerable, and all political possibilities of peaceful settlement have been exhausted, I have decided upon a *solution by force.*
2. *The attack on Poland* will be undertaken in accordance with the preparations made for "Case White," with such variations as may be necessitated by the buildup of the Army, which is now virtually complete. The allocation of tanks and the purpose of the operation remain unchanged.
Date of attack: September 1, 1939. Time of attack:—

In the draft orders, the time of attack was deliberately left blank. When the orders were issued, it was inserted in red: 0445.

This time also applies to operations at Gdynia, in the Bay of Danzig, and at the Dirschau Bridge.
3. *In the West* it is important to leave the responsibility for opening hostilities unmistakably to England and

France. . . . Attacks on the English homeland are to be
prepared, bearing in mind that inconclusive results with
insufficient forces are to be avoided in all circumstances.

Signed: Adolf Hitler

★   ★   ★

In Danzig, large crowds had turned out to admire and gawk at
the cruiser, in port for a courtesy visit. A long banner strung over
the fronts of warehouses welcomed her: *Wilkommen, Schleswig-
Holstein*. At 5:00 P.M., Captain Karl Dönitz, head of the U-boat
arm of the Reich navy, moved from the eastern U-boat command
headquarters in Swinemünde to a plain wooden barracks on the
outskirts of Wilhelmshaven, designated as his western command
headquarters "if *Fall Weiss* should develop into a major war." In
the German capital, seeing that Hitler was in a noticeably genial
frame of mind, Admiral Albrecht approached him diffidently
and ventured his opinion that England must inevitably be drawn
into the conflict. He never understood the Führer's reply: *"Ich
höre den Friedensengel rauschen"* — "I hear the wings of the angel of
peace."

There were few sandbags in Berlin, nor was there any evacuation from it. The atmosphere in the city was no different from
any other day of the past four weeks. Had it been otherwise, an
event taking place at the same time in another part of the city
would have been inconceivably surreal: Göring, Henderson,
Dahlerus, and Ogilvie-Forbes were having tea together.
Dahlerus had already treated Göring to an elaborate meal at the
Hotel Esplanade, where the brandy was of such outstanding
quality that the plump Field Marshal insisted on removing two
bottles for later use. Dahlerus's latest brainwave was that Göring
should meet a Polish representative somewhere in Holland.
Göring, whose gastronomic content served to remind him what
personal loss might be at stake, hoped it might be possible, and
Henderson agreed that he would submit the proposal to the
Foreign Office. Privately, though, the British ambassador consid-

ered that, if Göring could spare so much time right then, it could only be a bad omen. He would not bother to send the message.

Their discussion was still going on at 6:30, when Ambassador Lipski was at last permitted to see von Ribbentrop. Once again, Paul Schmidt was present, and, in all his years as a diplomatic interpreter, the meeting was the shortest he had ever attended.

"Have you authority to negotiate with us now on the German proposals?" von Ribbentrop asked.

"No," Lipski replied, as the Reichsminister had known he must.

"Well, then," said von Ribbentrop, "there is no point in our continuing this conversation." And that was that. At the same moment, a message was sent from the German High Command to the U-boats waiting at their Atlantic stations. Hostilities with Poland would begin at 4:45 A.M., but "attitude of Western powers still uncertain," so there were to be "no attacks against English forces except in self-defense or by special order." Very soon after, Lipski got back to his embassy and tried to call Warsaw. He could not; the line had been cut.

"A calm twilight," wrote Harold Nicolson, "under which the garden stretches itself at ease. The flag hangs limply on its flagstaff. It is odd to feel that the world as I knew it has only a few hours more to run."

*   *   *

"But why?" With the Duce's agreement, Count Ciano was talking to Sir Percy Loraine and committing a deliberate political indiscretion. "Why do you want to start the irreparable? Can't you understand that we shall never start a war against you and the French?" There had been no reply at all from London about the idea of a peace conference; this was the only way the Italians could think of to transmit their determination to keep out of things while appearing, as Hitler's allies, to make ready. Loraine, almost in tears, gripped Ciano's hands in his. He had guessed that two weeks ago, he said, and had so informed London, but he was delighted to hear it direct from the Count. "He shook my hand again," Ciano wrote, "and left happy." At 7:00 P.M. — nine minutes after sunset in Britain — London cut its communications with Italy.

Exactly one hour later, German-speaking people listening to the broadcasts from Gleiwitz were horrified out of their evening routine by the sound of gunfire from their radios. There were shouts, crashes, and more shots, and through the commotion, for three or four minutes, a voice yelling in Polish. Heydrich's nasty little stunt was going precisely according to plan: Scattered outside the radio station, the customs house at Hochlinden, and other border points, lay a dozen drugged and dying men in Polish uniforms.

Returning home on the blue-lit train, there was nothing for Jack Woodward to do but, despite himself, listen to the girls in his carriage: "They've got whisky, brandy, meat extracts, and everything down in our basement . . . If it weren't so serious, it wouldn't half be funny." He thought with dread of the sudden popularity of air-raid shelters: *Haven't seen any lying around in gardens the last two days* . . . Andrew Hole, true to his name, had spent the day getting further into the intractable Sheffield clay. Four feet down, he had had enough, but, because there had been no word from Germany published throughout the day and considering that there was no obvious reason for this delay, he felt more hopeful than before. After a bath, he went out with his wife to see some friends. Donald Richardson could not get home from London — the evacuation traffic was too heavy — so in spite of his guilty trip to the movies at lunchtime, he went to see another film, *Double Crime on the Maginot Line.* Coming out, he saw three news vendors doing a good trade and bought a paper. There was nothing new, but "somehow," he wrote, "it seems as if anything might have happened in the interval, it seems so long."

Derek Silver was very alarmed by the evening paper placard — "Mobilization Order" — and breathed a great sigh of relief when he found it applied only to reservists. His chatty landlady told him that she had been that day to see a wealthy friend who had spent five pounds [$23.40] on sandbagging her house. Neither woman had stored any extra food. "Well, you'd be too young to remember, Mr. Silver, but there was plenty to eat in the last war."

At 9:00 P.M., all radio stations in Germany interrupted their scheduled programs and broadcast, word for word, the Sixteen Points. The broadcasts omitted to mention that 1.5 million fully armed German soldiers were in forward positions on every one of the common borders with Poland, that tank units were with them, and that every German military airfield was alive with final preparations. To William Shirer, an American journalist resident in Berlin, and to all his foreign colleagues, the Sixteen Points sounded eminently reasonable.

Within minutes, the proposals were being received in Great Britain, and there the reaction was the same or stronger. Derek Silver thought so, although "still we are kept in the air as to the next step." Andrew Hole and his wife returned home to a sight they found "horribly ominous" — by the light of hurricane lamps, neighbors were continuing to build his mother's air-raid shelter. But, when they heard the broadcast of the Sixteen Points, "though we knew it might be false, we embraced it with joy."

★   ★   ★

The world turned, and darkness spread from the east. Each in its different mood, the nations of Europe slept. Niusia Zamecka slept in happy innocence; in happy ignorance, Zofja Olszolwska slept. In Devon, tired from the work on the farm, Kit Dennis slept; in the orchard below her window, Mary the lamb slept; in London, wrapped in the security of an unshakable faith, the cycling pilgrim Francis Vanek slept peacefully. In the distant Shetlands, on the remote island of Foula, fragrant well-banked peat fires smoldered and the Smith family — Willie, Lizzie, and their three daughters — all slept and dreamed of wind and work and heather and salt sea spray.

The world turned, and darkness was on the face of the deep. Sunset came to eastern America, and night beckoned. In the Schoharie Rest, with an ideal escape from Mrs. Seidel's well-meant inquisitions, Ernest Kroll and Heinz Lindt read aloud to each other from the works of Alphonse Daudet and William Shakespeare — *A Midsummer Night's Dream,* "the perfect text," said Kroll, "for August nights in the country." In Oakland, Maine, Barkley Goodrich snuggled down under his blankets in the big old bed on the cottage porch, wondering hazily if the thunder would come rumbling across the East Pond again. Not many miles away, little Libby Tufts was sound asleep already; at eleven years, two months, and three days, to be awake at 11:45 was utterly beyond her.

Strangely enough, the small town in which she slept was named South Poland. At 11:45 on Thursday, August 31, 1939, in South Poland, Maine, U.S.A., it was 4:45 the following morning in the country of Poland. And there, at that moment, the darkness was shattered.

17

Time limit?

As he reached his office in the Horse Guards on Friday, September 1, General Sir Edmund Ironside could hear Big Ben striking 10:00. Inside, the telephone was ringing; it was Winston Churchill, calling from Chartwell. "They've started," the familiar gruff voice announced. "Warsaw and Cracow are being bombed now."

"Great God in heaven! Thank you for telling me, Winston, Good-bye."

Without hesitation, Ironside telephoned the War Office to speak to General Lord Gort, Chief of the Imperial General Staff. Gort was an officer of exceptional gallantry; during the Great War he had been mentioned in dispatches nine times and, in addition to the Military Cross and Distinguished Service Order with two bars, had won the Victoria Cross. But today, complaining to Ironside that he was off to a meeting, he did not believe what he heard. "Well, it's true," Ironside repeated testily. "You'd better tell Belisha." Gort did so, and within minutes Leslie Hore-Belisha, the Minister for War, was seen rushing to Number Ten Downing Street. A sudden thought came to Ironside. Telephoning Churchill, he asked him how he had got the news. "From the Polish ambassador an hour and a half ago," Churchill replied. "He was absolutely definite. I'm afraid you don't need to doubt it."

Ironside assured him he had had no such doubts and hung up. But, as he gazed out of the window, he said to himself, "How could the War Office possibly be ignorant of this?"

It was a hot, misty morning in London. West of the Horse Guards' Parade, Saint James's Park, Green Park, and Hyde Park stretched into the haze, two and a half miles of almost uninterrupted urban garden. In another Hyde Park, some 3,000 miles further west, at the precise moment of Churchill's call to Iron-side, Eleanor Roosevelt was awakened by the telephone. For her, the time was 5:00 A.M. "It was my husband in Washington," she wrote a little later, "to tell me the sad news that Germany had invaded Poland and that her planes were bombing Polish cities. He told me that Hitler was about to address the Reichstag, so we turned on the radio and listened until 6:00 o'clock."

"... *Dieses möchte ich der Welt erzählen* ..." In spite of the hiss and crackle of static interference, the harsh, metallic voice from the Kroll Opera House in Berlin came over clearly: "... I should like to say this to the world. I alone was in the position to make such proposals . . . . For two whole days I sat with my Government and waited . . . . I can no longer find any willingness on the part of the Polish Government to conduct serious negotiations with us . . . . I have therefore resolved to speak to Poland in the same language that Poland for months past has used toward us . . . . This night for the first time Polish regular soldiers fired on our own territory . . . . We have been returning the fire, and, from now on, bombs will be met with bombs."

Among all the lies and distortions, the Führer said one thing that day, and one thing only, that was true: "I now want to be nothing but the first soldier of the German Reich. Therefore, I have once more put on that uniform which was once most sacred and dear to me. I will not take it off again until victory is secured — or I will not live to see the outcome."

It was intended to sound heroic, and perhaps to some it did; but few Germans stopped to think what it actually meant. After leading the nation into war, Hitler acknowledged with those words that he could not stomach the possibility of defeat. If that came, he would be dead, leaving Germany to sort itself out without him.

Outside the Opera House, under a sultry sky overcast with low gray clouds, the streets of Berlin were almost deserted. All newspapers had been rushing out extra editions since early morning, but, to his surprise, William Shirer noticed that hardly anyone was buying them. The Berliners seemed not to be interested or even to care, and it occurred to him they might just be too dazed — *dazed,* he thought, *by waking up to find themselves in a war which they had been sure the Führer would somehow avoid. They cannot quite believe it, now that it has come.* He was right — so right, indeed, that elsewhere in Berlin and also in Düsseldorf, his thoughts were being echoed almost exactly. Ulrich von Hassell heard Hitler's speech in his hotel room and dismissed it in one word: "weak." Throughout the capital, he found "only official enthusiasm over the closing of the border . . . . The feeling that war is really here has not yet penetrated the public mind. They are for the most part apathetic and still look upon it as a sort of Party project."

Similarly, after listening to Hitler's broadcast, the young soldier Bernt Engelmann drove with an army motorcycle courier named Pliechelko into Düsseldorf. "No crowds had gathered," Engelmann wrote later. "We saw no trace of rejoicing, certainly none of the wild enthusiasm that Germans had shown when war broke out in August 1914. Here and there small groups of people clustered around the newsstands, talking quietly among themselves, depressed and anxious. No one waved to us soldiers or pressed bouquets into our hands . . . . 'They don't believe it yet,' Pliechelko said. 'They probably thought everything would turn out all right this time, too.'"

★ ★ ★

Zofja Olszolwska's reaction was identical. That section of the Polish population fortunate enough to live in the heart of the country, away from borders and cities, heard the appalling news over the radio. The one at Moniaki had a huge horn-shaped loudspeaker, like the one in the *"His Master's Voice"* advertisement; and, like the little dog, she and her family huddled around, ears cocked in fixed, disbelieving attention. As the announcement ended, someone wailed, "How could it have been so easy for them?"

"Thank God Tadeusz is on his way to Britain," said someone else, and Zofja, suddenly feeling she might vomit, remembered that her husband was traveling via Riga in Russia and that, to get there, he was flying in a German plane.

Niusia's first hint of the invasion was at 9:50. She was returning from the privy when she heard airplanes and, looking up, saw
two machines circling each other. "I thought it was maneuvers.
Then I heard some machine guns and everybody came out of the
house to see what was happening. Grandpa said, 'My God! It's
war!' and rushed indoors to switch on the wireless . . . . Everybody was stunned. With ears glued to the loudspeaker, we were
trying to catch the fading words. The battery or the accumulator,
or both, were packing up. When we could no longer hear even a
whisper from the wireless set, Grandpa turned the switch off
and looked at our anguished faces. He knelt down in front of the
picture of Jesus Christ and started to pray aloud. We repeated
after Grandpa, 'Our Father, Who art in Heaven, hallowed be Thy
name . . .'"

It was the same in Britain, too: "Few people really thought it
would happen," wrote Ross Mackay. "Everywhere people stood
in groups discussing it. Schoolchildren arrived by the trainload,
all very subdued. The wireless confines itself to news bulletins
and instructions to the people, with gramophone records in
between. The Country has mobilized . . . ."

After his elation the night before on learning of the Sixteen
Points, Andrew Hole had no feeling left. He and his wife spent
the morning "packing up for the duration—a queer job; too
busy to be emotional; bunging all the valuable china into boxes
in the cellar."

For various reasons, some people did not hear the news at
once. Harold Nicolson was sitting in a deck chair at Sissinghurst
Castle, deeply engrossed in reading, when his wife Vita came
walking quickly down the path. "It has begun," she said, and told
him all she knew, including the fact that Parliament was recalled
for 6:00 P.M. He noticed it was exactly 10:45. Plenty of time to
finish his book. He carried on reading, and Miss Macmillan,
their secretary, brought him his gas mask.

Donald Richardson, the London solicitor, found all normal
work in his office had ceased, so he had a not very successful go
at *The Times* crossword and finished reading a novel. But then
rumors began to circulate; and, when at last he was able to

contact his wife, she was weeping so much she could not speak. Halfheartedly, he finished off his routine work "and waited for orders, and waited and waited . . . . After being for more than half an hour alone in my own office, I feel as though I have completely lost touch with events outside, yet I have the greatest reluctance to look at a paper or listen to the wireless. War seems absurdly remote for *me.*"

In spite of being a journalist, Derek Silver missed it as well. On the way to work, he passed a *Daily Mail* placard as usual, but all it said was "Hitler's 6:00 A.M. Proclamation." He did not know the Führer had made a broadcast to the Wehrmacht just before then, and, since war was not mentioned, he ignored the placard. Twenty empty buses were waiting at the station for evacuees; trestle tables were set out with tins of biscuits; but otherwise there was nothing unusual. By 11:55 he had been sitting in the Police Court for an hour and a half, taking notes on a case of such interminable dullness that for relief he had begun reading a volume called *Cheddar Gorge: A Book of English Cheeses.* Then the office boy from a rival paper came in with a note for his boss, who was chairman of the bench, and whispered to Silver something that sounded like "Thames . . . bombed." For an instant his stomach turned over, but the boy repeated more clearly, "Eight towns in Poland bombed."

With worldly-wise relief Silver whispered back, "Tell it to the Marines. Just exaggerated frontier incidents. They've been having frontier incidents all week and we aren't at war yet."

"We're not now, but we soon will be," the boy hissed in return. "It's real — it's on the wireless now." He left the court, and, hastily packing his papers together, Silver hurried after him.

In fact, the Marines had been among the first in Britain to know. One of them was Sandy Powell, seventeen and a half years old, six-foot-three with a forty-eight-inch chest. In Whale Island, the naval gunnery school in Portsmouth, he was on parade at 8:30 A.M. with about 100 other men of C Company, when the adjutant, Captain Pickton-Phillips, informed them of the invasion. "The Germans," Pickton-Phillips added, "have two or three days to get out of Poland. If they do, well and good; if they

don't, I have no doubt you are all ready." They were; remaining
rigidly at attention, not one Marine showed any reaction until
the parade was dismissed.

★   ★   ★

During his phone call just after 10:00, Ironside must have
misinterpreted Lord Gort's reaction and the Minister of War's
hasty departure for Number Ten because, as early as 5:30 A.M.,
Leslie Hore-Belisha had received the first terse intimation:
"Germans are through." At 7:00, Sir Alexander Cadogan had
been awakened by a telephone message; at 9:00 he had picked up
Lord Halifax from Eaton Square and gone to Downing Street. At
10:30 Count Edward Raczynski, the Polish ambassador, was the
first foreign diplomat to see Halifax. Even he had no written
evidence, only telephoned information, but, he said, "the Polish
Government considers this to be a case of aggression under
Article 1 of the Anglo-Polish Treaty of Mutual Assistance."
    "I have very little doubt of it," Halifax replied. Soon after, he
summoned Theo Kordt, the German Chargé d'Affaires, for an
interview. It was completely unproductive: Halifax did not know
exactly where Poland had been invaded, and Kordt, who was
certainly not going to tell him, suggested his information might
be mistaken. At 11:30, the Cabinet met under, as the Prime
Minister said in his opening address, "the gravest possible conditions. The event against which we have fought so long and
earnestly has come upon us. But our consciences are clear, and
there should be no possible question now where our duty lies."
    Before noon, therefore, both in the Polish embassy and the
Cabinet Office in London, it was taken virtually for granted that,
within a very short period, Britain would fulfill its guarantee to
Poland. Instead, another international conflict began — blood-
less, but as fraught with danger as the undeclared war that had
been raging since dawn; and Chamberlain's government found
itself on the brink of overthrow.

★   ★   ★

"In all the break-up of the office routine, there is a distinctly holiday-adventure feeling apparent with everyone," Donald Richardson wrote. He wished he could share the mood. "Behind it all, at least as far as I am concerned, however, there is a cold fear that keeps popping into my heart — chiefly," he noted wryly, "through my ears. All yesterday and today my hearing has been keenly on the alert, however absorbed I may have been in any job, and at least once an hour I hear a backfire, or what seems like gunfire, and my whole being leaps at it."

At noon in Berlin, Göring took Birger Dahlerus to see Hitler in the Chancellery. A little earlier, Sir Nevile Henderson had made the ridiculous suggestion to London that Marshal Smigly-Rydz should come at once to Berlin — as if the Polish Commander-in-Chief might not be sufficiently busy, or as if he would contemplate an action that would be tantamount to surrender. Sir Nevile had also informed London that, after the Opera House speech, Hitler had begun to address his generals but had broken down and been unable to finish. However, the Führer had recovered somewhat by the time he received Dahlerus, and opened the interview by thanking the Swede for all his efforts. But then, blaming Britain for the failure of these efforts, he had begun once again to grow passionately excited. Poland, he declared, would be crushed and annihilated as a nation. If Britain still wished to talk, he was willing to do so, but, gesticulating violently, he began to shout, "If England wants to fight for a year, I shall fight two years . . . If England wants to fight for three years, I shall fight for three years . . ." Crouching low and clenching his fists, his voice rose to a shriek: "And if it is necessary, I shall fight ten years!"

Another shriek echoed through Chelmsford market, a terrible, high-pitched, wailing scream that did not stop. Seeing the crowd, Derek Silver pushed his way through. "Press!" he called out. "Excuse me — press!" A man looked at him in surprise as he elbowed past. "Nothin' 'ere for the papers, mate," he said. "It's only a pig 'avin' its teeth off." Sure enough, struggling against ropes and the firm grip of several men, a large pig was being crudely operated on, its front teeth being cut off with a hacksaw.

To Silver's amazement, the crowd seemed to be enjoying the spectacle. He backed off with distaste and, as the creature's cries pursued him, muttered to himself, "Well, war shouldn't bother them too much."

★ ★ ★

In the dining room of the Schoharie Rest, Ernest Kroll and Heinz Kordt tucked into an extra-hearty breakfast. It was the last morning of their holiday, and Mrs. Seidel wanted to stoke them up for the journey back to New York. Through the closed kitchen door, the sound of the radio came only as an ominous vibrating hum. Whatever it was saying, it was sure to be bad news, and they did not want to hear. "I expect she'll tell us anyway when she brings the pancakes in," Ernest muttered somberly.

For once, however, she did nothing of the sort, but bustled around in a motherly way, making sure that they had every comfort possible and bringing them packs of sandwiches for the downriver boat trip. But there was evidently something on her mind. "Look," she said, "why don't you boys stay a little longer? When will you have such a good time again?"

Sincerely wishing they could, they bade her farewell with affection; for all her gossipy ways, she was a kindhearted woman, and they would both remember her and the Schoharie Rest with fondness. Yet work called; their week was up, and Otto Bettmann was running his photographic archive with the help of only one secretary. Mrs. Seidel took them to the bus stop. From there they retraced their route to Catskill, boarded the *Governor Clinton,* and, sitting on the vessel's open top deck, steamed sedately down to Manhattan.

That was where they learned the news they had been avoiding. Descending the gangplank, they heard newsboys shouting, saw them holding up placards with huge black headlines: "HITLER INVADES POLAND." Heinz stopped. Ernest could see he had tears in his eyes. "Now it's just a matter of time," said Heinz, his voice choked. "Hitler will come here."

Ernest could still hear those words the following morning when he reported for work at the archive. Herr Bettmann was already there, and he greeted his employee with a weird smile. "Kaput," he said, "Europe is kaput." Using the surname with which Hitler's illegitimate father had been born, he went on, "Nobody would stand up to that Schickelgruber. Ach, that Chamberlain! Now we shall all have to pay the price. America, too. America will be alone — without the will — without even the strength — to stop the Nazis." Rubbing his hands one inside the other to stifle a shiver, he sighed deeply and said, "Why did not someone stand up in the beginning to that Schickelgruber?" It was by then only the second day of war between Germany and Poland, but, with sinking apprehension, Ernest Kroll realized that at least two people in America had already mentally surrendered.

★ ★ ★

But would there actually be a war between Britain and Germany? If so, when — and why not immediately? These were the questions unexpectedly exercising the British Cabinet during the afternoon of Friday, September 1. The first hesitations were expressed in the Cabinet itself by ministers whose names were not recorded, but who argued that their information was insufficiently firm to allow the irrevocable step of declaring war. Birger Dahlerus had been on the telephone to Cadogan, requesting permission to come to England again and return to Berlin with General Ironside as a mediator. He would not accept Cadogan's refusal, demanding that the suggestion be put to the Cabinet. Their answer was robust: "Out of the question. The only way in which a world war can be stopped is (1) that hostilities be suspended and (2) German troops should be immediately withdrawn from Polish territory." So much for that one. The Cabinet's agreed communication to Germany said much the same, with the added observation that, if the conditions were not instantly met, the British "will without hesitation fulfill their obligations to Poland."

It was Chamberlain who pointed out that the conditions might not be met. The only remaining option would be to declare war. The governments of Britain and France had already agreed that such a declaration should come from both simultaneously. But, as Germany's blitzkrieg smashed more and more deeply into Poland, it transpired that, although the French Cabinet — meeting at the same time as their British counterparts — had decided on immediate mobilization, the French Parliament was not going to be recalled until 3:00 P.M. the next day, Saturday, September 2. The implications of this were considerable. Only Parliament could pass a war budget, without which war could not be declared; and only Parliament could permit the inclusion of a time limit in any warning, since that would amount to an ultimatum.

Thus, when the House of Commons convened at 6:00 on Friday evening, the Prime Minister's speech, firm as it was, fell short of expectations. It was a dramatic, twilit scene: The lights were dimmed, the blackout curtains were drawn tight shut, and, as Chamberlain and Arthur Greenwood, deputy Leader of the Labour opposition, entered together, they were loudly cheered by all Members. In the Distinguished Strangers' Gallery, the Polish and Russian ambassadors found themselves sitting side by side, as, in the dim chamber below, the Prime Minister described what measures had been taken so far. When he told the House that the Sixteen Points ("which Hitler claims to have been rejected") had never even been communicated to the Poles, there was an audible gasp on all sides, and, in ringing tones, Lady Astor exclaimed, "Well, I never did!" But, when he read out the text that, in a few hours, Sir Nevile Henderson would give to Hitler, one Member cried out, "Time limit?" There was none.

"He is evidently in real moral agony," Harold Nicolson wrote, "and the general feeling in the House is one of deep sympathy for him and of utter misery for ourselves."

In Chelmsford, hearing reports of the speech, Derek Silver found in it "a loophole of hope . . . . We are giving Hitler a last chance to turn back." But, he reflected, "every hour we waste is an hour gained by him in his invasion." Close by, children dancing on sheets of corrugated iron were making a great racket that did not stop until they were driven indoors by rain. Thereafter, there was no sound except hammering as people nailed up blackout curtains.

Later in the evening in London, walking through "a perfectly black city," Harold Nicolson began to wonder why no time limit had been given; and, within twenty-four hours, the House's attitude to Chamberlain had swung completely around.

★ ★ ★

"Aren't we a very old team?" At half past midnight on the morning of Saturday, September 2, Winston Churchill was wide awake and writing a letter to the Prime Minister. As a matter of course under the exceptionally threatening circumstances, the entire Cabinet had resigned in order to allow Chamberlain to form a much smaller, more compact War Cabinet. Churchill had at long last been invited to rejoin, and, although he would be without portfolio — without, that is, a specific area of responsibility — he accepted with pleasure. By midnight, though, he had heard nothing more from Chamberlain. His letter began in a semijocular way, a complaint against old age. The six Cabinet members he knew of, including himself, aggregated 386 years — "an average of over sixty-four! Only one year short of the Old Age Pension!" — and he wished to urge the inclusion of some younger men, particularly Anthony Eden. But, far more seriously, by the time he wrote his letter, he had heard — even though the Poles had been under heavy attack for thirty hours — that there was talk in Paris of sending yet another note to Germany. "I trust you will be able," he wrote, "to announce our Joint Declaration of War at *latest* when Parliament meets this afternoon. . . . I really do not know what has happened during the course of this agitated day, though it seems to me that entirely different ideas have ruled from those which you expressed to me when you said 'the die was cast.'"

Many others were awake in Britain, among them Donald Richardson, too frightened to sleep — "one could not dream it could be so dark in London" — and Derek Silver in Chelmsford. With a sudden intimation of mortality, he had become very preoccupied with the thought that he and his girlfriend had never made love. "In view of the circumstances," he wondered if he might broach the subject, and then realized he would have to buy a contraceptive — something he had never done before. The thought of future embarrassment blended with a tingling anticipation and, feeling a sudden need for fresh air, he switched his light out, opened the blackout curtains and the window, and returned to his virginal bed.

The uncertain hours of darkness passed in peace for Britain, while for Poland, the war continued. Sunrise on Saturday came at 5:12 A.M. London was soon warm and humid; it would be a close, muggy day. During the morning, Lord and Lady Halifax went walking again with Sir Alexander Cadogan, grateful for the extra security of their new environment — the king had given Halifax a key to the gardens of Buckingham Palace. Absentmindedly, they admired the purple autumn crocuses blooming on the lawns, but, as Cadogan wrote later in the day, there had been "no answer from Germans. We are simply waiting."

So, too, in Berlin, were Ambassadors Henderson and Coulondre. The night before, both had presented their countries' notes to von Ribbentrop, although not simultaneously as they had wished. The Reichsminister had not allowed it and had seen Henderson first, at 9:30, and Coulondre half an hour later. Henderson's staff had already moved from their houses to a hotel adjacent to the embassy and had burned ciphers and confidential documents, while he had asked the American Chargé d'Affaires to be "good enough to take charge of British interests in the event of war." But so far, there was not a hint of a reply from either the Chancellery or the German Foreign Office.

Donald Richardson awoke to a magnificent sense of safety, mainly because neither he nor, it seemed, anyone else had expected there would be quite so many barrage balloons. On his way to work, he counted 150 floating over the city. Thrilled to imagine how many more there were that he could not see, he determined not to have another empty anxious day like yesterday and, since there was no legal work to be done, persuaded his boss to let him act as doorman for the Town Hall. As he pointed out, many people were coming in unidentified, and "any ill-disposed IRA man could blow the place to bits with impunity."

He was kept happily busy the whole day long, sorting out hundreds of callers, mostly people wanting gas masks. A high percentage were foreign refugees; others wanted to volunteer for the forces. One old man of at least eighty tottered in "to see if he was wanted." A very old lady in nurse's uniform, charming to look at and charmingly mannered, "stoutly declared she had been right through the last war and was ready to face the next: 'I may not be young, but I'm still active.'" But others were less cooperative, such as the woman who accepted ARP night duty, then refused when — although there were more than six hours before her duty began, plenty of time to get home on her own for warm clothes — no official car could be provided for the task. Then there were the pathetic ones, the most difficult to handle — the crippled man with a crippled wife and a six-day-old baby, just sent home from the maternity hospital in order to make way for casualties and somehow left out of the evacuation schemes; and another young woman, "her face showing long suffering," asking about evacuation plans for her parents, both aged over eighty. "Sorry," he had to say, "nothing doing yet."

"Never mind," she replied. "I'm sure there's not going to be a war."

Good for you, he thought, and wished her luck.

The British Parliament was going to meet at 2:45, expecting to hear of firm decisions taken in conjunction with France. It was at 1:30 in the afternoon of September 2 that the real trouble with the French government began, an hour and a half before their Parliament met. Their general staff had advised them that forty-eight hours were still needed to complete evacuation and general mobilization; their Foreign Minister Georges Bonnet therefore insisted that, if an ultimatum were given to Germany, it should not be less than that time and should begin from noon on September 3. Lord Halifax told Sir Edward Phipps, British Ambassador to Paris, that the apparent delays and the French government's attitude were causing "some misgiving here" and added, "We should be grateful for anything you can do to infuse courage and determination into M. Bonnet."

No sooner was this message conveyed than another telephone call came from Count Ciano, which, though well meant, only increased British nervousness about the French. Ciano explained that he had approached von Ribbentrop again with a suggestion for a five-power peace conference; that von Ribbentrop had rejected it with the assertion that Britain and France had, in their notes of the night before, made an ultimatum to Germany; that Ambassador Attolico had raced around to those countries' embassies and received confirmation that no ultimatum was involved; that Hitler had then been willing to consider a conference and would reply by noon on September 3; and, finally, that the French government had already agreed to the proposal. (Indeed, in his diary the Count wrote privately that he had proposed the conference as a result of French pressure and that, judging from Bonnet's tone of voice when told of progress in Berlin, it "produced lively satisfaction in Paris.") Now, he wondered, what did the British think of this?

The short answer was "not much." Sir John Simon, Chancellor of the Exchequer, was due to speak on Chamberlain's behalf in the Commons with a prepared statement saying that no reply had come from Germany, that Britain was unwilling to wait longer, and that, as soon as the French Parliament had finished its session, an ultimatum would be sent. He was just going into the Chamber to say this when Halifax, rushing over from the Foreign Office, managed to stop him with a breathless warning to "make no statement at all about the international situation."

"I never remember spending such a miserable afternoon and evening," Halifax wrote later. "From 3:00 to 5:30 we were telephoning to Bonnet, who I suspect had committed himself rather further than he was willing to admit to the conference." It was an appalling quandary. "You seem to me," Halifax told Bonnet cogently, "to believe that one can resuscitate a corpse with holy water!" When a message from Colonel Beck to Bonnet became known in London, the French Foreign Minister's attitude seemed even more extraordinary: The day before, Beck had told him plainly, "We are in the thick of war as a result of unprovoked aggression. The question before us is not that of a conference but the common action that should be taken by the Allies to resist."

That was precisely the British government's view, yet the immediate decisiveness and essential cooperation expected from France were missing. However much anyone in London might want peace, it was never again to be peace at any price; everyone from Chamberlain down was firm on that. The alliance with Poland would not be sold out. But, by the same token, the alliance with France could not be ignored; the agreement for joint action must be honored. Britain could not make a unilateral declaration; yet, if a conference was undertaken while German troops were still in Poland, how wretchedly timid it would appear! If it were even suggested, Chamberlain's government would certainly fall, and all the while, though Bonnet appeared to ignore it, their mutual ally was under attack.

The Cabinet met at 4:15 in what Halifax delicately described as an "extremely difficult mood." The weather matched them; inside and outside the Cabinet Room the air was hot and humid with intermittent rumbles of distant thunder. Halifax summarized the communications with Ciano and Bonnet and gave the provisional conclusions on which he and Chamberlain had agreed — to allow the Germans until noon or possibly midnight next day for their reply, which must accept an armistice, and to insist as a precondition for a conference that German troops must be withdrawn from Poland. But hardly anyone in the Cabinet would support those ideas. A heated argument began as one Minister after another demanded no further delay. Malcolm MacDonald, Secretary of State for the Colonies, remarked bitingly, "The Germans can make up their minds quickly enough on occasion and have been known to ask other people to make up their minds in a very short time."

Chamberlain realized he had severely misjudged his Ministers' frame of mind. A personal message from the Polish ambassador and a telegram from Warsaw strengthened them further: The message, which Chamberlain read out, was a plea for an

immediate honoring of Britain's obligations. He read the telegram aloud as well: "Battle today over the whole of the front has
increased in intensity and has acquired a very serious character.
Our troops are opposing strong resistance. The whole of German air force is engaged against Poland. Villages and factories
bombarded. The engagement of German aircraft by Allied forces
of greatest urgency."

That settled it. The Prime Minister and Cabinet together
agreed that Hitler would be informed he could have until
midnight that night to decide on all the questions facing him,
and the Cabinet accepted that Halifax and Chamberlain would
work out the communication's precise wording in conjunction
with the French. Members of Parliament would be informed
that evening.

★   ★   ★

Packed and tense, the House of Commons was waiting for
Chamberlain — *exactly like a court,* thought Harold Nicolson,
awaiting the verdict of the jury. At 7:35 the Clerks entered and took
their places; two minutes later, Mr. Speaker came in and the
Honorable Members stood in silence. It was not a pleasant
silence. At 7:42 Chamberlain and Greenwood came in together,
and at 7:44 the Prime Minister began to speak.

"We expected one of his dramatic surprises," Nicolson wrote
afterward, "but none came." His speech lasted only four minutes; he sounded ill. "Amazement turned into stupefaction,"
wrote General Spears, "and stupefaction into exasperation."
Cabinet members saw and shared the House's reaction: "Our
own people were flabbergasted," wrote Evan Wallace, the Minister of Transport, "and the Opposition infuriated." Nicolson put
it simply: "It was evident when he sat down that no decision had
been arrived at." No ultimatum; no time limit; not even any
agreement yet with Paris. Elsewhere, in unhappy anger, Cadogan
was writing his notes: "We couldn't budge the French. Awful
evening." In the House, every Member felt with Nicolson the
same surge of fear: "Was there to be another Munich after all?
Then Greenwood got up."

The Deputy Leader of the Opposition was not accustomed to the kind of reception he was given. Nicolson described it: "His own people cheered, as was natural; but what was so amazing was that their cheer was taken up in a second and greater wave from our benches." And in an "astonishing demonstration" — one that has usually, and wrongly, been attributed ever since to Leo Amery — "Bob Boothby cried out, '*You* speak for Britain.' . . . Greenwood almost staggered with surprise."

But he did speak for Britain: "There is a growing feeling, I believe, in all quarters of the House that this incessant strain must end sooner or later — and in a sense the sooner the better." This was the kind of thing the House had hoped to hear from Chamberlain. "I am gravely disturbed. An act of aggression took place thirty-eight hours ago. The moment that act of aggression took place one of the most important treaties of modern times automatically came into operation. There may be reasons why instant action was not taken . . . . That delay might have been justifiable, but there are many of us on all sides of this House who view with the gravest concern the fact that hours went by, and news came in of bombing operations, and news today of an intensification of it, and I wonder how long we are prepared to vacillate?" They cheered him to the rafters for that. "If," he continued, "deeply though I regret it, we must wait upon our Allies, I should far have preferred the Prime Minister to have been able to say tonight definitely, 'It is either peace or war.' . . . There shall be no more devices for dragging out what has been dragged out for too long. The moment we look like weakening, at that moment dictatorship knows we are beaten. We are not beaten. We shall not be beaten. We cannot be beaten; but delay is dangerous . . . . I cannot see Herr Hitler making any deal which he is not prepared to betray."

The tension, said Nicolson, became acute: "Here were the P.M.'s most ardent supporters cheering his opponent with all their lungs. The front bench looked as if they had been struck in the face . . . . We feel that the German ships and submarines will, owing to this inexplicable delay, elude our grasp. The P.M. must know by now that the whole House is against him."

★ ★ ★

In a pub in Portsmouth, Sandy Powell sat drinking with a group
of other neatly uniformed Marines. The room was crowded, and
most people were talking together, but quietly; there was none of
the usual raucous Saturday evening jollification. Even the piano
in the corner was closed; no one felt like playing or singing. The
morning in Whale Island had been spent cleaning kit — washing,
pressing, and polishing — and the afternoon in sport. The mood
then had been mixed, some of them getting edgy, others talking
big. Now, deeply aware that this was likely to be their last run
ashore for some time, the young Marines wanted to get drunk
but could not. Instead, as they drank, they discussed the possibilities ahead of them — which ships they might be with, where
they might have to go, whether anyone would be lucky enough
to get some cushy number. One young man, an expert soccer
player, expected to be asked to stay and continue playing for the
corps. But all were subdued. Eventually, although time had not
been called, Sandy said, "Well, lads — reckon I'll thin out.
Church parade in the morning." Although he was not yet eighteen, his six-foot-three made him a dominating figure anywhere,
and standing in uniform he seemed to fill the whole pub. "I'll
come, too," said another. One by one they downed the last of
their pints and headed for the door; and, as they did so, one of
the civilians called out, "Good luck!" and raised three cheers for
the Marines. In a sudden tremendous outburst of encouragement, everyone picked it up, clapping and banging their glasses.
The young men grinned and waved, and stepped out into the
dark.

At the Tunbridge Wells' Repertory Theater there was a play on
that evening called *Idiot's Delight*. Saying he thought it sounded
appropriate, Derek Silver's girlfriend's brother took his own
girlfriend to see it. Derek himself had other things in mind,
which did not include extra company. He had cycled the fifty
miles from Chelmsford that morning, pausing on the way to buy,
for the price of a shilling, his first contraceptive sheath, and that
evening he took his girl to see the film *Jesse James*. A few hours

later, somewhat despondently, he wrote that the movie had gone "all right, with hand-holding accompaniment." But that had been all. Coming out of the cinema into a pitch-black town center had been strange. Cloudy and raining, it had been very, very dark — their first experience of full blackout. Huddling close together under one umbrella, they had hurried for home and, around midnight, they had each gone to bed — alone.

As a further mark of the serious situation, the cricket club at Walton-on-the-Naze had canceled its scheduled Saturday match. All day long, Ross Mackay had expected a declaration of war to come at any minute, but, when nothing had happened by 9:00 P.M., he wondered if there might still be time to go to London and see his family. Night driving under blackout was difficult — car headlights had to be covered with layers of newspaper with only a tiny slit, giving barely more than a glow — so he decided to go at dawn.

In London, because the evacuation traffic had quieted down, Donald Richardson was able to get home for the first time in three nights. It was only a temporary place, but his wife was there, and traveling out in the darkened Tube he felt rested and content; yet, when he reached home and saw her, for a few minutes he was suddenly completely overcome. Holding her tight, he wept and shook with emotion; it was, he said, "a horrible reaction . . . . Although having done very little for the past three days (or perhaps because of that), the tension must have been deeper than I knew. I felt as though I were on leave from the front."

Sir Alexander Cadogan was halfway through dinner when the summons came from Downing Street. He was wanted there "at once: at once." He drove as quickly as possible; it was not easy, for in addition to the hazards of the blackout, it was raining. At Number Ten he found the Prime Minister and Annie Chamberlain dining with Lord Halifax and Sir Horace Wilson, and gratefully joined in the meal. "P.M. told me about the House and the trouble with his own colleagues," he wrote later that night. It was a terse enough description: The Prime Minister's speech in the Commons had, without warning to the ministers, overturned the agreement with them, and afterward Chamberlain had faced open revolt.

One of the rebels, Sir Reginald Dorman-Smith, the Minister for Agriculture and Fisheries, later recalled, "It didn't seem real. We were on strike." This was literally true. As soon as the session had ended, Dorman-Smith and thirteen other Ministers had gathered in one room and decided they would not move from it until war was declared. It was not a large room, and with fourteen angry men it it, "as we waited, we got scruffier and sweatier." Eventually the Chancellor of the Exchequer, whose room it was and who was another of the rebels, had decided they must confront the Prime Minister. They had done so forcefully, and, following the verbal challenge with a letter, had returned to Sir John Simon's room.

Cadogan's diary summarized the events that evening in Number Ten, as thunder grumbled over the capital: "We got Corbin [the French ambassador] and telephoned to Daladier, and then to Bonnet. But couldn't move them. Finally agreed we must act." Britain would declare war independently of France. The ultimatum would be delivered next morning at 9:00 A.M. with a deadline of 11:00 A.M. "My suggestion," Cadogan noted in brackets in his diary. It was becomingly modest for a man who had just stipulated the moment when war would begin.

Nevertheless, it was as well a decision had been reached — assuming, of course, that it was stuck to — because while the Cabinet rebellion was going on, a rebellion had been growing among ordinary Members, too. Its focus, of course, was Churchill. Through the day he had waited at his flat in Morpeth Mansions expecting a call from Chamberlain. None had come, and, after the inadmissible further delay announced by the Prime Minister in the House, Churchill's parliamentary supporters had gathered in his flat to debate their own next move. They knew his national popularity, the degree of support his stance of consistent antiappeasement enjoyed. Should he now bolster the Prime Minister or stand against him? Either could split the country.

The rebellious Cabinet Ministers were summoned to Number Ten. When they arrived in the Cabinet Room ("really scruffy and smelly," Dorman-Smith remembered) they found Cadogan on the telephone to Bonnet with a secretary—the only other person who could speak French well—listening and taking notes. Outside, the thunderstorm gathered force. "Cadogan was saying that, naturally, we would like to go in with the French at the same moment," Dorman-Smith's memoir continued, "but Paris was saying that, if you start war now, we cannot get our young people out of Paris . . . . They were horrified and terrified at our determination for an immediate ultimatum and said, 'Are you going to have all our women and children killed?'"

The Prime Minister was "calm, even icy-cold, all the time we were there. . . . But now, facing a sit-down strike, he had no alternative. The climax came most dramatically. The P.M. said quietly: 'Right, gentlemen, this means war.' Hardly had he said it when there was a most enormous clap of thunder and the whole Cabinet Room was lit up by a blinding flash of lightning . . . the most deafening thunder-clap I've ever heard in my life. It really shook the building. I felt in a different world."

On the other side of London, Donald Richardson jerked upright in bed, eyes wide, staring into the darkness. Outside came another shattering crash. Even through the heavy blackout curtains, the livid flicker of lightning was visible. He tottered to the window, drew the curtain aside, and stood for some minutes gazing at the downpour before returning, trembling, to bed. He noticed his pajamas were damp—he was sweating as if he had a high temperature, but he was icy cold. His wife did not awaken. He lay as still as he could.

18

All that beautiful Sunday

The night's heavy rain had washed the air clean. It could not have been a more lovely morning, and it was Sunday, the day of rest. In her bedroom at Winsor Farm, near Plymouth in Devon, Kit Dennis hummed quietly as she brushed her hair. Elsewhere in the house, her mother, gloves already on, was choosing a hat; her father, his gold watch ready and waiting to be slipped into a waistcoat pocket, was struggling with his stiff white detachable shirt collar; downstairs, her sister Margaret, whose turn it was to stay home and cook lunch, was at work in the kitchen; outside — even though it had been completely cleaned the day before, as usual — her brother Henry was giving the family car a final polish, to make up for not going with the others. A last pat of the hair, a straightening of a hat, a satisfied jingle of a watchchain, and the Dennises were ready to leave for church.

At the other end of the country, on the island of Foula in the Shetlands, the kirk had fallen into some disrepair, but there was a Church of Scotland chapel, run by a lay preacher (or as the islanders called him, a missionary). Often they would also gather in the Smiths' house, the schoolhouse, where Lizzie would lead their singing with the school piano. The service in the chapel took place at noon. This morning, however, Nanette and her sisters were told they would not be going; at 11:00 there was to be an important broadcast on the wireless, all the way from London. They could play in the garden until then.

In Nottinghamshire in the Midlands, Oscar Baker and his sister Theresa were already on their way to worship at Saint Philip Neri's, the nearest Roman Catholic church; the five-mile walk from their village usually took nearly two hours, and they always set off early. It was particularly fortunate they had done so today, for to their astonishment they were stopped, though only briefly, by three soldiers who asked where they were going.

In Bradford, in the West Riding of Yorkshire, Elspeth Harmes was also walking early to Saint Stephen's. It was only a few months since she had been confirmed, and her regular attendances at the Victorian Gothic building were as much to do with the leading choirboy, Eric Jones, as with the forceful, forward-looking character of the vicar, Donald Foster, an outspoken pacifist. His Sunday evening "talking parties," loosely structured debates for young people, stimulated her immensely. She knew she had acquired a reputation for questioning anything to do with established thinking, a reputation that she rather liked and that he encouraged. As for Eric, it was simple: He and Elspeth were in love and had been so for eight years.

At 9:00 in Whale Island, C Company's church parade began, every Marine—Sandy Powell among them—spotlessly turned out in peacetime No. 1 kit, complete with pith helmet. From the parade ground, they marched with faultless rhythm out through the main gate, a sturdy, deliberate public show, to worship.

At the same moment in Berlin, Sir Nevile Henderson marched as deliberately up the front steps of the German Foreign Office. Neither Hitler nor the Reich Foreign Minister Joachim von Ribbentrop was prepared to receive him. The task had been delegated to Paul Schmidt, and that morning of all mornings, the hard-pressed interpreter had overslept; he was very nearly late for the momentous appointment. As his taxi hurtled over the Wilhelmsplatz, he could see the British ambassador entering the building by the front door. Schmidt raced around to a side door and ran to von Ribbentrop's empty office. Just as 9:00 struck, Henderson was announced.

Although Henderson shook hands, he refused to sit down. Standing in the middle of the room, he said—and Schmidt could hear the deep emotion in his voice—that he had come on the instructions of his government to present an ultimatum to the government of Germany. Both he and Schmidt remained standing as he read it out loud. It was not long:

"More than twenty-four hours have elapsed since an immediate reply was requested to the warning of September 1st, and since then the attacks on Poland have intensified. If His Majesty's Government has not received satisfactory assurances of the cessation of all aggressive action against Poland, and the withdrawal of German troops from that country, by eleven o'clock British Summer Time, from that time a state of war will exist between Great Britain and Germany."

Two hours to go. With a hollow sensation in his stomach, Schmidt listened to history happening and gazed sadly at Henderson. They had always got on so well together. The ambassador finished his short speech and presented the document to him; then, with some words of personal regret that Schmidt sincerely reciprocated, Henderson formally bade him good-bye.

★   ★   ★

Sandy Powell was in good voice and, before sitting to hear the Chaplain's address, joined in the three hymns with vigor. The prayers were different from usual. Normally they were for the health of the King and Royal Family, the prosperity of the Empire, and so on. Today there was an extra one—for peace. Shifting his gun to a more comfortable position (for church parade, they only wore side arms, but they kept them on all the time), he knelt and joined in. Couldn't do any harm.

Others in Britain did not get to church that morning at all. In South Wales, Tom Elliott never had any intention of going; he had arranged with some friends to spend the time playing nap, their favorite card game. In North Shields, Lionel Tomlinson had come home in exasperation; although the business needed it, he could do no fishing today—not because of its being Sunday, but because it had become virtually impossible to persuade a full crew to go out at all. Further up the river, Molly McAndrew would normally have gone to Saint Lawrence's in Byker, but not today: Ernie, her fiancé, had got his converted lifeboat *Monarch* ready for a day out on the Tyne. While they were chugging contentedly downstream, Mike Warbreck-Howell and his family were halfway through a major house move from one side of the Pennines to the other; predicting gasoline shortages, Mike's father had decided they must leave their large house in Wilmslow and live closer to his work in Halifax. At the same time, Ross Mackay arrived in London from Walton-on-the-Naze to find the capital "amazingly empty"; half a million people had been evacuated, and another half-million, like Gerald and Betty Hawker, had taken themselves off voluntarily. Posters dotting the capital showed a soldier in full combat gear talking to a small boy: "Leave this to me, sonny," said the caption. "You should be out of London."

★　★　★

As soon as Henderson had left the German Foreign Office, Paul Schmidt took the British ultimatum to the Chancellery. It was difficult to get through to Hitler's office; the room outside was packed with senior Party officials and members of the Cabinet, all urgently demanding to know what had happened. In the past, Schmidt had been in the habit of referring to international diplomats as his "classroom"; now his only answer to the worried inquiries was "Classroom dismissed."

At last he managed to push his way through. Inside the inner office Hitler sat at his desk; von Ribbentrop was there, too, standing silently, staring out of the window. Both looked expectantly at the interpreter when he came in. Schmidt stopped several feet short of the Führer's desk, took a deep breath, and began to read. Von Ribbentrop resumed his stare out of the window; Hitler gazed fixedly at the top of his desk. When Schmidt had finished his translation, there was a long silence. Von Ribbentrop continued to look out of the window as if all this had nothing to do with him. Hitler sat immobile and silent. Then, with a savage glare, the Führer turned abruptly toward his Foreign Minister and, in a voice that was a snarl, asked him the simplest and most difficult question: *"What now?"*

Von Ribbentrop paused before quietly giving his answer: "I assume that the French will hand in a similar ultimatum within the hour."

★ ★ ★

As long ago as February, a Housing and Local Government
Report had stated with gloomy frankness: "In a country the size
of England, there is, in the condition of modern war, no place of
absolute safety." Nevertheless, evacuation of the urban centers
was common sense, and, heartbreaking as it was for parents to see
their children tagged like parcels and crowded into the trains, the
nationwide program had been phenomenally successful: In less
than four days, 1,473,391 evacuees, including escorts and
teachers, had arrived in their reception areas, carried from seventy-two stations by 4,000 special trains, without a single accident or casualty. The government paid their train fares, and,
almost without realizing it, British people undertook the greatest
single migration of population in the history of their kingdom.
For many city-born children, it was their first sight of the
countryside: for many of the country dwellers, it was their first
contact with such children. "FN" written on a child's documents meant "few nits," "N" meant the child had some head
lice, and "V" meant they were visibly crawling. Many village
shops ran out of dust combs and even sheep-dip, and soon it
seemed host families were trying to outdo each other with tales
of pathetic ignorance and strange squalid habits. Derek Silver's
editor entertained the office with the questions put to him by an
East End boy who had never seen vegetables growing and who
thought cabbages, and then carrots, must be potatoes; stories
were legion of children who would not eat unless they were
allowed to sit, as they were accustomed to, on the floor, or who
refused to sleep in beds. Much of it was true, as were many of the
tales the other way around of grotesque exploitation of the
evacuees by their hosts; later the Prime Minister admitted that
neither he nor his Cabinet colleagues had had any concept of the
desperate conditions in urban working-class areas. Perhaps Silver was overly optimistic when, seeing the lawn of a mansion
covered with evacuated children, he called the evacuation
"democracy in action"; but he was certainly correct when he
observed that "whatever happens next, Britain will never be the

same after this." And it could bring great happiness, as one couple in Northampton testified.

"We got our two little evacuees," they wrote. "We've always wanted children, and it's been our life's sorrow that they've been denied us. Now our home is alive for the first time. We've a boy and a girl, eight and six . . . . They scream and race about the place, and yesterday, the little girl was sick on the drawing-room carpet, but that's what we've always wanted. Thank God for our little evacuees."

One person who had not left London, and did not, was Francis Vanek. After early Mass on the morning of Sunday, September 3, he was in Hampstead, preparing for another cycle club meeting. And one who had deliberately returned was David Howarth. On September 1, Richard Dimbleby had reached him with the long-expected phone call: Would David care to come back and go on "a trip?" He certainly would. With a suitcase ready in the office, he gave his car to his secretary and left Ireland the same day, not even returning to the Porter Lodge. Now, in Broadcasting House in central London, simultaneously frightened and excited, he waited for 11:00.

*   *   *

During the previous night, Georges Bonnet, the French Foreign Minister, had made one last attempt to avoid the spread of war. Count Ciano had been asleep when the imploring message had been brought to him: Could he not at least obtain a symbolic withdrawal of German forces from Poland? He did not even bother to tell Mussolini. Saying simply, "Nothing can be done," he had thrown the message in the wastepaper basket and went back to bed. "This shows that France is moving toward the great test without enthusiasm and full of uncertainty," he wrote on Sunday morning. "A people like the French, heroic in self-defense, do not care for foreign lands and for nations too far away."

He could have added that, though not entirely honorable, the central cause of French reluctance was understandable: If British and French declarations of war were followed by an immediate German attack, France would have to fight alone for some indeterminate, perhaps long, period before British forces could assist. Because of that hesitation, von Ribbentrop's last prediction to Hitler (like so many of his other predictions) turned out to be wrong; the French ultimatum to Germany was not presented until more than three hours after the British one. Had the French General Staff had their way, it would have still included a forty-eight hour deadline. As it was, Prime Minister Daladier had forced an earlier deadline, first to 5:00 A.M. on September 4 and then to 5:00 P.M. on the third. But, once Henderson had presented Britain's ultimatum, the questions of if and when the French one would come were academic. With or without them, the final countdown had begun. In the anteroom to Hitler's office, Göring heard Schmidt's news and turned pale. "If we lose this war," he said to the interpreter, "then God have mercy on us!"

★ ★ ★

It was the busiest weekend John Landells had ever known. Since Friday morning, the Creed machines in the office had been chattering out tickertape reports from Reuter's, and his paper, the *Shields Evening News,* had churned out one special edition after another. The local sports program continued, with the cricket season ending and the soccer season starting, but local news was thrust aside; it seemed unreal, and anyway no one could guess what next weekend might bring. Sunday presented a problem: Weekday papers like his cost twopence, but Sunday papers cost fourpence. On this particular Sunday, it was inconceivable they should not publish, but, if they did so, at twice their normal price, how would that affect their sales? There was a short but lively argument before a solution was found that satisfied everybody in the office. On Sunday, September 3, 1939, there were three special editions of the *Shields Evening News,* sold at the usual weekly price of twopence – and every one was dated Saturday.

As far as the rest of Europe was concerned, it was definitely Sunday and, for the Reverend Bob Leaney, vicar of Mountfield in Sussex, one of the busier days of the week; yet, in contrast to the highly charged, hectic goings-on elsewhere, his morning was utterly placid. After an early cup of tea, he conducted Communion at 8:00 A.M., then returned home for breakfast. Around 10:30, leaving his wife Liz in the vicarage sitting room, sewing and listening to the wireless, he went back to the church to make sure everything was ready for Matins at 11:00. The inside of the building looked lovely, decked out with harvest festival flowers. Any chance visitor could only have admired the pretty displays and wondered at this evidence of the villagers' depth of piety. In fact, out of a population of about 600, Bob's congregation usually amounted to no more than thirty, and practically the whole of the harvest decorations were supplied by the squire. Privately Bob had to admit it was a bit of a sham, but he was not going to complain. One day he might persuade the villagers to contribute more; in the meantime, it was far better that the church should be decorated than not, especially when the squire was such a regular attender. There he was now, coming to take his customary seat in the front pew, ready to read the lessons as he always did. The great clock on the tower ticked ponderously toward 11:00. The last notes of the summoning bells faded; then, heavy and resonant, audible throughout the village, the clock struck the hour.

★　★　★

Ten minutes earlier, Birger Dahlerus had made his last appeal, a frantic telephone call from Berlin to the British Foreign Office. With despairing, obsessive optimism, he still believed the situation could be saved. He had tried once already that morning, protesting then that, with a bit of give-and-take, everything could be arranged: The German government was anxious to satisfy the British and willing to give assurances that the independence of Poland would not be violated. Somehow skating over in his mind the fact that this violation had already occurred, he had explained that German troops could not be expected to withdraw at once: "Never in world history has an army withdrawn before negotiation." In his final call, at 10:50, he suggested that, as a last resort, Field Marshal Göring should fly over at once for discussions in London. It was preposterous. Cadogan's formal record of the conversation stated that Lord Halifax "sent a reply to the effect that our position had been known to the German Government for some time, and we could not now delay our procedure." In his own diary, Sir Alexander was more succinct: "Dahlerus rang up 10:50 . . . . I said 'Rats.'"

In the Cabinet Room, set up for the broadcast, the BBC announcer Alvar Liddell was with the Prime Minister. Mr. Chamberlain, he thought, looked "crumpled, despondent, and old." By 11:10 no reply had come to London from Germany. At twelve minutes past, a definite message was received from the British embassy in Berlin that no reply had even reached there; and, at a quarter past precisely, the Prime Minister began the declaration of war: "I am speaking to you from the Cabinet Room at Ten Downing Street . . ."

From thousands of wirelesses the dreadful words reverberated: "This morning the British Ambassador in Berlin handed the German Government a final note, stating that, unless the British Government heard from them by 11:00 that they were prepared at once to withdraw their troops from Poland, a state of war would exist between us."

In her drawing room in the Yorkshire town of Rotherham, Dr. Kennerley's wife Eleanor stood clutching their baby son. Her husband was with his Territorial Army regiment, the York and Lancaster, somewhere in Norfolk, as far as she knew. With eyes wide and heart pounding, alone with the infant, she listened in a paralysis of fear, completely unable to move.

"I have to tell you now that no such undertaking has been received and that consequently this country is at war with Germany."

In North Shields, Lionel Tomlinson watched his mother's face go ashy white. Apparently unperturbed, his father sat puffing his pipe. They listened in silence, and Tomlinson knew that he and his brothers would have to go and fight.

"... You can imagine what a bitter blow it is to me that all my long struggle to win peace has failed ..."

In Mountfield Vicarage, Liz Leaney's sewing fell from her hands as she listened, feeling sick with shock. Bob, for a few minutes more of blessed sanctuary and ignorance, was in church and did not know—but he, too, would have to go to war.

"... We have done all that any country could do to establish peace. The situation in which no word given by Germany's ruler could be trusted and no people or country could feel themselves safe has become intolerable ..."

In Tunbridge Wells, sitting on the floor back to back with his girlfriend, Derek Silver listened, feeling strangely detached from reality—analytical, almost light-headed. It was such a lovely morning: blue sky, white clouds, green and beautiful garden. Compared to the words he was hearing, his surroundings seemed incongruous, almost ridiculous, for invisibly, over it all, lay the actuality of war "which we've so long regarded as the final horror." In time he would grasp it, but he simply could not do so yet.

"... We have resolved to finish it. It is the evil things we shall be fighting against—brute force, bad faith, injustice, oppression, and persecution—"

In his temporary home in Middlesex, his father-in-law's boss's house, Donald Richardson listened and felt the same dreamlike sense of separation from the actual world.

"—and against them I am certain that the right will prevail."

Impossible to grasp, impossible to banish or cancel or undo, the speech ended and the National Anthem was played. Automatically scrambling to his feet, Richardson glanced outside and saw, on the golf links by the house, at least a dozen golfers carrying on with their games, oblivious to the reality he was being asked to accept. Somehow it seemed reassuring—quite in the tradition of Drake. The anthem ended; somebody switched off the wireless. There was a silence of about twenty seconds. "Well," said his father-in-law, "now we're for it."

"Now *someone's* for it, you mean," said the owner of the house. That caused a laugh, and for a few minutes they felt cheerful again. And then the air-raid sirens began.

The sirens were the first that Molly McAndrew knew of it. With a small group of friends and with Ernie, her fiancé, she was happily bobbing around in *Monarch,* fishing idly, when the wailing from shore sprang up. "My God!" said Ernie. "They've landed!" With the clumsiness of haste and anxiety, he started the boat's engine, and, as fast as possible, they motored toward the mouth of the Tyne.

In London, Francis Vanek had had no more idea than Molly or Ernie of the imminence of war. Muttering in irritation and assuming that this was yet another exercise, he rode his bicycle into a school playground. It contained the nearest shelter he could see; not until he was inside with other people did he learn that Great Britain was at war.

Oscar Baker and his sister Theresa learned it in Saint Philip Neri's church in Nottinghamshire, when Father McNicholas interrupted the service. Kit Dennis also learned it in her church in Devon, when the Reverend Lucas told his flock; so, too, did Elspeth Harmes in Bradford, when the Reverend Foster mounted the pulpit steps and, pacifist to the core, informed the congregation that the very gravest situation imaginable had come to pass. Declaring that all should pray for the earliest possible return to peace, he asked them to rise and join him in a hymn— "Let There Be Light." Looking up toward the choir stalls, six-teen-year-old Elspeth saw Eric Jones stand up, and gazing at him as he did at her, she sang, though she felt her heart would break.

In Mountfield, the service of Communion proceeded without any interruption. Neither the people in church nor the Reverend Bob Leaney had the faintest idea that anything untoward had happened. Around midday, after shaking hands with each of his outgoing parishioners — only two dozen, he noticed, with a collection of less than three pounds — Bob stood by the roadside with the squire, waiting for a busload of evacuees that were supposed to be coming down from London. Commander Eger-ton was in an exceedingly bad humor. "Really, Vicar," he exclaimed, "it just isn't good enough. There are the Poles, who are meant to be our allies, being pounded by the Hun — for three days now — and here are we, who are meant to have guaranteed them; and what are we up to? Hmm? What's the Prime Minister about? What I'd like to know is, why on earth haven't we declared war?" Though he did not say it, it occurred to the Reverend Leaney that Commander Egerton took it as a personal insult still to be at peace. "What's the reason for it, eh?" Egerton continued. "You're a man of the cloth. Can you see any sense in this at all? I'm damned if I can, none at all."

To Leaney's relief, he suddenly heard the rumble of an engine and the toot of a horn. "I'm sure you're right, Commander," he said mildly. "But I think these may be our evacuees arriving. Shall we be ready to welcome them?" Grunting in dissatisfaction, the Commander turned toward the bus and gave a beaming smile.

★   ★   ★

It soon transpired that the air-raid warning was a false alarm, but that did not change the new truth. "All that beautiful Sunday," wrote Ross Mackay, "we were practically confined indoors." Overhead hovered a host of barrage balloons. At last the time came when, if he was not to face the problems of driving under blackout, he had to leave and head back for Walton-on-the-Naze. "As my family were going to the south coast and I to the east, it was a sad farewell, for we could not tell whether we would be together again."

From the Admiralty, two short signals were sent in plain language to the whole British fleet. One was a statement of fact: "Winston is back." Instead of being a Minister without Portfolio, Churchill had entered the War Cabinet as First Lord of the Admiralty. Bearing no further comment or elaboration, that first signal to the fleet could be read either as a warning or a message of encouragement; Churchill himself chose to take it as the latter and saw it as a personal compliment. The other message was even shorter and had no ambiguity: "Total Germany." Among others who picked it up was the radio operator in Wilhelmshaven, the western headquarters of U-boat command. In minutes it was rushed to Captain Dönitz. He stared at the message in stunned, blank amazement, and his aides heard him whisper, *"Mein Gott! Also wieder Krieg gegen England!"* — "My God! So it's war with England again!"

By the evening not only Britain but France as well was formally at war with Germany. Despite the Pact of Steel, Italy had contrived to remain neutral and at peace; yet in his home, the Palazzo Chigi, Count Ciano was plunged in gloom. "In what way can France and England bring help to Poland?" he wrote in his diary. "And, when Poland is liquidated, will they want to continue a conflict for which there is no longer any reason? The Duce does not believe so. He believes rather that, after a short struggle, peace will be restored before the clash, which in any case he considers impossible from a military point of view."

Mussolini, however, had not yet heard the speech Churchill had given that afternoon. In London, the new First Lord had been absolutely clear: "This is not a question of fighting for Danzig or fighting for Poland," he had declared. "We are fighting to save the whole world from the pestilence of Nazi tyranny, and in defense of all that is most sacred to man."

Ciano had not heard the speech either. But, sitting alone in Rome that night, he divined the future more accurately than his father-in-law had done. "I am not a military man," he wrote despondently. "I do not know how the war may develop, but I know one thing — it *will* develop, and it will be long, uncertain, and relentless. The participation of Great Britain makes this certain. England has made this declaration to Hitler. The war can end only with Hitler's elimination, or the defeat of Britain."

About the same time as Count Ciano wrote his prophecy, John Landells was making his way home to Jarrow, worn out with the efforts of the day. Three special editions had been pumped out, and he had taken part in any and every job that needed doing — he had been copyboy, he had typed, he had even gone to get sandwiches. Physically exhausted, he was still mentally fully alert. What news, what news! The image of those specials being pasted up was as vivid as if it was still happening. The first edition had carried Britain's declaration, the second the text of a stirring speech by the king, and the third the news of France's declaration. His Majesty had called it "perhaps the most fateful hour in our history." *It certainly is in mine,* John thought. He had been very struck by something else the king had said: "For the second time in the lives of most of us, we are at war." It was the first time for John Landells. Before reading the speech, he had never really considered how lucky he had been; born just a few months after the Armistice that had ended the Great War with Germany, he had never until today known anything but peace.

Now, looking out from the bus as it went bumping along through the darkening streets of South Shields, he watched the sun going down on the first day of the new war with Germany, and he made a promise to himself. On the first day of peace, whenever it might come and wherever he might be, he would be alive and awake at dawn, and he would see the sun rise again.

Epilogue

Nowadays, everyone knows what happened eventually; but, at the time, Hitler's question to von Ribbentrop — *What now?* — was the only one that anyone anywhere could ask, and the one that no one could answer at all. Day by day, the impenetrable future became the dreadful past, part of the heritage of each nation and individual. Now we, the inheritors, know what happened next and, like unwise gods, may choose to dispense judgment on those fallible people; at the same time, we make our own mistakes and grope blindly forward into our own future.

But what of their future, now the past? The fates of the public figures are well known: Chamberlain's unhappy death; Stalin's repulsive life; Churchill's defeat in the polls when peace was won; Hitler's cowardly suicide, the fulfillment of his promise to Germany that he would never witness the conquest of his nation; Mussolini's execution of his son-in-law, Count Ciano, and his own execution at the hands of Italians, followed by his being hung upside-down from a girder; Göring's suicide; all the trials at Nuremberg and the almost incomprehensible charge of 6 million humans going up literally in smoke from the chimneys of Treblinka, Dachau, Auschwitz. What an inheritance for the "master race," or even for the human race. We may hope we would never have done it ourselves; we can never be certain.

The individual fates of many in this story must remain a mystery, particularly those who wrote diaries for Mass-Observation — a great prewar and wartime experiment of social recording. Their names have been changed here but they may (if they have survived) recognize themselves and remember the words they wrote all those decades ago. Other witnesses of the time continued to try their best and, for the most part, succeeded. In March 1942 Oscar Baker joined the merchant navy, took part in

Operation Torch and many convoys, including the delivery of Liberty ships. Chronic ill health contracted during Torch forced him to leave his post as a Master Mariner in 1953; nevertheless, he fathered a happy family of six and remained as a supply officer to the National Health Service until his retirement in 1984. Molly McAndrew married her sweetheart Ernie on December 23, 1939. In 1953, imbued with politics of the socialist tradition, she became a member of Wallsend council and ten years later was the town's mayor. Nine years after that, in 1972, "strangers" were voted in—people from outside the locality, with far-left militant views—and in 1980 her husband Ernie decided to try and buy their council house. Molly herself took the application to the town hall, and there, while she and Ernie were on holiday, it was "leaked" (in her words) to leading councillors. When she and Ernie returned home, she was "interrogated" by those councillors—people who were later expelled from the Labour Party. But Ernie was never able to buy his council house. He was already ill, and his worries for her during this time precipitated a heart attack, from which he died on July 8, 1981, two months short of his sixty-fifth birthday. Molly left the Labour Party and twice since then has stood and been elected as an Independent Labour councillor. By 1988, she was the longest-serving member with unbroken service on Wallsend council.

Kit Dennis, the farmer's daughter in Devon, married her near neighbor from Plympton, Joseph Clifton. They had no children but prospered in other ways. Joseph's 127-acre farm and his farmhouse with its leaky roof were eventually sold for redevelopment; retiring to a centrally heated, fully carpeted modern house, they could only be amused when later generations yearned for the "simple life." Like them, Dorothy Williams, the South Wales schoolteacher whose spinster future had seemed assured, never left her home district; but, in June 1941, she, too, married and was blessed with two children. Dreaming in Vacationland, U.S.A., Barkley Goodrich met, fell in love with, and married Libby Tufts, the little girl from South Poland; they, too, produced a fine family, of some academic distinction. Claud Kennerley, the Yorkshire doctor, never properly recovered from the war: it temporarily destroyed his practice and permanently impaired his health. Having contracted an illness from treating members of the British Expeditionary Force, he was invalided out of the army late in 1942 and rebuilt his practice from scratch; but in 1972, he died of heart failure. In America, Ernest Kroll went on, as his friends had predicted, to become a poet and unexpectedly gained a most unusual distinction: Some lines of his were engraved in stone in Washington, D.C., along with those of other poets, but he was the only living one; the authorities who had chosen his work were inexplicably under the impression that he, too, was dead.

John Landells had foretold that his protégé, Bill Hardcastle, would become a famous journalist, and he did. Landells himself survived to keep his private promise; after seeing military service in Europe, northern Africa, the Near East, and the Mediterranean, he was in Brussels on V.E. Day and climbed to the roof of a high building to see the sun rise on the first day of peace in Europe. Thereafter, he, too, returned to journalism, ending his career in 1984 as Chief Press Officer to British Shipbuilders. As an intellectual Christian, Bob Leaney found the ideal way of life once war was done and became in time a Professor of Divinity. In Birmingham, alert to the huge inequities of the existing social system, Dr. Haigh's later life followed a similar, though not identical, course, and he became an Emeritus Professor of Social Medicine.

Niusia Zamecka, the ten-year-old Polish girl, spent four years in German-occupied Warsaw. From there, after the uprising in 1944, she was taken to prison in Germany. With the Allied victory, she ended up recuperating in England, and there became Janine Philips, for she met and married an Englishman. The war separated Zofja Olszolwska from her husband Tadeusz for five abominable years; although she was allowed to remain in Moniaki, the family home was taken over by the Germans for a command post, and from it — in a ghastly inversion of the biblical image — she could see "a pillar of smoke by day and a pillar of fire by night," unerasable plumes from the furnaces of the

Belzec extermination camp. Reunited after the war, the Olszolwskis also settled in England, and Tadeusz lived until 1988.

Sandy Powell, the youthful, towering Marine, remained in the
corps until 1953. His wartime record included Mediterranean,
Atlantic, and Russian convoys, "D-Day and all that carry-on,"
and special work that remains secret. He was also in Malta,
Palestine, and Suez, before spending twenty-five years in the
police force and a decade in charge of a center for the elderly,
handicapped, and sick. By 1988 he was proud to say he had done
thirty-five years of work for the community, and four of his eight
children carry that on as members of the Royal Navy, the Royal
Marines, the Women's Royal Naval Service, and the police.

Lionel Tomlinson, the trawlerman, also did much wartime
convoy work and afterward returned to fishing until 1965, when
he took up the supply of oil rigs in Nigeria, Angola, and the
North Sea, prospering sufficiently to be able to retire at sixty-two
back to his hometown. Mike Warbreck-Howell was delighted
when the war came; he was able to leave Cambridge University
and join the Fleet Air Arm as a pilot, much more to his liking.
John Scott, who had been an adolescent Communist in Birmingham, threw that off during the war and achieved respec-
tability: He became a headmaster. He also married Elspeth
Harmes, who, despite her early departure from school, eventually graduated in theology and whose childhood love for the
choirboy Eric Jones turned into a fond memory. Charles King,
the Australian Communist, found the Russian invasion of Finland too much to stomach. On writing an editorial condemning
it, he was expelled from the Party and returned to teaching and
the study of poetry. Ironically, when he died in 1966, he was
working on a history of the Communist party in Australia.

Richard Richter, whose mother had been imprisoned by the
Gestapo in Vienna, achieved two of his wartime ambitions: He
joined the British Army and, as a member of its interrogation
squad, located the man who had "shopped" his mother. The
culprit was a rather pathetic clerk who had been acting under
considerable duress. Richter's interrogation work gave way after
the war to a life in business, yet some things remained

unfinished: In 1988 he still possessed, from his interrogations, firsthand evidence of a Nazi war criminal who by then was living, prosperous and still unpunished, on the outskirts of Hamburg.

During the war, Willie Smith, the Shetland fisherman, found new employment both in running the Foula mailboat and in fishing; his wife Lizzie, "the Teacher," continued in her profession; and, in the course of the war, on their tiny island of Foula, David Howarth met them and their three daughters, Stella, Nanette, and Jessamine. His own prewar BBC work changed, after some months as a war correspondent with Richard Dimbleby, to naval work, and, as a member of the Special Operations Executive based in those remote islands, he established a spy network that became known as the Shetland Bus. And he fell in love (though he had not expected it) not only with the islands and their people, with whom he lived and worked after the war as a boatbuilder, but also with Nanette Smith, though she was nearly fifteen years younger than he. They married, David changed his profession from boatbuilding to writing, and they had a family of three girls and a boy.

Francis Vanek, the cycling pilgrim, spent a large part of the war welding bridges. When it was all over, he was able to return to his real profession, at which he was far more skilled — the art of ladies' tailoring. He, too, married, in a match that has lasted; he fathered two daughters and a son and has proved to be one of those who only with the utmost reluctance has considered retirement.

★   ★   ★

So, for better or worse, their lives panned out — a few of those millions who lived through August 1939. Fifty years later, of course, the mood of those last four weeks of peace has become remote but not forgotten. Memories remain, sometimes humorous, often painful and bitter, yet almost always astonishingly vivid. Now, though, as that summer fades into history, and from history into legend, all that those born later can do is to try and imagine what it meant to be alive at that time, when the only real, living questions in everyone's mind were utterly unanswerable. Early in September 1939, the *Picture Post* asked those questions of its readers:

"The war is on. How long will it last? What will it lead to? How much suffering will be undergone, how many lives will be lost, how many nights such as this will we go through before peace comes once more?"

Chronology

Wednesday, August 2   After a lengthy debate the British House of Commons votes itself a summer holiday. The House will rise on Friday and will not expect to return until 21 October. In America, Albert Einstein writes a letter to President Roosevelt, warning him of the possibility that Nazi Germany might be attempting to build an atom bomb.

Thursday, August 3   In the Free City of Danzig a dispute flares between Polish customs officials and members of the Nazi-dominated Senate. In Germany a detailed forecast of U-boat needs clearly does not anticipate an early war. In Moscow the German ambassador, Count Friedrich von der Schulenberg, secretly meets Vyacheslav Molotov, Soviet Commissar for Foreign Affairs; and in London a similarly secret meeting takes place between Ambassador Herbert von Dirksen and Sir Horace Wilson, the Prime Minister's closest adviser.

Friday, August 4   The 25th anniversary of Germany's invasion of Belgium and the declaration of war by Britain against Germany. In Danzig the customs dispute continues. In Britain the Bank Holiday weekend begins, and the Commons rise for the summer recess.

Saturday, August 5   The first British transatlantic air mail service is inaugurated. A joint Anglo-French military delegation led by Admiral Sir Reginald Plunkett-Ernle-Erle-Drax and General Joseph Doumenc leaves Britain, traveling by sea to Leningrad, for discussions with Molotov. At Balmoral Castle in Scotland, two hundred boys are entertained to tea by the king and queen, while Albert Förster, Nazi Gauleiter of Danzig, flies to Berchtesgaden to confer with Adolf Hitler. The Danzig customs

284

dispute is temporarily resolved, but its resolution is seen in other countries as a Nazi climb-down, infuriating Hitler.

Sunday, August 6   The Feast of the Transfiguration. In Rome, fearing Germany will go to war with Poland, the Duce Benito Mussolini, and Count Galeazzo Ciano, his son-in-law and Foreign Minister, discuss possible ways to evade the terms of the Pact of Steel, signed with Germany on 23 May. The pact commits them to aiding Germany, but Italy is three years short of readiness for war.

Monday, August 7   Bank Holiday Monday in England and Wales. Count Ciano asks to see Joachim von Ribbentrop, Hitler's Foreign Minister.

Tuesday, August 8   Winston Churchill makes a fifteen-minute radio broadcast to America, warning of the increasingly serious threat of war in Europe and the likelihood of American involvement.

Wednesday, August 9   At Weymouth, on the south coast of England, King George VI inspects the Reserve Fleet immediately prior to its mobilization. Ambassador von Dirksen, preparing to depart on leave to Germany, visits the British Foreign Secretary, Lord Halifax. An official warning concerning the Polish attitude to Danzig is sent from Berlin to Warsaw, where it is viewed as an unwarranted interference in internal Polish affairs. Admiral Drax and his colleagues arrive in Leningrad late at night.

Thursday, August 10   Nighttime air war exercises are conducted over England on a larger scale than any since the Great War. Drax and the other delegates spend the day sightseeing in Leningrad, while in Berlin Julius Schnurre, head of the Economic Policy Department of the German Foreign Ministry, picks up discussions with Georgi Astakhov, Chargé d'Affaires of the Soviet Embassy, sounding out the possibility of a pact between Germany and Russia.

Friday, August 11   The Anglo-French delegation finally arrives in Moscow. It is agreed to start talks next day. In Britain the Foreign

Office learns that Germany will be in a state of complete military readiness on the 15th. While Gauleiter Förster warns Danzig Nazis to be prepared for anything, Karl Burckhardt, Commissioner of the League of Nations in Danzig, is summoned to see Hitler in Berchtesgaden. Ciano and von Ribbentrop meet in Salzburg, and when Ciano asks von Ribbentrop whether Germany wants the "Polish Corridor" or Danzig, von Ribbentrop replies, "Not that any more. We want war."

Saturday, August 12   In Scotland the grouse-shooting season opens. In Moscow the Anglo-French-Russian military talks begin. Ciano goes to Berchtesgaden to see Hitler, while Astakhov sends Schnurre new information from Moscow indicating Russian willingness to open political negotiations with Germany.

Sunday, August 13   On holiday in Scotland, Neville Chamberlain, the British Prime Minister, complains of his poor luck at fishing. Ciano returns to Rome, disgusted at the attitudes of von Ribbentrop and Hitler.

Monday, August 14   Chamberlain and Halifax receive details of Ciano's meetings and consider the idea of sending a German-speaking Briton to negotiate directly with Hitler. Meanwhile in Moscow Ambassador von der Schulenberg receives instructions for a meeting with Molotov next day, and Marshal Kliment Voroshilov, Commissar for Defense, puts his central question to the Anglo-French delegates: Will the Red Army be allowed to march across Poland? Knowing it is almost impossible that the Poles will agree, Drax is unable to answer.

Tuesday, August 15   The Feast of the Blessed Virgin Mary. Churchill begins a tour of the Maginot Line, France's main land defensive barrier against Germany. At last given permission by their political masters, the British Chiefs of Staff eagerly draft new instructions for Drax, while the Foreign Office and the Quai d'Orsay put pressure on Poland to allow Russian forces into Poland if necessary. In Moscow Molotov is highly interested in von der Schulenberg's proposals; von der Schulenberg in turn is surprised and pleased at the Russian's moderate conditions. Captain Karl Dönitz, head of the U-boat arm of the German Navy, is recalled unexpectedly early from leave. In Berlin, von Dirksen's own leave is uninterrupted; although he wishes to see von Ribbentrop, the Nazi Foreign Minister will not receive him. Von Dirksen also discovers that the Italian ambassador in Berlin, Bernardo Attolico, believes Germany is about to go to war with Poland, ignoring Britain's attitude. Von Dirksen is convinced Attolico is wrong.

Wednesday, August 16 The British Deputy Chiefs of Staff report that "it is perfectly clear that without early and effective Russian assistance, the Poles cannot hope to stand up to a German attack on land or in the air for more than a limited time." Von Ribbentrop cables von der Schulenberg, telling him that all Molotov's conditions can be met. Captain Dönitz arrives at Kiel, the main U-boat base, and begins to implement plans for *Fall Weiss,* Case White, the projected attack on Poland.

Thursday, August 17 In Moscow Molotov is highly gratified by the Germans' obvious haste to achieve a political agreement, and to Drax's outrage, Marshal Voroshilov — by now sure that neither the French nor the British mean business — dismisses their delegates for four days. For some time, American Intelligence has been far better informed than its British counterpart about developments between Berlin and Moscow, and now Sumner Welles, Under Secretary of State, passes the information to British Ambassador Sir Ronald Lindsay. Lindsay immediately telegraphs London, confident his message will be in the Foreign Office first thing in the morning, London time. It is, but is not deciphered for four days. Meanwhile the British Ambassador in Warsaw, Sir Howard Kennard, fails to move Colonel Joseph Beck, the Polish Foreign Minister; and Hitler orders Admiral Canaris, the head of German Intelligence, to obtain Polish uniforms for a "special SS operation."

Friday, August 18 Placards have been appearing in London with a simple but ambiguous question, "What price Churchill?" Now

The Times prints a letter signed by 375 academics urging the Prime Minister to include Churchill in his Cabinet. As the Foreign Office learns that a German attack on Poland is threatened to take place in two weeks' time, Sir Nevile Henderson, the British Ambassador in Berlin, begs Chamberlain to write personally to Hitler.

Saturday, August 19 Henderson notes unhappily that while Churchill is inspecting the defenses of France, Chamberlain is still fishing in Scotland. However, Lord Halifax and his advisers agree that the Prime Minister should be enabled to stay on holiday. Sending a telegram to Mussolini, who played a prominent part in the "Munich agreement" of 1938, they begin to draft a letter for Chamberlain to send to Hitler. At the same time in Warsaw Colonel Beck replies to French pressure with *"un 'non' catégorique"*; and after two further meetings with von der Schulenberg, Molotov suddenly produces a draft Russo-German pact and invites von Ribbentrop to come to Moscow.

Sunday, August 20 In the early hours of the morning an agreement is signed between Germany and Russia. Hitler, suspecting Molotov might cause delays in its ratification, sends a personal message to Stalin urging all speed. Lord Halifax telegrams Kennard in Warsaw, requesting him as urgently to try once more to gain Polish permission for Russian forces to enter their country. Churchill, resting at the château of a friend, paints a picture of the building and remarks that it will be the last picture he paints in peace.

Monday, August 21 Chamberlain reaches London early in the morning, having traveled overnight from Scotland. British Intelligence suggests that Field Marshal Hermann Göring, founder of the Gestapo and head of the Luftwaffe, should come to London for discussions. But just as Drax and Doumenc decide to dispense with Polish permission and on the responsibility of their own governments allow Russian forces to enter Poland, Marshal Voroshilov — knowing of von Ribbentrop's impending arrival — postpones indefinitely any continuation of the Anglo-French-Russian talks.

Tuesday, August 22   Hints of a Russo-German Pact are everywhere. Chamberlain recalls Parliament for the 24th. *The Times* announces the massing of German troops on the Polish border. There are heavy losses of British gold reserves. The telegram from Ambassador Lindsay in Washington is finally deciphered, and Ambassador Kennard and his French counterpart Léon Noël try for one last time to make Colonel Beck change his mind. Sir William Seeds, British Ambassador in Moscow, accuses Molotov of negotiating in bad faith, and Chamberlain gives a fighting speech, to be broadcast by the BBC, saying it is unthinkable that Great Britain should not carry out its obligations to Poland. Nevertheless Hitler addresses his generals, ordering them to be ready for war on the morning of the 26th.

Wednesday, August 23   French citizens are advised to leave Paris. King George leaves Balmoral and returns to London. Churchill leaves France and also returns to London. A personal appeal from Chamberlain is delivered to Hitler at Berchtesgaden. Sir Percy Loraine, British Ambassador in Rome, is confident that the Italians will not fight, and Mussolini declares himself ready to mediate. At last Colonel Beck relents; but early in the evening von Ribbentrop arrives in Moscow, and there, late at night, the Russo-German Pact is concluded.

Thursday, August 24   Hitler has predicted that the Chamberlain government will fall; but it does not. While Marshal Voroshilov goes duck-shooting, in London Parliament reconvenes and immediately passes the Emergency Powers Act, which is given the Royal Assent the same day. The British Fleet is ordered to war stations. Göring has a meeting with Birger Dahlerus, a businessman from neutral Sweden, and proposes that Dahlerus, who has good connections in Britain, should act as a go-between. From Berlin Ambassador Henderson urges that Poland and Germany should reestablish contact, saying that it is the "*last* hope, if any, of peace: if there is a last hope."

Friday, August 25   For the first time in seven and a half years, the base rate of the Bank of England is increased, from 2 percent to 4 percent. The city of Coventry is bombed by IRA terrorists. Dahlerus arrives in London. Many border incidents take place in Poland, and a treaty of mutual assistance is formally signed between Poland and Great Britain. Ambassador Attolico tells Hitler that Italy will not support Germany without German help with the hardware of war. On hearing of this, Hitler cancels his invasion date, 0430 the following morning. To some it seems that war has been averted by a matter of hours; others are sure this is only a postponement.

Saturday, August 26   In France, horses, cars, and some property are requisitioned. The pope issues a general appeal for peace. In Britain the soccer season opens, and from Italy Mussolini submits a preposterous list of Italian requirements to von Ribbentrop. During the morning, Dahlerus sees Halifax again, flies back to Berlin with a letter for Göring, and returns to London later that afternoon. "If things turn out badly," Queen Elizabeth tells her lady-in-waiting, "I must be with the King." She goes to London — like many of their subjects, she prefers the idea of being bombed at home, if one must be bombed at all. Robert Coulondre, French ambassador in Berlin, sees Hitler and appeals to him as one old soldier to another. When Coulondre cites the probable fate of women and children in any war, Hitler hesitates visibly, but von Ribbentrop strengthens him again. In the course of a Cabinet meeting in London, the Chiefs of Staff advise that the earliest possible date for any ultimatum to Germany is September 1.

Sunday, August 27   Ciano recommends British acceptance of Hitler's latest offer. The British Cabinet learns for the first time from Lord Halifax of "Mr. D," Birger Dahlerus, and his efforts. Colonel Beck agrees to consider an exchange of population between the predominantly German and predominantly Polish areas, and by midnight Dahlerus is back in Berlin.

Monday, August 28 During the early hours Dahlerus meets both Göring and Sir George Ogilvie-Forbes, Counsellor of the British Embassy in Berlin, before breakfasting again with Göring. Colonel Beck refuses to go to Berlin, and Poland mobilizes. Rationing is imposed in Germany; gold reaches £8 sterling an ounce; Chamberlain has another audience with the king, and Arthur Greenwood, Deputy Leader of the Opposition, visits Number Ten four times. Colonel Beck at last accepts the principle of direct negotiations; but toward midnight he tells Ambassador Kennard that Polish mobilization is proceeding.

Tuesday, August 29 Ambassador Attolico suggests to von Ribbentrop that a peace conference should be held; von Ribbentrop rejects the idea with contempt. In the House of Commons Chamberlain makes a firm, uncompromising speech. Ambassadors Kennard and Noël persuade Colonel Beck to postpone any further mobilization, and Hitler, angry at British interference, grudgingly accepts direct negotiations with Poland, but demands that a Polish plenipotentiary must arrive in Berlin by the end of the following day.

Wednesday, August 30 There is sudden optimism on the London Stock Exchange; Hitler is said to have studied Chamberlain's speech with care. In Berlin, however, Ambassador Henderson is informed from Britain that Hitler's demand for the arrival of a Polish plenipotentiary that day is unreasonable. In Warsaw Beck tells Ambassador Kennard that Polish mobilization will resume at midnight. Military guards are posted on all British railway stations; many D-notices are issued to newspapers, forbidding publication of specified aspects of news. Henderson and von Ribbentrop meet again, and this time come close to blows: von Ribbentrop "gabbles through" Hitler's latest proposals and refuses to give Henderson a copy of the text.

Thursday, August 31 During the night, Göring reads Hitler's new demands to Dahlerus, who telephones Ogilvie-Forbes at the British Embassy. Ambassador Henderson passes the information to Josef Lipski, the Polish ambassador, and breakfasts with Ulrich von Hassell, an ex-diplomat and now a prominent anti-Nazi, before seeing Attolico. London children are evacuated from the capital, and Ciano calls Halifax to confirm that Italy will not fight either Britain or France. Nevertheless, during the afternoon Hitler orders the SS as *agents-provocateurs* to attack a German radio transmitter near the Polish border, and issues "Directive Number 1 for the Conduct of the War."

Friday, September 1   Before dawn, German forces invade Poland. At 5:40 A.M. Berlin radio broadcasts Hitler's proclamation to his army; the invasion has been launched "in order to put an end to this lunacy." At 7:28 A.M. the British Foreign Office learns of the invasion. At 10:00 A.M. Hitler is driven through an abnormally silent Berlin to the Reichstag, from where he broadcasts the news to the world. At 2:00 P.M., while Colonel Beck formally breaks relations with Germany, British mobilization starts. The House of Commons is summoned for 6:00 o'clock that evening, with all blackout curtains drawn; yet there is no immediate declaration of war against Germany. Instead, only a warning is sent to Berlin.

Saturday, September 2   By 4:30 P.M. Poland has been at war for thirty-six hours, but no reply has been received in London from Berlin. In the Cabinet Room, Neville Chamberlain reads out a message from the French government: They want 48 hours more delay. At 6:00 P.M. Halifax calls Ciano and Parliament meets "in troubled silence." At 7:30 P.M. a call is made from the Cabinet to Édouard Daladier, the French Prime Minister, resulting in their agreement to restate Britain's position to Germany, without a time limit. At 7:44 P.M. Chamberlain relays this to the House of Commons, where it is received as half-hearted: Arthur Greenwood demands "no more devices." By then, over thirty Polish towns and cities have been bombed with more than 1,500 casualties of Polish women and children, while the IRA has launched a series of attacks on individual soldiers in the British Territorial Army. At 8:50 P.M. von Ribbentrop informs Attolico that there will be no German withdrawal from Poland; at 9:30 P.M. Sir Percy Loraine calls London from Rome to say that Mussolini is abandoning his efforts for peace. Churchill, expecting at any minute to be invited to join the War Cabinet, has waited all day for a message from Chamberlain. A violent thunderstorm is raging over England, and a deputation from the House of Commons confronts Chamberlain demanding no further delay. "Right, gentlemen," the Prime Minister answers. "This means war." Nevertheless some people hope it may not yet be too late. Dr. Fritz Hesse, Press Councillor to the German Embassy in London, comes to Sir Horace Wilson, Chamberlain's chief adviser, with an invitation from von Ribbentrop for a secret meeting, "heart to heart." Wilson refuses, but repeats that if Germany withdraws from Poland, bygones will be bygones; and the French Foreign Minister, Georges Bonnet, contacts Ciano to try and arrange a symbolic German withdrawal. But Ciano, perhaps more realistic, ignores the message, throwing it in the wastepaper basket before returning to bed. Lord Halifax calls Paris to establish a time limit; and at 10:30 P.M. Chamberlain's peacetime Cabinet begins its final meeting. An absolute ultimatum will be sent to Germany.

Sunday, September 3 At 9:00 A.M. the ultimatum is sent. It will expire in two hours. Worn out by the enormous efforts of the past few days, Paul Schmidt, Hitler's interpreter, oversleeps and arrives at the Foreign Office only just in time to slip in by a side door as Ambassador Henderson enters from the front. Neither von Ribbentrop nor Hitler will receive Henderson; the task is delegated to Schmidt. The brief meeting between interpreter and ambassador is painful for both men, who have an honest respect for each other. Schmidt brings the ultimatum to Hitler and reads it slowly and carefully in English and German. Von Ribbentrop stares out of the window; Hitler turns to him with a savage glare and barks: "What now?" His plans had been made in the belief, encouraged by von Ribbentrop, that neither Britain nor France would fight. Now von Ribbentrop predicts correctly that a French ultimatum will follow soon.

By 11:00 A.M. no reply has been received in London from Berlin. With great sadness and great determination Chamberlain broadcasts his tragic, historic declaration: "I have to tell you now . . . that this country is at war with Germany." People throughout the nation hear the message with shock and incredulity, mixed sometimes, now that there is a definite course of action to follow, with an odd sense of relief. The briefest of signals is sent to the Fleet, "Total Germany." Picked up in Wilhelmshaven, it is passed to Captain Dönitz, who reacts with despair and disbelief: "My God! So it's war with England again . . ."

Newly reappointed as First Lord of the Admiralty, Churchill immediately states his fundamental policy: "This is not a question of fighting for Danzig or fighting for Poland. We are fighting to save the whole world from the pestilence of Nazi tyranny, and in defense of all that is most sacred to man." That evening, with most of Europe at war, Ciano writes a frank and accurate prophecy in his diary:

> I am not a military man. I do not know how the war may develop, but I know one thing — it *will* develop, and it will be long, uncertain and relentless. The participation of Great Britain makes this certain. England has made this declaration to Hitler. The war can end only with Hitler's elimination or the defeat of Britain.

Notes on Sources

The majority of interviews with witnesses of August 1939 were conducted over the winter and spring of 1987–88 in a wide variety of locations and by correspondence. Some of the interviewees' names have been changed at their request, and to maintain a degree of privacy for them I do not feel I should specify precise dates and places. Moreover, since I have made use of the results in every chapter, it would be needlessly repetitive to include them again below; and for the same reasons I feel I should not make it explicit which of the unpublished diaries came from the Mass-Observation Archive. However the following notes on other source material may be useful.

1 *Take your gas mask with you*
Churchill awakening: William Manchester, "At home with Winston Churchill," *Illustrated London News* (May 1987); his letter to Wolmer: Martin Gilbert, *Winston S. Churchill* (hereafter *Companion*), V, *1936–39 Companion* (Heinemann, 1982), p. 1580. Parliamentary proceedings: *Hansard. Parliamentary Debates*, fifth series, vol. 350, cols. 2425–26 (hereafter *Hansard*). Paul Schmidt in Norderney: Paul Schmidt, *Hitler's Interpreter*, ed. R. H. C. Steed (Heinemann, 1951). Von Dirksen and Lord Kemsley: *Documents and Materials Relating to the Eve of the Second World War*, II, *1938–39* (hereafter *Dirksen Papers*), Ministry of Foreign Affairs of the USSR (Foreign Languages Publishing House, Moscow, 1948), pp. 113–15. Ronald Cartland in Parliament: *Hansard* vol. 350, col. 2495; and Harold Nicolson, *Diaries and Letters 1930–39*, ed. Nigel Nicolson (Collins, 1966), pp. 407–8. Background history of Poland: Norman Davies, *Heart of Europe: A Short History of Poland* (Clarendon Press, 1984); and O. Halecki, *A History of Poland*, rev. ed. (Dent, 1955). Einstein and Szilard:

Banesh Hoffman, with H. Dukas, *Albert Einstein: Creator and Rebel* (Hart-Davis, MacGibbon, 1973), pp. 204–8.

2 *The earth's a good place*
Fresdorf and Dönitz: Peter Padfield, *Dönitz — the Last Führer* (Panther, 1985), pp. 209–11. Cadogan: *The Diaries of Sir Alexander Cadogan 1938–45* ed. David Dilks (Cassell, 1971), pp. 168, 193, 237. Molotov and von der Schulenburg: Sidney Aster, *1939: The Making of the Second World War* (Deutsch, 1973) pp. 298–300. Wilson and von Dirksen: *Dirksen Papers*, pp. 116–25. Kubizek and Hitler: John Toland, *Adolf Hitler* (Doubleday, 1976), pp. 457, 534.

3 *The keys of peace and war*
Mussolini's remarks on Nazism and Hitler: Toland, *Adolf Hitler*, pp. 326–27, 354–55. Ciano on Attolico: *Ciano's Diary 1939–43*, ed. M. Muggeridge (Doubleday, 1946), August 3–4, 1939. H.G. Wells on King George, royal visit to USA: Robert Kee, *The World We Left Behind* (Sphere, 1985), pp. 11, 252. Greenwood on Danzig: *Hansard*, vol. 350, col. 2430. Chodacki's confrontation with Danzig senate: Aster, *1939*, pp. 320–21.

4 *Holiday time, ladies and gentlemen!*
Church services: Roman Catholic Missal for August 1939. Ciano and Mussolini: *Ciano's Diary*, August 6–8, 1939. Wilson and von Dirksen: *Dirksen Papers*, pp. 116–25. Cadogan's note: *Cadogan Diaries*, p. 193. Caribou flight, IRA suspects, Jewish refugees, air crash, Princess Elizabeth, Claude Viviers: in *South Wales Evening Post*, August 8, 1939. Churchill: Gilbert, *Companion*, p. 1583; and Charles Eades [Compiler], *The War Speeches of Winston Churchill*, vol. 1 (Cassell, 1951), pp. 102–5.

5 *Different worlds*
Fleet inspection: *The Times*, August 5, 1939. Von Dirksen and Halifax: *Dirksen Papers*, pp. 126–32. Beck and Danzig dispute: Aster, *1939*, p. 321. Drax and Voroshilov: Aster, op. cit. p. 301. Wood and Churchill: Winston S. Churchill, *The Second World War, I, The Gathering Storm* (Cassell, 1948), pp. 183, 302. Schnurre and Astakhov: Aster, op. cit. pp. 296–300. Niusia Zamecka: Janine Phillips, *My Secret Diary* (Shepheard-Walwyn, 1982), pp. 34–35. Von Hassell: *The Von Hassell Diaries, 1938–44*,

(Hamish Hamilton, 1948), p. 57. Förster: cited Kee, *The World We Left Behind*, p. 289. Ciano and Ribbentrop: *Ciano's Diary*, August 11, 1939. Hitler and Burckhardt: Toland, *Adolf Hitler*, p. 536.

6 Can the Red Army march across Poland?
President and Mrs. Roosevelt: J.P. Lash, *Eleanor and Franklin* (Deutsch, 1972), p. 582. Drax and Voroshilov: Aster, *1939*, pp. 301–2; Roger Parkinson, *Peace for our Time* (Hart-Davies, 1971), p. 173; A.P. Adamthwaite, *The Making of the Second World War* (Allen and Unwin, 1977), pp. 218–19. Ciano and Hitler: Toland, *Adolf Hitler*, p. 539; Schmidt, *Hitler's Interpreter*, pp. 132–33; *Ciano's Diary*, August 12–14, 1939. Cadogan: *Cadogan Diaries*, p. 195. Niusia: Phillips, *My Secret Diary*, pp. 11–12, 36. Chamberlain and Syers: Aster, op. cit. p. 323. Von Hassell: *Von Hassell Diaries*, pp. 58–59. Schmidt: Schmidt, op. cit. p. 133.

7 This is no time for half-measures
Von Dirksen and Attolico: *Dirksen Papers*, pp. 132–35. Dönitz: based on Padfield, *Dönitz*, pp. 170, 212; and others. Moscow talks: Aster, *1939*, pp. 304–10; Toland, *Adolf Hitler*, p. 540; Parkinson, *Peace for our Time*, pp. 174–75; *Cadogan Diaries*, pp. 195–96. Churchill: Gilbert, *Companion*, pp. 1588–89.

8 In order to escape
Heydrich: Toland, *Adolf Hitler*, pp. 567–68; Parkinson, *Peace for our Time*, p. 171. Kennard, Moscow talks: Aster, *1939*, pp. 309–11; Lindsay, ibid. pp. 314–17; and Parkinson, op. cit. p. 176. HMS *Formidable: South Wales Evening Post*, August 17, 1939. Ciano: *Ciano's Diary*, August 17, 1939.

9 The present unusual situation
Cadogan: *Cadogan Diaries*, pp. 196, 207–8. King: Aster, *1939*, p. 317n; Noël, ibid. p. 311. Dönitz: Padfield, *Dönitz*, pp. 212–13, 220. Ciano: *Ciano's Diary*, August 18, 1939. Loraine, Beck, Henderson, Ribbentrop: cited Parkinson, *Peace for our Time*, pp. 176–77. Smigly-Rydz: cited Churchill, *The Gathering Storm*, p. 305. Henderson-Livesey, Churchill in Dreux: Gilbert, *Companion*, pp. 1590–91. Halifax *et al.* in FO, his letter to Chamberlain: *Cadogan Diaries*, pp. 197–99. Schulenburg and Molotov: Aster, op. cit.

p. 310; Parkinson, *Peace for our Time*, p. 178; William Shirer, *The Rise and Fall of the Third Reich* (BCA, 1968), pp. 637–38.

10   *I have them!*
Hitler to Stalin: Aster, *1939*, p. 310; Parkinson, *Peace for our Time*, pp. 178–79. Ciano: *Ciano's Diary*, August 19–21, 1939. Halifax to Kennard: Aster, op. cit. p. 311; *Cadogan Diaries*, p. 199. Hitler's health: Shirer, *Third Reich*, p. 639. Dönitz: Padfield, *Dönitz*, pp. 212–13. Nicolson: *Diaries and Letters*, pp. 409–11. Stalin to Hitler: Shirer, op. cit. p. 640. Hitler's reaction: Toland, *Adolf Hitler*, p. 541. Maze on Churchill: Gilbert, *Companion*, p. 1591.

11   *The day is charged . . . and full of threats*
Reactions to impending Pact: Churchill, *The Gathering Storm*, p. 307; Hore-Belisha, cited Parkinson, *Peace for our Time*, p. 179; Schmidt, *Hitler's Interpreter*, p. 134; 'Uncle Franz,' Bernt Engelmann, *In Hitler's Germany* (Methuen, 1988), p. 149; *Von Hassell Diaries*, p. 62; Nicolson, *Diaries and Letters*, p. 411. The Berchtesgaden speech: Adamthwaite, *The Making of the Second World War*, pp. 219–21. Göring at Nuremberg and Town Clerk's warning: cited Parkinson, op. cit. p. 181. Churchill en route to and in Paris: Gilbert, *Companion*, pp. 1592–93. Speaker's recall: *House of Commons Journal*, vols. 194–95, Session 1938/40, p. 401. Cabinet meeting: Parkinson, op. cit. pp. 182–83; *Cadogan Diaries*, pp. 199–200. Preparations for Pact: Schmidt, op. cit. pp. 134–39. Voroshilov to Doumenc: Aster, *1939*, p. 312; Shirer, *Third Reich*, p. 651; Churchill, op. cit. pp. 305–6. Seeds to Molotov: cited Parkinson, op. cit. p. 183. Nicolson in Plymouth and London: Nicolson, op. cit. pp. 411–12. Kennedy and Halifax: Aster, op. cit. pp. 334–35. Ciano: *Ciano's Diary*, August 23, 1939. Niusia: Phillips, *My Secret Diary*, p. 42. Hitler to Chamberlain: N. Baynes (ed.), *Hitler's Speeches, April 1922–August 1939*, (II) OUP for RIIA, 1942, pp. 1682–85. Stalin to Ribbentrop: Aster, op. cit. p. 313. Halifax and Cadogan: *Cadogan's Diaries*, p. 200.

12   *Action will begin*
King and Ciano: *Ciano's Diary*, August 24, 1939. Niusia: Phillips, *My Secret Diary*, pp. 42–43. Henderson to Halifax: Toland, *Adolf Hitler*, p. 550. Nicolson to Vita Sackville-West: Nicolson, *Diaries*

and Letters, p. 413. Cadogan to Halifax: *Cadogan Diaries,* pp. 200–1. Dahlerus and Göring: Aster, *1939,* pp. 339–40. Cazalet, Channon: Gilbert, *Companion,* pp. 1596–97. Commons vote: *House of Commons Journal,* p. 401. German return from Moscow: Schmidt, *Hitler's Interpreter,* pp. 139–41. Cadogan: *Cadogan Diaries,* pp. 200–1. Ciano: *Ciano's Diary,* August 25, 1939. Hitler's reaction to Chamberlain speech: Schmidt, op. cit. pp. 141–43; and to Anglo-Polish Treaty, ibid. p. 144; and with Coulondre, ibid. pp. 144–45; and with Attolico, ibid. pp. 145–46. IRA bombing: Kee, *The World We Left Behind,* pp. 300–1. 'Uncle Franz' and Hitler's cancellation: Engelmann, *In Hitler's Germany,* p. 150.

13 *To measure the unknowable*
Seeds' reaction: Aster, *1939,* p. 319. Voroshilov to Drax: ibid. p. 313. Ciano: *Ciano's Diary,* August 26, 1939. *Von Hassell Diaries,* p. 63. Roberts: cited Richard Lamb, *The Ghosts of Peace 1935–1945* (Michael Russell, 1987), p. 112. Cadogan: *Cadogan Diaries,* p. 202. Radio team: Engelmann, *In Hitler's Germany,* p. 150. Ribbentrop and Attolico, and Hitler to Mussolini: Toland, *Adolf Hitler,* pp. 555–56. Cabinet and earliest possible ultimatum: Aster, op. cit. pp. 341–42; Parkinson, *Peace for our Time,* p. 190. Dahlerus and Hitler: Shirer, *Third Reich,* p. 691; Toland, op. cit. pp. 556–57; Padfield, *Dönitz,* p. 214.

14 *What's the use of worrying?*
Strange man: Kee, *The World We Left Behind,* pp. 304–5. Von Hassell: *Von Hassell Diaries,* pp. 62, 64. Hitler to Daladier: Schmidt, *Hitler's Interpreter,* pp. 147–48; Toland, *Adolf Hitler,* p. 558. Dahlerus and Chamberlain: *Cadogan Diaries,* pp. 202–3; Toland, op. cit. p. 559; Parkinson, *Peace for our Time,* pp. 191–92; Aster, *1939,* pp. 343–44, 349. Ciano to Halifax and to Mussolini: *Ciano's Diary,* August 27, 1939; on British note, ibid. August 28, 1939. Oster: Shirer, *Third Reich,* p. 681. Nicolson: *Diaries and Letters,* p. 413. Henderson and Hitler: Aster, op. cit. pp. 350–51; Toland, op. cit. p. 560; Parkinson, op. cit. pp. 195–96; Schmidt, op. cit. p. 148.

15 *And still we wait from day to day*
Cadogan *et al* in Park: *Cadogan Diaries*, p. 204; on plebiscite and
Corbin, ibid. pp. 204–5. Nicolson: *Diaries and Letters*, pp. 414–15.
Churchill on Eden: Churchill, *The Gathering Storm*, p. 201.
Chamberlain's speech: *Hansard*, vol. 357, cols. 111–16. Niusia:
Phillips, *My Secret Diary*, p. 46. Henderson and Hitler: *Cadogan
Diaries*, p. 204; Schmidt, *Hitler's Interpreter*, pp. 148–49; Shirer,
Third Reich, p. 699; Parkinson, *Peace for our Time*, pp. 198–99.
Mrs. Roosevelt: Lash, *Eleanor and Franklin*, p. 583. Ciano: *Ciano's
Diary*, August 29, 1939. Kennard: Parkinson, op. cit. p. 200.
Halder: Aster, *1939*, p. 365; Parkinson, op. cit. p. 201. Von
Hassell: *Von Hassell Diaries*, p. 64.

16 *I hear the wings of the angel of peace*
Ribbentrop and Henderson: Schmidt, *Hitler's Interpreter*, pp. 150–
53; Aster, *1939*, p. 359; Parkinson, *Peace for our Time*, pp. 202–3.
Dahlerus and Göring: Parkinson, op. cit. p. 204; Lamb, *The
Ghosts of Peace*, p. 115; Shirer, *Third Reich*, p. 705. Kennard and
Lipski: Aster, op. cit. pp. 360–61; Shirer, op. cit. pp. 706–7; and
Henderson: ibid. p. 708n. Ciano: *Ciano's Diary*, August 31, 1939.
Henderson and Malhomme: Aster, op. cit. p. 361; and von
Hassell: *Von Hassell Diaries*, pp. 67–68. Churchill: Churchill, *The
Gathering Storm*, p. 313; Gilbert, *Companion*, p. 1601. Göring and
von Hassell: *Von Hassell Diaries*, pp. 68–69; and tea party: Parkin-
son, op. cit. p. 205; Shirer, op. cit. pp. 715–16. Henderson,
Dahlerus, Lipski: Aster, op. cit. pp. 361–62; Parkinson, op. cit.
p. 204; von Hassell, *Von Hassell Diaries*, pp. 69–70; Shirer, op. cit.
pp. 710–11. Wilson and Dahlerus: Toland, *Adolf Hitler*, p. 566;
Aster, op. cit. p. 363; Parkinson, op. cit. p. 204. Lipski and Beck:
Aster, op. cit. p. 364; and Ribbentrop: Schmidt, op. cit. p. 154.
Niusia: Phillips, *My Secret Diary*, pp. 46–47. Naujocks: Parkinson, op. cit. p. 205; Shirer, op. cit. pp. 718–19. "Directive No. 1":
ibid. pp. 712–13; *Hitler's War Directives 1939–45*, ed. H.R. Trevor-
Roper (Sidgwick and Jackson, 1964), p. 3. Dönitz, and Hitler to
Albrecht: Padfield, *Dönitz*, p. 215. Nicolson: *Diaries and Letters*,
p. 416. Shirer: Shirer, op. cit. p. 704.

17 *Time Limit?*
Churchill to Ironside: Gilbert, *Companion,* p. 1602. Mrs. Roosevelt: Lash, *Eleanor and Franklin,* p. 583. Hitler's speech in Opera House: Shirer, *Third Reich,* pp. 722–24. Reactions to it: ibid. p. 721; von Hassell, *Von Hassell Diaries,* p. 71; Engelmann, *In Hitler's Germany,* pp. 151–52. Niusia: Phillips, *My Secret Diary,* pp. 47–48. Hore-Belisha, Raczynski, and Halifax: Aster, *1939,* pp. 368–69. Cadogan: *Cadogan Diaries,* pp. 211–13. Dahlerus and Hitler: Toland, *Adolf Hitler,* p. 571; and Cadogan: Aster, op. cit. p. 370; Shirer, op. cit. p. 726. French Parliament: Aster, op. cit. p. 372. British Parliament: ibid.; *Hansard,* vol. 351, cols. 126ff; Nicolson, *Diaries and Letters,* pp. 416–20; Aster, op. cit. pp. 378–80; Parkinson, *Peace for our Time,* pp. 214–15. Churchill to Chamberlain: Gilbert, *Companion,* pp. 1605–6. Halifax to Phipps: Parkinson, op. cit. p. 212. Italian intervention: *Ciano's Diary,* September 2, 1939. Bonnet and Halifax: Aster, op. cit. p. 375; and Beck, ibid. p. 376; Shirer, op. cit. p. 73 on. "Extremely difficult" Cabinet: Aster, op. cit. pp. 376–78; Parkinson, op. cit. pp. 213–14. Cabinet rebellion: Aster, op. cit. pp. 380–83, 385–87.

18 *All that beautiful Sunday*
Presentation of British ultimatum: Schmidt, *Hitler's Interpreter,* pp. 156–58; Shirer, *Third Reich,* pp. 739–40. Evacuation: Carlton Jackson, *Who Will Take Care of our Children?* (Methuen, 1985), pp. various. Ciano: *Ciano's Diary,* September 3, 1939. Dahlerus and Cadogan: *Cadogan Diaries,* pp. 212–13; Parkinson, *Peace for our Time,* p. 218. Liddell on Chamberlain: Aster, *1939,* p. 389. Chamberlain's broadcast: ibid.; *Cadogan Diaries,* p. 213; Parkinson, op. cit. p. 218. Dönitz: Padfield, *Dönitz,* pp. 216–17. Churchill on Danzig: Eades, *Churchill,* pp. 106–7.

Epilogue
"The one real, living question": *Picture Post,* September 16, 1939, p. 30.